Kasey Mairosney

I'm Just Here For

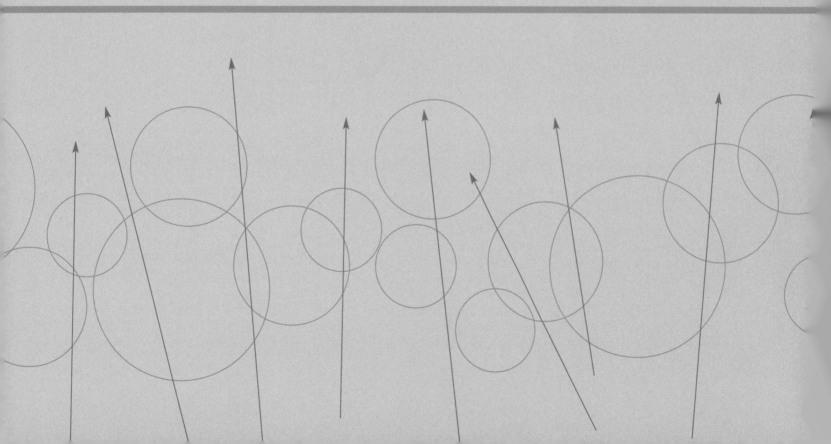

> Curiosity is a willing, a proud, an eager confession of ignorance.
>
> —LEONARD RUBENSTEIN

Let's get one thing straight right up front. I am not a chef. I don't have much interest in creating tantalizing new dishes, which is a good thing because I don't have the talent for it. What I am interested in is making food make sense. I want to understand what makes food tick and how to control the process known as cooking. In that regard I'm more a mechanic than I am a cook.

In the bigger scheme I'm a student, which is ironic since I spent seventeen years as one of the worst students in the history of public education. The reason I barely made it out of high school and wasted the better part of a decade in college is that most of the classes—biology, math, history, and chemistry—just didn't mean anything to me. I couldn't relate to the garble of formulas, equations, dates, and . . . stuff. Now, through the miracle of modern food tinkering, things are starting to make sense to me. After all, food is about nothing if not chemistry, physics, math, biology, botany, history, geography, and anthropology. Yes, there are formulas and equations and even a symbol or two—but now I think they're kind of cool. And the best part is that it all leads to dinner.

Of course the more I learn, the more I realize I don't know. At some point, I hope to learn enough to realize that I know nothing at all. Then maybe I'll be able to snatch a pebble from Julia Child's hand.

the **FOOD**

Food + Heat = Cooking

ALTON BROWN

Stewart, Tabori & Chang
New York

Contents

A Mission—of Sorts

If I could choose to have any job title, it would be culinary cartographer.

Let's say I invite you to lunch. You've never been to my house so you ask for directions. I fax you a very precise list of instructions designed to get you where you're going. Distances are calculated to the tenth of a mile and landmarks are described in Proustian detail. You arrive without a hitch.

But do you know where you are? If a tree had fallen in the road or a road suddenly closed, would you know what to do? Unless you have a global positioning system in your pocket, I'm eating lunch alone.

If only I'd sent you a map instead.

This is what's wrong with recipes. Sure, they can get us where we're going, but that doesn't mean we know where we are when we get there. And it would be a real shame to make it all the way to a soufflé without realizing that scrambled eggs are just over the next hill and meringue's just around the corner.

Do you have to know how to scramble an egg before you can make a soufflé or how to sear a steak to make a beef stew? No. A halfway decent recipe can get you to either of those destinations. But unless you understand where you are and how you got there, you're a hostage. And it's hard to have fun when you're a hostage.

Of course, to gain the kind of knowledge I'm talking about, we must start at the beginning—the very beginning:

Cook (v.) – to prepare food for eating by means of heat.

A car is not defined by CD changers, mud flaps, or leather upholstery. A car is defined by wheels, a chassis, and an engine. Likewise, cooking is not defined by seasonings, glazes, sauces, infusions, dusts, rubs, or relishes. It is defined by the application of heat. Since most of us live in a world where heat is conjured by the stroke of a switch or the twist of a knob, we're not inclined to give it much thought.

That is unfortunate. Because until a cook (the noun, that is) comes to terms with the intricate tango of matter and energy that defines cooking, he or she will remain in a world of darkness and doubt.

Case in point: I recently dined at the home of a friend who must remain nameless lest I never get invited there again. The entrée featured the breast of a free-range chicken encased in a nutty, herby crust and drizzled with a citrus reduction that hinted at Gewürtztraminer. Despite the fact that half a dozen different flavors had been invited to the party, they lacked any unity or leadership and thus could not cover the fact that there was not one drop of moisture left in the meat. Were I a Fletcherite,[1] I'd have been there all night.

When I asked my hostess to share her inspiration for the dish, she enthusiastically presented a glossy food magazine in which a page was devoted to a picture of the dish and half a paragraph to the recipe, which included everything short of freeze-dried yak essence. And yet when it came to the engine and wheels, the skimpy instructions simply said "salt to taste" and "cook 45 minutes or until done." Fashionably salt-fearing and unable to recognize "done," my hostess had followed her recipe straight to oblivion. This sad end could have been sidestepped if only she had tempered her blind recipe faith with a dose of Baron von Rumohr,[2] who wrote that there are three elements the cook must learn to control: **salt, water, and (above all) heat**.

This book is the result of my own desire to "get" the basics; to really understand why a steak that tastes great when seared is gross when boiled. Or why broccoli is better blanched than steamed. Or why brining is just about the best thing you can do to pork.

I know there are those who would say "who cares? As long as I know how, why bother with why?" I can only offer that for me, until I deal with the why, I don't really know the how . . . if you know what I mean.

This book is divided by cooking method rather than food type. That's because when it comes to cooking, I think a mushroom has more in common with a steak than with other vegetables. The recipes herein involve the application of heat to foods such as plants and animals. Foods that we ourselves manufacture—such as batters, custards, and doughs—are, alas, another book.

---

[1] Followers of Horace Fletcher (1849–1919), American businessman and mastication promoter who believed that the secret to health lay in chewing each bite of food until no discernable mass remained. Fletcher himself claimed to chew every bite thirty-two times.

[2] Nineteenth-century foodie/philosopher whose 1822 *The Spirit of Cookery* kicks the pants off anything Brillat "you-are-what-you-eat" Savarin ever wrote.

How to Read a Recipe

Before I had knowledge, I cooked from recipes. Unfortunately I treated them with the same lack of respect that I had for the instructions to countless model kits as a child. (Hey, I don't need anybody telling me what the *Jupiter 2* looks like. I know what it looks like. You just glue this here and this here and... and...) I read recipes like a nine-year-old boy tearing through the instructions to a Ravel 1:20 scale model of an Apache attack helicopter he got for his birthday. As a result, I ruined quite a bit of food. But today, I know a better way.

Sit down in a comfortable chair and read through the ingredient list item by item and ascertain whether or not the required ingredients are indeed in-house. Nothing's more frustrating than putting together that peach pie only to find that you aren't in possession of peaches.

Now go through the parts list and note specifics like chopped, diced, crushed, cooked, drained, canned, fresh, and so on. Missing such details can lead to doom. Take a cup of black beans, for instance. Are they dry, soaked, cooked, cooked and drained, canned, or canned and drained? When added to a dish, each will render a different result.

Remain seated and read through the procedure as if it were a bedtime story. Those of you with children know what I'm talking about. No matter how sure you are of the story—of its beginning, middle, and end—you cannot paraphrase, omit, improvise, or rush. It is your duty to read the story word for word . . . slowly. The same goes for recipes. You may have baked a cake before, or braised cabbage, or roasted a leg-o'-beast, but that doesn't matter.

Do the instructions call for tools? If so, how specifically? A well-written recipe will be specific when it matters and general when it doesn't. If you lack particular gear, ponder substitutes. Generally speaking, pots and pans are exchangeable as long as the size (either dimension or volume) is close to the same. However, if a recipe calls for a non-stick pan, there's probably a good reason. Requests pertaining to glass or metal baking dishes should be heeded, as should those for the use of "non-reactive" vessels (see Reactivity, page 27). A whisk may be replaced by a hand mixer, though it usually doesn't work the other way around. A stick blender can often replace a bar blender, and a good food processor can often replace a chef's knife.

The one place you shouldn't substitute tools is in baking. Baking is all about Mother Nature, and as we all know, it's not nice to fool (or fool with) Mother Nature. If a cake recipe says "8-inch round cake pan," go to the store and buy three or four 8-inch round cake pans. You'll be glad you did.

Once you've pondered the materials, look over any times that are mentioned. Even if the time that a particular step takes is a little nebulous (Who can say how long it will take a pint of wine to reduce by a third?), a good recipe should give you approximates. If not, guess for yourself. Add all the times up and make sure you don't have any issues. Many novice cooks have decided at 5:15 P.M. to embark upon cassoulet and then went to bed hungry.

You're almost ready to go to the kitchen. I usually run down to the office and make a copy of the recipe and stash the book or magazine. Not only are copies easier to work with—ever tried holding a book to your exhaust hood with a magnet?—you can make notes on them without having to ponder posterity. When the dust clears you can write your summary on the back and stash the thing in a three-ring binder. (Nerdy yes, but this kind of thinking landed me a television show.)

Now to the kitchen. Assemble the *mise en place*. The concept is simple: wash, chop, and measure all ingredients (or **software**, as I like to think of it) and gather all **hardware** before you start cooking. It doesn't matter what you're cooking or whether you'll be doing it in five minutes or five hours, *mise en place* can save your hide. This is especially true when you're in a hurry (a quick dinner), bleary-eyed (breakfast), or busy being charming (a dinner party where everyone comes into the kitchen and demands that you be charming).

My own *mise en place* method concerns a tray and a bunch of small reusable rectangular containers. I measure each item into its own container and stack the containers on top of each other in the order they'll be used, so that the top box is the only one that needs a lid.

With *mise en place* in place, check the recipe once more for hidden dangers and booby traps. Overlooking a little phrase like "preheat oven" is an insidiously easy way to destroy a soufflé (which is in turn a great way to destroy your entire day). Recipe writers do err on occasion, and it's not unknown for an ingredient to pop up in the procedural text without

a fancy French way of saying "good to go."

having been properly announced in the parts list (Internet recipes are notorious for this kind of thing).

Walk up to a cold residential oven and turn it to any temperature—say 350° F. Depending on your model, within a few minutes the oven will politely chime, telling you that the target temperature has been reached. What exactly does it mean by that? It means that the air inside the oven has reached 350° F. The moment you open the door to slide in your edible, most of that heat takes a hike toward your ceiling. Recovering that temperature can take quite a while, especially if the item you placed inside is large (say a turkey) and cold (shame on you for not bringing it to room temperature, but more on that later). At the very least, your cooking time calculations are going to go whacko and at the very worst, your food (a batch of cookies for instance) could be ruined.

Luckily you can help your oven keep its word by allowing it to continue heating for twenty minutes after it tells you it's ready to go. That will give the mass of the oven—the walls, ceiling, and floor—time to get good and hot. Once that's happened, they will be able to lend heat to the cooler air, allowing it to "recover" much faster.

If your oven is a little light in the mass department, you might consider leaving a pizza stone in it all the time as a kind of thermal regulator.

End of lecture number one, beginning of lecture number two.

The most underused tool in the kitchen is the brain. I blame the food media (yes, that of which I am a part) who have lulled us into a state of recipe slavery. We don't *think* about recipes as much as we *perform* them.

As I have stated, I not only use recipes, I even try to memorize them from time to time so that I can ponder their finer points. But don't think for a moment that recipes can replace knowledge. For example, one of the best omelets I ever had started out as a busted hollandaise. You could collect egg recipes all your life and still miss the relationship between these two dishes.

Cooking requires not just knowledge (which can simply be absorbed and regurgitated) but understanding, and understanding requires thought. If that seems a little too Zen-like for you, try one of these experiments.

ADAPT SOMETHING

Take a recipe that you really enjoy and feel confident making and change it around.

• Change Veal Scalopini into Turkey Scalopini.

• Trade fresh mushrooms for dry in a pasta sauce.

• Cook something that's usually served raw, like lettuce.

HOST A "REFRIGERATOR ROULETTE" PARTY

Invite a couple of friends over and ask them to bring three food items. Put the food in the middle of a table and figure out what to do with it all. This is a home version of the game that chefs have to play when they audition for jobs—an applicant is given a selection of ingredients and a set amount of time to do something with it.

What I've come to understand is that a lot of folks don't want their own food. They want Mario Batali's food, Charlie Trotter's food, Thomas Keller's food. I like that food too, but I have no desire to cook it. I want *them* to cook it.

Taking control of ingredients is the first step in taking ownership of food. If I set out to execute a recipe and decide to substitute basil for mint, or use plums instead of peaches, or red wine rather than white, I am taking the first step toward laying claim to that food. Sure, there are times when measuring is darned important. As I've said, baking rewards the cavalier with flattened cakes, tunneled muffins, cookies that crack, and soufflés that suffer. But by and large, cooking is a highly flexible craft and unless you make a point of stretching it a little every now and then you'll never know what you or it are capable of. In the end, a cook must develop his or her own sense of proportion.

Recipes are written so that if you follow them to the letter the dish will succeed. This doesn't mean that if you don't follow them to the letter you won't succeed, either. And if you do mess up a few dishes in the name of education—hey, it's only food.

WHY BOTHER COOKING?

Early man ate critters raw, so why change? There are a couple of very good reasons. Heat breaks down meat and vegetable fibers alike, making them a heck of a lot easier to chew and digest. Heat kills parasites and microorganisms that can do nasty things. And heat makes foods taste better.

Many physical and chemical changes take place during cooking, from the caramelization of sugars to the coagulation of proteins. Cooking also causes chemical reactions by breaking down cell walls that normally keep reactive substances away from one another. When they do combine, these substances may give birth to a vast brood of new flavor elements. Garlic, for example, only tastes the way it does when it is cooked because two rather simple chemicals combine and then fraction to create hundreds of new compounds.

Finally, the tongue does a better job of tasting when the food to be tasted is warm. (If you don't believe this, take two scoops of ice cream and microwave one of them until warm and soupy. Taste it alongside the frozen scoop. The warm liquid will taste much sweeter.)

Heat

A lot of the ink in this book is dedicated to the pondering of heat. If cooking is itself defined by the application of heat, then it seems to me that a smart cook would want to know as much as possible about this force. Here's a brief primer.

At its most basic, heat can be described as energy. If an object is hot, you can bet its molecules are in motion. This motion can be set off by:

Chemical reaction. The temperature of the human body is the result of chemical reactions—our consumption and digestion of food is tallied in calories, which are actually units of heat.

Mechanical friction. Rub two sticks together and you get heat; get enough of it and you can make fire. Heat is also created by the friction of electrons moving through a metal coil that provides some resistance. The cigarette lighter in your car and the coils of an electric cook top work this way. And when you place a metal pan on that coil, electrons move through it and heat the pan as well (see page 25).

Radiant energy. Although those versed in quantum physics would argue the point all the live-long day, for the humble cook let it suffice to say that radiation simply refers to energy that travels in waves, be they visible (photoelectrons) or not (microwaves). Waves create heat by vibrating the molecules they hit. Light waves and infrared waves carry a lot of energy, but cannot penetrate very deeply. Microwaves can penetrate deeply into certain tissues, but they carry a relatively low dose of energy. Gamma waves carry a lot of energy and can penetrate very deeply indeed, which is why nuclear weapons have a nasty reputation.

THE LOWDOWN ON HEAT

Through the ages a lot of great gray matter has pondered the nature of heat and come up with the wrong answer. As recently as the late eighteenth century, heat was still thought to be a kind of invisible liquid, which was dubbed "caloric." Then, a guy named Count Rumford, who happened to be the war minister of Bavaria (even though he was an American), noticed that when cannon barrels were drilled, the same amount of heat was produced regardless of the amount of material involved. He deduced from this that heat and movement are closely related, and since heat can be harnessed to do work and can travel through a vacuum, it must be a form of energy. As a reward, Rumford had a baking powder named after him.

DEFINITIONS

Degrees (either Fahrenheit or Celsius) are units of heat measurement—not heat units. In the kitchen, the heat units we need to be concerned with are BTUs and calories.

A **BTU** (British thermal unit) is the amount of heat energy required to increase the temperature of a pound (pint) of water by 1° F.

A **calorie** is the amount of heat needed to raise the temperature of 1 gram of water from 58° to 60° F.

Although any heat-producing device from a refrigerator to a nuclear power plant can be rated in calories, the term is usually used to describe the potential heat energy of food. So the next time you feel bad about noshing on that 378-calorie candy bar, rest easy in the knowledge that your body can, through various chemical reactions, produce enough heat to warm 13.3356 ounces of 58° F water by 2°.

Physical reaction. Fire is a physical reaction wherein a fuel (oxygen) combusts in the presence of a catalyst (a chunk of charcoal).

When it comes to getting heat to food, there are really only two methods of transferal: radiation and conduction. Radiation works on food via waves, conduction is a little trickier.

Basically, conduction is what happens when a piece of matter that's hot comes into direct contact with another piece of matter that isn't. Since heat always moves toward areas of lesser heat, the hot matter makes the less-hot matter hotter. The transferal matter in question can be anything from air to a chunk of metal. However, different types of matter react differently when hot. Metal atoms, locked in a crystalline structure, can only vibrate and pass the energy along—like those funny contraptions you see in executive offices with the series of suspended metal balls; when you lift one and let it fall, the one on the far end swings up. The atoms that make up water and air are different: they're fluid and can move about freely—and this changes everything. Left to their own devices, hot gases and liquid molecules will expand and (becoming less dense) rise. As they give up their heat to other bodies, they cool and sink, thus setting up a natural convection current. Whether in an oven, a pot of water, or a desert the effect is the same.

The faster the convection current, the more hot matter comes in contact with the item to be heated—in our case, food. This means that a blast of 150° F air can cook faster than a 500° F oven. Don't believe it? Try this experiment:

Buy an ice cream cone on the hottest day of the year and eat it in your car in the parking lot with the windows up (no air conditioning please). The cone will indeed melt, but unless you're in Death Valley it won't happen so quickly that you can't keep up with it. Now, buy an identical cone on a cold day and eat it while driving with the windows down. The cone will melt much faster—so fast in fact that you probably won't be able to stay ahead of it. Even though the air is much cooler, more of it is coming into contact with the cone, so there is more transference of heat.

What we can take from this is that although the heat is still moving via conduction, the convection rate is actually an equal if not greater consideration. This is why convection is usually considered as its own classification of heat transference. Here it is in slightly different terms.

Let's say it's an average Wednesday night in the early Stone Age and you, an average *Homo erectus*, return to your cave with a nice big mammoth steak. You could chew it up raw, or you could:

a. Build a fire and hang the hunk a foot or so over the flames. This would be cooking via convection. That means that the vapor (smoke) and the surrounding air will absorb

THE LUCY MODEL 1

You place two pieces of food in a pot of water; one is big (Ethel, on the left), one is small (Lucy on the right). The temperature of the water (a measurement of its heat content) is represented by the number of candies on the conveyor belt. The speed of the conveyor belt represents convection—that is, the number of heat units (or candies) being brought in contact with the food (Ethel and Lucy) via movement of the medium, in this case water molecules. Time is, of course, time.

THE LUCY MODEL 2

Let's say the water is set in motion (convection) by being heated to 195° F (technically a simmer). Ethel and Lucy start suckin' in the heat, but since the convection rate is relatively slow, they don't fill up very fast.

the fire's heat, expand, and rise upward. Since hot always moves to cold, part of this thermal energy moves into the meat. The faster the air/gasses move past the meat, the quicker it will cook.

   b. Build a fire and allow it to die down to a bed of brightly glowing coals, then hang the meat next to but not above the coals. Now radiation is solely responsible for broiling the steak. (Unlike convection currents, which rely on the fact that heat rises, radiant energy moves equally well in all directions, which explains why food cooks under a broiler.)

   c. Build a fire and set a flat rock next to or over it. After an hour or so, slap the meat on the hot rock. That's cooking via conduction.[3]

THE LUCY MODEL 2 (CONTINUED)
Now if the water were 17° F higher, it would be boiling. That would mean a few more heat units on the old conveyor, sure, but more important, the water would be moving (convection) much faster, thus delivering more heat in less time. (Beyond the convection of the water itself, boiling water has additional movement due to the bubbles traveling upward from countless points on the bottom of the vessel). So, now you've got the same amount of heat moving into the foods in much less time. This seems like it would be a good idea, right? Well, that depends on the food.

THE LUCY MODEL 3
Let's say that in 5 minutes both Lucy and Ethel consume 20 candies apiece. Lucy's feeling a little full, but since Ethel has far more mass, she's not even warmed up yet. Eventually Ethel will be done, but by that time Lucy will be toast—that is, overcooked.

[3] Rock is a very slow conductor but it does get the job done. Several years ago, I was doing a poolside grilling demo at a nice home in Atlanta. I looked around for a place to fire up my chimney starter and settled on the middle of a wide gravel path that ran around the yard. So confident was I in the wisdom of my placement that I was quite shocked to return half an hour later to find that the heat radiated through 4 feet of gravel, melted a sprinkler line and set a railroad tie on fire. While I stood there marveling at the sight of thermodynamics at work, the soles of my sneakers melted.

THE DESERT AS OVEN

Radiant energy heats the rocks and the desert floor as well as the air itself which expands and rises in a natural convection. This rising current of air explains why birds can seem to float in the same space for hours without flapping their wings. They're riding thermals. If there's enough moisture around, these thermals will eventually build thunderheads.

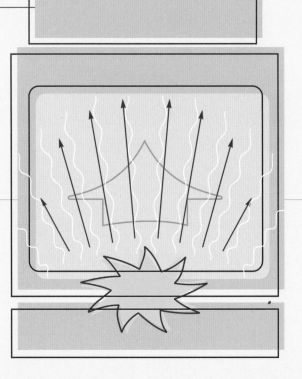

Of course methods may be combined and hybridized. If you hung that meat directly over glowing coals, you'd be cooking with both radiant energy and convection. If you were advanced enough to have a vessel in which to boil water, you could drop your meat in and cook it by conduction and, since the water would be moving, convection as well.

In today's kitchen, most cooking is from hybrid methods:

Oven Roasting/Baking	Radiation (from the walls and, in electric ovens, the calrod), Convection (from the air currents inside)
Broiling	Radiation (from the flame or calrod)
Boiling, steaming, frying, simmering, poaching, stewing	Conduction (from the fluid medium) Convection (of the fluid medium)
Braising	Conduction (from the fluid and from the vessel) Convection usually isn't an issue because what small amount of liquid exists is usually very dense and therefore doesn't circulate
Microwave	Radiation
Hybrid cookers such as "speed ranges" that combine microwaves with halogen light or "calrod ranges" that combine microwaves with halogen light or calrods	Radiation from multiple sources Convection

Addito Salis Grano[4]

Given the surfeit of flavoring agents available to the twenty-first century cook, the inclusion of salt in Baron Rumohr's big-three list with water and heat may seem quaint. But if you polled half of the world's chefs, I bet one in three would say that knowing how to handle salt is at the heart of cooking. Without it, you're dead.

What's so magical about NaCl, the only rock we eat? From whence does it get its power? Simple. Not only does it taste good, it makes just about everything it comes in contact with taste good. Not salty, but better.

What's even more interesting is that without salt's crystalline blessing even dry-aged Kobe beef grilled to medium-rare perfection would taste like a communion wafer. Sodium naysayers will tell you that the taste for salt has been programmed into us by the dark agents of industry. I think it was programmed into us by God. Why else would our tongues have receptors exclusively reserved for its recognition?

Think I'm whacked? Try to explain this: On average Japanese people consume twice as much salt as Americans yet they have the gall to live an average of ten years longer.[5]

Now, despite the fact that the 1970s tied salt to the stake, the 80s stacked the wood and the 90s lit the match, the guys

Low approach vector results in uneven seasoning. Yuck.

---

[4] "With a grain of salt."—Pliny the Elder

[5] The life expectancy of the average Japanese female is eighty-three years; male, seventy-seven.

in the white lab coats have finally gotten hip to what the guys in the white kitchen coats have known all along: salt is good . . . salt works. In fact, a healthy adult can pretty much put salt out of his or her mind as long as he or she (a) has two functioning kidneys; and (b) drinks plenty of water.

When it comes to the actual act of seasoning there are a couple of things to keep in mind:

- Salt all dish components separately. Just because you salted the dressing doesn't mean you shouldn't salt the greens.

- Salt should be added when it can do the most good: during or even before cooking. Liberally salt the water the potatoes cook in and they will be properly seasoned. Wait to season them at the table and you'll have flat-tasting potatoes covered in little rocks. In some cases salt can be added well before cooking, while in others it should be added just before.

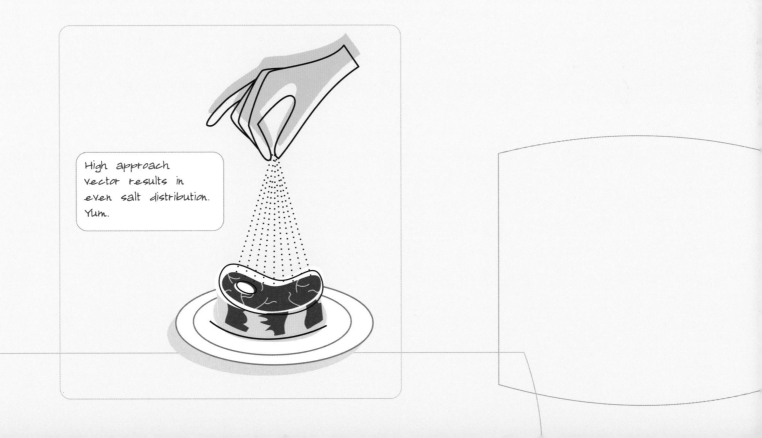

High approach vector results in even salt distribution. Yum.

IODINE AND SALT

If the human machine doesn't get enough iodine, the thyroid gland gets mad. Then it gets even by getting big and sprouting cysts, which give the unlucky victim the neck of a bullfrog in mid-croak. Although you're not likely to spot a goiter while strolling through your local mall, there was a time when goiters were a common site. In the early days of the twentieth century, goiter reached epidemic levels in the Midwest. The fix was to add iodine to something of universal use: salt. The problem deflated overnight. Actually, the best source of dietary iodine is seafood and since it's a lot more available than it used to be it's tough to find a good goiter . . . unless you travel to Africa, Asia, or parts of South America.

ME: I often season meats several minutes before cooking them.

YOU: Eeek. Don't you know that pulls juices out of the meat?

ME: Yes.

YOU: (stunned silence)

ME: Coaxing fluids to the surface of meat is not always a bad thing, especially if those fluids contain water-soluble proteins and the meat is headed for the searing pan. When they come into contact with high heat, these proteins contribute to the browning process.

CHEMICALLY SPEAKING: SALT

Any time you find an acid bound to an alkaline, you've found yourself a salt. Of course, in the kitchen we're really only concerned with NaCl, the molecular marriage of chlorine (an acidic gas) and sodium (a base metal). If you're into curing meats you might also be into sodium nitrite or perhaps even sodium nitrate. The two elements are united by an ionic bond, which means they've got one of those license plates that reads "2gether 4ever"—this is one of the strongest bonds around.

Different types of salt taste different not because of differences in the salt per se but because of the other stuff they're mixed up with. **Artisanal sea salt**, for instance, raked right off the beach, contains traces of salts other than NaCl, not to mention a host of other minerals. **Rock salt**, mined from the ground, can contain anything from iron to cobalt (a good reason to restrict its use to endothermic reactions). Most of the salt sold in the United States is very nearly pure, because it's harvested as a brine. Water is pumped into solid underground salt reserves, which then dissolve and are pumped back to the surface. The brine is stripped of other components (usually by physical rather than chemical means) and then concentrated by boiling. The brine is then cooled until tiny, perfect cubes of salt are forced out of the solution. Before these are marketed as **table salt**, they have a couple of things added to them: anticlumping agents and iodine (see Iodine and Salt).

If the brine is boiled and cooled in open pans, conglomerates of crystals grow downward from the surface like upside-down pyramids. These are separated out via centrifuge, then dried and sorted by size. The larger pieces (which may be rolled into flakes) are sold as coarse or **kosher salt**.

Kosher salt tastes better on food. The fact that kosher salt doesn't contain any additives may be a factor, but I suspect it has more to do with timing. Because kosher salt flakes are irregularly shaped and have a very low surface to mass ratio, they dissolve slowly, releasing their flavor like a time-release medicine. The tiny cubes of table salt attack the tongue all at once. I can always tell when food has been sprinkled with table salt because salt is the first thing I taste. Kosher salt works more behind the scenes and is therefore (to my tongue at least) a more effective seasoning.

Even if flavor wasn't an issue, I'd still prefer kosher to table salt because it is controllable. Since it's composed of irregularly shaped flakes, you can actually pinch kosher salt between your fingers and hold it there. Gently move your fingers back and forth and flakes gently fall. Stop moving and the salt stops falling. Table salt crystals are so small and so uniform, they tend to act more like a fluid than a solid, so even if you manage to get hold of a few, you're not going to get to decide where they go. Although kosher flakes are quite large, the crystals that make them up are actually very fine, so when a flake of kosher salt hits the moist surface of a food, it dissolves quickly and spreads out across a wider area.

THE SPICE KING

Black pepper is the king of spices. Back in the Middle Ages, pepper was a currency: a family's wealth was determined not by how much money they had in the bank but by how many peppercorns they had in their pantry. Black, white, and green peppercorns all come from a small berry that grows in clusters on a vine native to India. When these berries are picked young, dried, and fermented, they become black peppercorns, whose hot spice is tempered by a touch of sweetness. White peppercorns are mature berries that have been dried and rubbed from their skins. They are less pungent than darker pepper. Green peppercorns are brined or freeze-dried and have a slightly sour character, similar to capers. Whole peppercorns can be stored up to a year in a cool, dry place, but their essential oils disperse quickly when ground, so use a pepper mill rather than a pepper shaker. (For more on spices, see Spice Rubs, page 191.)

The fastest way to get heat into food short of dipping it in hot lava...tastes better, too.

CHAPTER 1 | Searing

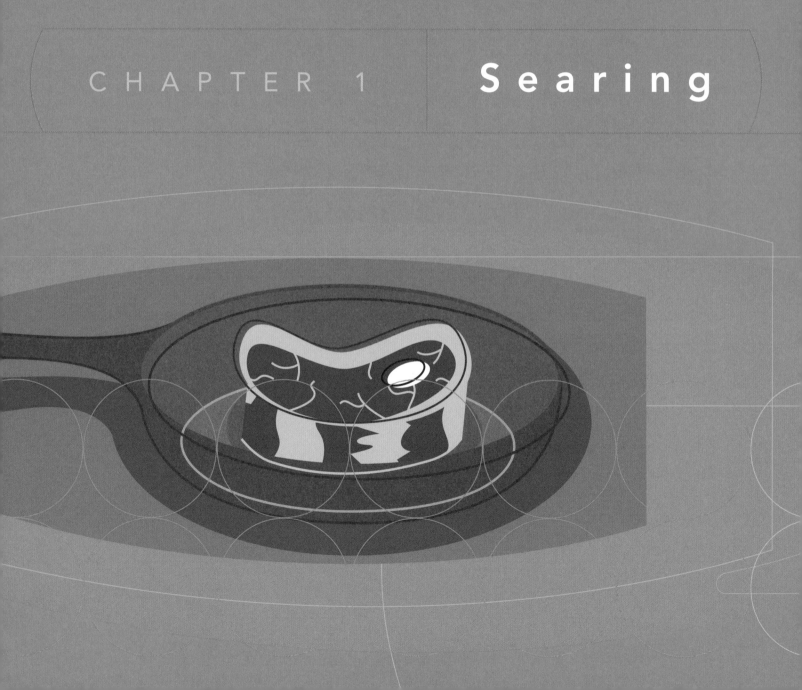

King Sear

This method creates a flavorful brown crust on the surface of many foods, the mere mention of which has been proven to activate saliva production in human test subjects (a fact not lost on the food service industry). What searing does not do is "seal in flavors" or "seal in juices."

If you feel it necessary to seal in juices you should buy a laminator.

HERE'S WHAT YOU NEED

A source of high heat. The average electric cook-top coil tops out at 2000° F. A gas flame—my personal favorite—can reach 3000° F. Searing can also be executed in a pan on the floor of a hot oven or on the exhaust manifold of a Formula One racing car (yes, it's been done).

A perfect vessel

Not only does the ideal searing surface (pan, skillet, and so on) have to get very, very hot, it has to get evenly hot all over and it has to be able to maintain that heat even in the face of foods. Several materials are ruled out from the get-go. Wood and paper make lousy searware because they tend to become fuel before they get hot enough to actually sear anything. Glass and ceramics are such lousy conductors of heat that they're called "insulators." Come to think of it, all the really great heat conductors are also great electrical conductors and they're all metal. What's so special about metals? Besides the fact that they can be molded, cast, and forged, they have a unique, crystal-like molecular structure. The atoms are locked in a uniform geometrical pattern, which makes metals (except mercury) pretty darned tough to bend or break. But their outer electrons are so weakly bound that they just wander around throughout the surface like quantum Flying Dutchmen, which is exactly what makes metals such good conductors. So when the electrons meet the heat on the bottom of the pan, they vibrate through to the other side, thus conveying the hot stuff to the cool stuff. Of course, this leads to the question: Which metal sears the best?

Copper is the hands-down winner when it comes to conductivity—that's why we make wire out of it (that, and the fact that it's easily extruded). Trouble is, purchasing copper cookware often requires taking out a small loan. And since copper is toxic in large amounts it has to be lined with either steel or tin, which tends to wear off. Save copper for where it's really needed: a bowl (see Reactivity, page 27).

Aluminum is also a righteous conductor. It's economical and it's light, but that's a problem, because being light it lacks the density to hold a lot of thermal energy. That means it's going to need some recovery time when something cold comes to call. Aluminum also reacts chemically with certain ingredients and eventually warps, so I'd skip it altogether.

Stainless steel is bright and shiny, durable, relatively inexpensive, and relatively easy to clean. Did I mention that it's bright and shiny? But it's not a great conductor because it's an alloy, a mixture of several metals. And that means that instead of a neat and tidy molecular structure it looks something like this:

This makes it tough for electrons to get around. I still think stainless steel makes a swell sauté pan, but for searing I'll hold out for iron.

Iron is dense—really dense—which makes it a relatively slow conductor. But that density also allows for even heating, and once it gets hot it stays hot.[6] Iron is very economical, and cooking with it supplies dietary iron, which a lot of us (especially women) tend to run short on. Cast-iron pans must occasionally be seasoned, or cured, with a thin layer of hot fat in order to seal the

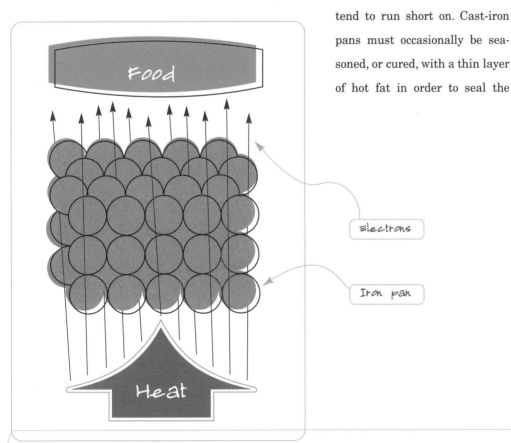

THE MAKING OF CAST IRON

To cast iron, a pattern is made (a positive image of a pan, pot, or what have you). Then a mixture of sand and clay is packed around it under high pressure creating a mold, or cake. Molten iron is poured through a small opening in the cake. After the iron has solidified, the cake is broken open, revealing the newborn cookware. The sand is then broken up and reused.

[6] Since the handles on cast-iron pans get almost as hot as the rest of the vessel, I strongly suggest turning the handle away from the edge of the stove, especially if children are about. (I've burned myself on the handle of a cast-iron pan half an hour after it came off the heat.) The density of iron at 293k = 7.86 g/mc3

CAST IRON FEEDING INSTRUCTIONS

1. Place the pan to be cured on the top rack of a cold oven and place a sheet pan or baking sheet on the bottom rack.

2. Turn the heat to 350° F.

3. When the pan is warm but still touchable, remove the pan and spoon in a dollop of solid vegetable shortening, which is more refined than other oils and won't leave a nasty film. As the shortening melts, use a paper towel to smear the fat all over the pan, inside, outside, handle—everywhere.

4. Place the pan back in the oven, upside down. This prevents excess fat from pooling in the bottom and botching the cure.

5. Bake for 1 hour, then kill the heat and let the pan cool for a few minutes. (Use fireproof gloves when you remove the pan from the oven.)

6. Wipe the pan clean but don't wash it until after you've used it.

That's it. To clean a cast-iron pan, I usually add a little fat to the still-hot pan, toss in some kosher salt, and rub it with paper towels. If that doesn't do the trick, I'll wash it with mild detergent, warm water, and a sponge. I re-cure my cast-iron pans every New Year's Day, whether I need to or not.

surface against rust (see Cast Iron Feeding Instructions). Some folks sneer at the maintenance required, but considering that ours is the very culture that nurtured Sea Monkeys, Chia Pets, and Pet Rocks, taking care of an iron skillet shouldn't be a problem.

ADDITIONAL SEAR GEAR

Spray bottle Your standard buck-fifty drugstore pump bottle is the perfect tool for applying a thin coat of lubricant (cooking oil) to the surface of the food to be seared. Beware of fancy-looking mister bottles. I've had three and worn out three with only moderate use.

Spring-loaded tongs A pair of these is like having a big metal hand. Muzzle with a rubber band for low-profile storage. I keep a short pair for the kitchen and a long pair for the grill.

Instant-read thermometer Heat control is the cook's primary directive, and yet there are a lot of cooks out there who do not own this simple device. This is like riding a motorcycle without a helmet, or owning a pit bull but not homeowner's insurance, or

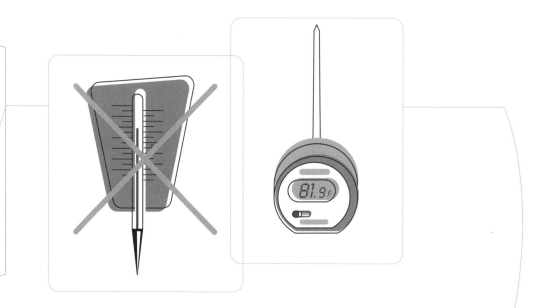

working a government job without a shredder. It's crazy. I'm not talking about the old metal-tipped glass tube with the metal paddle on it that you could have tapped a maple tree with. I am talking about a slender metal probe topped with a digital readout of some type. Analog models are also available, but they're easily swayed out of concentration, so use them at your own risk.

Welding gloves Potholders are for sissies and mitts are for baseball. If I'm gonna grab a five hundred–degree pan, I want protection that reaches halfway to my elbow. Skip the kitchen shop and head to the hardware store.

Splatter guard As the pan gets hot it's going to turn into a radiator. The air around it is going to get hot, expand, and rise, taking microscopic drops of grease with it. If you've got a really strong ventilation hood these drops may get caught up in the draft and get on out of the house. Odds are, though, the air is simply going to cool down as it rises, allowing the particles to fall down onto any horizontal surface they can find. The best way to prevent this is by using a splatter guard. It's basically a screen door for your pan.

Make sure you buy one wide enough to cover your widest sauté pan, because you definitely don't want to pan fry without this device in place. Besides preventing clean-up nightmares, it's also your own best protection against flying grease. (Don't think this is an issue? Try frying bacon naked sometime.)

Fresh air Any time you get animal protein around very high heat there's going to be some smoke. How much depends on the fat content of the meat. So turn your exhaust fan on, and if you don't have one, open a window and maybe a door. If for some reason you have a smoke detector right over the cook top (though I can't imagine why you would), take the battery out until you've finished cooking.

REACTIVITY

When we talk about "reactive" metals these days, we're talking about aluminum and maybe copper. Metals such as stainless steel are actually surrounded by a very thin layer (a few molecules thick, tops) of gas, an oxide that is created at the point where metal and air meet. Despite the fact that it's technically gas, this film creates a formidable barrier between food and pan.

The film around aluminum is very vulnerable to acid. When acidic foods are cooked in aluminum, traces of the metal leech into the food. This is why every tomato sauce recipe written in English demands that we cook it in a "nonreactive" vessel. And although researchers haven't been able to pin the cause of Alzheimer's disease on aluminum despite years of trying, there does appear to be a relationship. Anodized aluminum appears to be safe. (Anodizing uses electricity to deposit an oxide film on a metal, thus rendering it nonreactive.) The film, however, can be scratched, which is why I just stay clear of aluminum cookware altogether. I do allow aluminum foil to come in direct contact with food, which some folks would argue is as bad as snorting the stuff uncut. Sorry, but aluminum foil is just too darned important a tool in my kitchen. I'll give up antacid tablets and even deodorant first (both of which contain whopping doses of aluminum).

Copper is also reactive, but almost all copper cookware is lined with tin (which does have to be replaced every now and then). A century ago, when pennies were 100-percent copper, it was a common practice to drop one in a pot of cabbage soup to keep it green (copper ions, you know). Copper ions also bring stability to egg foams, which is why I whip egg whites in a copper bowl. Of course, in very large amounts copper is even more toxic than aluminum. Life's complicated.

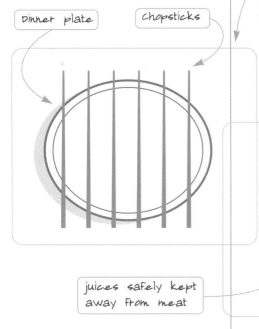

Dinner plate

chopsticks

juices safely kept away from meat

Wooden chopsticks If you're not going to rest your meat, you might as well not cook it. Make your own resting rack anywhere, anytime, with these amazing sticks! Take your average dinner plate. Place five or six chopsticks thusly:

Now you've got the perfect place to rest a wide variety of your favorite meats. You should, of course, keep them cozy under a loose layer of foil.

juicy steak resting

APPROPRIATE FOOD

Searing is unique in that it is not only used to cook food to doneness, but as an opening act for other cooking methods. Why? Because it's the fastest way to get heat into food so it's the fastest way to brown the surface of food. Brown is good. Brown works. Of course, if you wish to attain a delicious, golden brown crust you must choose your food wisely. To do so, it helps to understand the reaction responsible for browning.

Any carbon-based life form (and all food used to be alive at some point) will turn black if exposed to enough heat; in other words, it turns to charcoal. However, in order to brown, the food in question must contain high levels of either carbohydrates, which brown via caramelization, or proteins, which brown thanks to the chemical chaos that is the Maillard reaction (see below).

THE MAILLARD REACTION

When certain carbohydrates meet up with certain amino acids in the presence of high heat, dozens if not hundreds of new compounds are created. Some create flavor, others create color. Left to run amok, the Maillard reaction leads directly to the condition commonly known as "burned," which has its own flavors and colors—none of which are good.

So we need a food containing amino acids and carbs. And since we want to get this crust on as much of the food as possible, a food with a flat surface would be helpful, especially if you intend to sear it until it's cooked to completion. What we need is meat.

But it should be the right kind of meat. Some cuts of meat are quite tough and require prolonged cooking in order to break down connective tissues. Stew meat, lamb shanks, and chuck roast, for example, can be seared to add that "browned" flavor, but then should be slowly braised or simmered until done.

THE TROUBLE WITH SEARING

Doneness is a big issue. If the meat is thin enough, by the time the first side has earned its golden crust the interior will have cooked halfway through, so you flip. By the time the second side reaches maximum crustage (a minute or two longer than it took the first side, since the pan isn't as hot) you should have a perfectly cooked piece of meat.

However, the great majority of the meats that present themselves to the cook are not the perfect shape or size and therefore will not be done on the inside by the time the outer surfaces have reached golden brown and delicious status. The way I see it, you're left with three solid choices:

1. Change the thickness of the food.

2. Sear to attain a yummy crust then finish cooking by another method.

3. Stick with foods that are natural-born searers.

BIG RED BOOK O' BLUE

I like filet of tenderloin steak as much as the next guy. A good one is at least 1½-inches thick, though, and if you try to sear it to doneness (meaning medium-rare, of course) the outside will look and taste like a meteorite.

The solution: butterfly it. Lay out the meat and find the edge that's kind of flat. Pick up your boning knife and turn the steak so that the flat side is facing away from the knife. Carefully slice the steak horizontally through the center, cutting through to the flat edge. Then open it like a book.

Liberally season the steak and sear one side. Flip and repeat. Now just look at what you've done. You've doubled the flavor by doubling the seared surface area (and how about adding a bit of blue cheese in the center, too?)

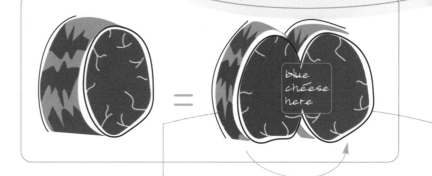

SEARING: THE SHORT FORM

1. Decrease the difference in temperature between refrigerated meat and your oven before starting the process; counter the meat for up to 30 minutes, depending on the size.

2. Don't be afraid to let the pan get hot. Heat the pan over high heat for 2 to 3 minutes if the food is small (a single duck breast) or 5 minutes if the food is large (a flank steak). Consider several small pieces (four duck breasts) to be one big piece.

3. Season the meat with salt as soon as you put the pan on to heat.

4. Double-check everything before you start because once the food hits the pan, there is no turning back.

5. Examine both sides of the target food—whichever side looks best goes down first. When you turn the food, the pan isn't as hot as it was when you started, so the second crust doesn't form as quickly. This means it probably won't look as gosh-darned delicious as the first side, which is why you cooked the handsome side first.

6. When you place the food in the pan there is going to be noise and maybe some smoke. Many people who cook respond to this by grabbing the food and moving it around. This is not a good thing to do.

7. The food is hot, it's juicy, the kitchen smells great, the table's set—time to dig in, right? Wrong. Heat is still applying pressure to the meat, and any slicing or poking will result in a rapid exodus of juicy goodness. Place seared meat on a resting rack, covered with a large bowl or loosely tented with foil. Wait 5 minutes. This will give you time to ponder a pan sauce (see Sauces, page 198).

Master Profile: Searing

Heat type: dry

Mode of transmission: 100-percent conduction

Rate of transmission: very high

Common transmitters: metal pans and griddles

Temperature range: the widest range of any cooking method, from very low to very, very high

Target food characteristics:

• low surface to mass ratio

• wide, flat shape

• high protein foods that profit from a contrast between surface and interior doneness: beef steaks, tuna steaks, scallops

• starchy batters: pancakes, crepes, and so on

Non-culinary use: branding cattle (and in some cases, fraternity members)

As long as you've read the section called Cleanliness is Next to... and put safe habits into practice, that is.

Skirt Steak: The Master Recipe

Skirt steak is flat, uniform in thickness, and rarely longer than a 12-inch pan is wide. Not only was it born to be seared, it is one of the leanest cuts of meat suitable for searing.

Application: Searing

Prep the meat. Remove the steak from the refrigerator, pat dry and place on rack for at least 15 minutes. (Less difference between meat and oven temperature.)

Lube the meat. The goal here is to barely coat the surface of the meat with a thin film of oil. This will hold the salt to the meat, provide no-stick insurance, and serve as a heat conductor for all those nooks and crannies that don't actually come in contact with the pan. The trick is to make this layer skimpy. Too much oil and the salt will wash away. Oil also likes to splatter and even burn when faced with high heat, so I say use as little as possible. To that end, I employ a drugstore spray bottle. I don't put anything in it but peanut or safflower oil and I keep it set for "spray" rather than "stream" at all times.

Season the steak on both sides liberally with kosher salt and pepper. What the heck does "season liberally" mean? Truth is, most folks under season their food before cooking, which usually drives them to over salt at the table. In the case of skirt steak, I go with at least ¼ teaspoon of salt per side.

Grind pepper onto each side (I go with half as much pepper as salt), and then **use your hand to really rub the seasoning into the meat**. Rubbing is the only way to make sure you've got good salt-to-meat contact. Once the massage is over, go wash your hands, and allow the meat to sit for at least 5 minutes. This allows some juices to come

Software:

1 skirt steak (see Critter Map, page 240)

1 tablespoon vegetable oil

Kosher salt

Freshly ground black pepper

Hardware:

Spray bottle for the oil

Cast-iron skillet

Resting rack

Aluminum foil or a large bowl

continued on next page

to the meat's surface—and those juices are what will give the steak a nice crust when seared.

Heat the pan. Place your largest cast-iron skillet on the cook top over high heat. Allow 3 minutes for the pan to reach cooking heat.

Turn on your stove's exhaust system. If you do not have an exhaust system, open a window. Hold the steak so that the bottom edge hangs down right at the closest edge of the skillet and **lay the steak down into the pan.** This isn't so much to prevent splattering as to make sure that you get the whole thing in the pan without sliding it around. This is important because moving the meat around in those first few moments can cut down on crust production.

Leave the meat absolutely alone for 3 minutes, then flip it over and cook for another 3 minutes—uninterrupted, please. This will result in a perfectly medium-rare steak. Want it more done than that? No, you don't … really, you don't.

Remove the steak from the skillet and let it rest on a resting rack for 5 minutes, covered loosely with aluminum foil or with a large bowl. Do not skip this step.

Now, skirt steak is not a very tender piece of meat. It's lean and fibrous and flat-out tough unless you slice it correctly—meaning thin. By slicing thin across the grain, you present the prospective chewer with short muscle fibers rather than long ones, which creates a far more tender mouth feel. The problem with thin, however, is that a skirt steak is not very thick to begin with, so if you cut straight through it you end up with something that looks like meat fettuccine, which may taste good but looks a little … weird. Thus the bias cut—across the grain. **Slice the steak on an angle** and you get it all: short muscle fibers and great-looking slices. The leftovers are delicious cold, by the way.

one of those strange, food-industry terms that attempts to describe something you can't really describe

Cast-Iron Duck

I'm chronically depressed about the puny amount of duck we eat in this country. It's just plain wrong. Besides being downright American, duck is without question our tastiest poultry. If we're to eat less red meat, I say let's eat more duck.

This sear is a little different than the basic method because it starts with medium rather than high heat in order to render out some fat without burning the duck skin. Since it depends on rendering out subcutaneous fat, proper searing also translates to a more healthful dish.

Application: Searing

With a sharp knife, trim excess fat and sinew from the breasts and score the skin in a crosshatch pattern, being very careful not to cut into the muscle. Pat the breasts dry with paper towels. The less moisture the better: it will result in a crisper skin—and crisp skin is essential. Season the breasts with salt and pepper. Heat a well-seasoned cast-iron skillet over medium heat for about 3 minutes. Using a spray bottle, lightly coat the pan with oil. Gently lay the breasts into the pan, skin side down. Resist the urge to move them around, as you'll want them to brown. Once you've achieved a golden brown skin, using tongs, flip the breasts away from yourself, using easy motions so you don't splash hot oil on yourself. Cook for another 3 minutes. Remove the breasts to a resting rack and loosely cover with foil. Letting the meat rest will allow the juices to redistribute throughout the meat. After about 5 minutes, with the skin side up, slice the breasts on a bias. Fan the meat over a tasty side dish—how about Red Flannel Hash (see next page)—and enjoy.

Yield: 4 servings

Software:

4 duck breasts

Kosher salt and freshly ground
    black pepper

Canola oil

Hardware:

Sharp knife

Paper towels

Spray bottle for the oil

Cast-iron skillet

Tongs

Resting rack

Aluminum foil

Red Flannel Hash

This dish is best with the delicious Cast-Iron Duck.

Application: Searing

Preheat the oven to 400° F.

Using a paring knife, peel the beet under cold running water, cut into medium dice (to yield 1 cup), and place in a cold-water bath as you go; this will help keep your clothes from getting stained. Peel and dice the potatoes (to yield 3 cups) and put them in a second cold-water bath after cutting them; this will keep them from oxidizing and turning brown. Drain the diced beet, and coat with 1 tablespoon duck fat. Spread the beet pieces out on a baking sheet and season with salt and pepper. Roast for 8 minutes, or until they are slightly tender. Drain the potatoes and put them in the pot of boiling water. When the water returns to a boil, drain the potatoes and plunge them into an ice-water bath to stop the cooking. Drain, rinse, and spin them in a salad spinner. Heat a cast-iron pan over medium heat for 3 minutes. Add the remaining duck fat and toss in the garlic. Cook the garlic for about 45 seconds, just to flavor the oil. Add the onion and cook for another 45 seconds. Add the potatoes and beets and cook until crisp with a minimal amount of stirring. Be sure not to overcrowd the pan or you'll never get that crispness you're after—work in batches if you must. Season with salt and pepper, add the chives, and stir to distribute. If you're really adventurous, crack a duck egg atop the hash and cover with a lid. Cook until the egg is at your favorite degree of doneness.

Yield: 4 servings

Software:

1 medium red beet

4 medium red potatoes

3 tablespoons duck fat or oil

Kosher salt and freshly ground
   black pepper

2 tablespoons minced garlic

1 Vidalia or other sweet onion,
   diced

1 tablespoon chopped chives

1 duck or chicken egg (optional)

Hardware:

Paring knife

2 cold-water baths

Baking sheet

Large pot of boiling salted water

1 ice-water bath

Salad spinner

Cast-iron pan

Wooden spoon

Bar-B-Fu

Nobody said that the protein to be seared has to be meat. Pound for pound, tofu is the cheapest form of complete protein around.

Just about every market around today carries a couple of hardnesses of regular or Chinese tofu: soft and firm. Soft tofu can be crumbled like a soft cheese, whereas firm tofu is what you want when you're going to cook a chunk of the stuff. It acts like a sponge, soaking up whatever liquid it meets, especially if it's wrung out first. And remember, surface-to-mass ratio determines marinating time, so cut first, then soak (see Have a Soak, page 181).

Application: Searing

Slice the tofu lengthwise into 4 equal parts and set on a baking sheet lined with paper towels. Place a couple of paper towels on top and lay a second baking sheet on top. Put a couple of cans of food on top of that to weigh it down. Set aside for at least 30 minutes.

Meanwhile, mix the garlic, chiles, barbecue sauce, and vinegar. Season the tofu "steaks" with salt and pepper, place the tofu in a zip-top bag, and pour in the barbecue sauce mixture. Allow to marinate for at least 1 hour or overnight.

Drain the marinade off the tofu and reserve. Heat a non-stick pan for about 3 minutes over medium flame. Shake off any excess marinade and add the tofu to the pan. No oil is needed. Don't move the "steaks" or they will not brown. Using tongs, flip after 2 minutes and allow to brown on the other side. Remove the tofu and place on the rolls. Pour the reserved marinade into the hot pan and add the beer. Allow to reduce to sauce consistency. Pour over the "steaks" and enjoy with some spicy and vinegary slaw. Wash down with the rest of your beer. Isn't health food great?

Yield: 4 sandwiches

Software:

1 pound firm tofu

1 tablespoon minced garlic

1 tablespoon minced serrano chiles

⅓ cup of your favorite barbecue sauce

¼ cup apple cider vinegar

Kosher salt and freshly ground black pepper

4 white hoagie rolls (make sure the bread is sort of firm and definitely flavorful; the bread can make or break this dish)

¾ cup of your favorite beer, preferably dark (I use Shiner Bock)

Hardware:

2 baking sheets

Paper towels

Cans of food for weighting

Gallon-size zip-top bag

Non-stick pan

Tongs

Blackened Tuna Steak

I have always suspected that the whole "blackening" phenomenon that crept out of the Bayou a decade ago was a clever way to serve burned fish. That said, this powder does turn pretty dark. And yes, it tastes mighty good, too, especially when applied to a fish that can be seared and left darned near raw on the inside—meaning tuna and salmon, but mostly tuna.

This recipe comes from Patrick Matecat, a very American albeit French chef who tolerated my presence in his kitchen for more than a year.

Application: Searing

Combine all the spices and salt in a jar or other lidded container and shake well to combine.

Heat a cast-iron skillet over high heat until it's hot enough to make a drop of water jump, not just sizzle. Lightly lubricate each piece of tuna with canola oil. Dredge the fish in the powder and shake off all possible excess.

Spritz the pan with oil right before adding the fish. This will assure even heating as the crust forms. A 1-inch steak cooked for 2 minutes on each side will be perfectly colored on the outside and just warm on the inside. If you like your tuna cooked a little more, you can remove the pan from the heat, cover loosely with foil and give it another minute on each side. Don't worry, the pan will stay plenty hot. Thicker steaks should also be seared on the sides by setting edgewise in the pan.

Serve the steak whole or slice thin and fan around a mound of coleslaw.

Note: If you don't like the look of what your market has cut in the case and if you're planning on serving at least 4 people, ask the fishmonger if he has any whole loins. If so, buy one that's about 8 inches long and have it sliced into 4 steaks. Never, ever be afraid to ask a butcher to cut something special for you. That's why he's there.

Yield: 1 steak

Software:

2 tablespoons paprika

1 tablepoon plus 2 teaspoons kosher salt

2 teaspoons onion powder

2 teaspoons garlic powder

1 teaspoon cayenne pepper

1½ teaspoons white pepper

1½ teaspoons black pepper

1 teaspoon dried thyme

1 teaspoon dried ginger

1 teaspoon ground cumin

Canola oil

1 tuna steak, 1-inch thick

Hardware:

Glass jar or other lidded container

Cast-iron skillet

Spray bottle for the oil

Pan-Seared Portobello Mushrooms

I tried several approaches before choosing this method of preparing mushrooms. This method produces a nice meaty texture and great mushroom flavor.

Application: Searing

Cut the mushrooms into ¼-inch slices without removing the gills. Heat a cast-iron pan over medium-high heat for about 3 minutes. Mist the mushrooms with oil and season with salt and pepper. Using a paper towel, spread about 1 teaspoon oil in the pan. Lay the slices of mushroom in the pan without overlapping, and sear, without moving them, for 5 minutes. Flip them over, cook for another 5 minutes, and serve. Some things are as simple as they seem.

Yield: 2 appetizer servings

Software:

2 portobello mushroom caps

Olive oil

Kosher salt

Freshly ground black pepper

Hardware:

Cast-iron pan or heavy sauté pan

Spray bottle for the oil

Paper towel

Tongs

There are a great many things one can learn to do without actually doing them.
Grilling is not one of them.

CHAPTER 2   Grilling

A View to a Grill

I am sitting here in a 28-foot Ambassador-class Airstream trailer. Constructed of shiny clean aluminum in 1978, its curvy interior, overhead storage, and pop-out tables epitomize modern design. I am typing on a Macintosh G4 Titanium Powerbook, which is roving through my MP3 collection like a digital whirling dervish. When I need to speak to someone, which isn't very often since the G4 is wirelessly connected to the Web through a device in the house, I do so on a Nokia cell phone capable of trading files with my Palm V, which I really should replace since it's so 1999. When I need a break I torture my dog by tracing designs on the wall with the mini–laser pointer on my key chain. Soon, though, I will go outside and set a fire in a contraption that looks like Sputnik, and cook a piece of cow. The point is: I am a modern guy but the cooking I enjoy the most is the kind that's been around the longest—over fire.

Why have a laser on a key chain? Because you can, of course.

Cooking over open coals, a process which, depending on who you ask, is called either broiling, grilling, or roasting, has been around since the first caveman noticed that the rack of mammoth hanging by the fire didn't turn green and stinky as quickly as the one left by the door. Drying and the curative powers of smoke were no doubt responsible, but it didn't take long for some Cro-Magnon klutz to drop dinner in the fire. And it was good. A lot less chewy and kind of yummy. Sure, it was gritty from lying in the coals, but soon (a thousand years, tops) some Og or Ogetta stuck a spear in the meat and, well, any Boy Scout or Girl Scout knows the rest. Grilling is huge to this day, but don't think for a minute that this has to do with flavor or getting outdoors or any other culinary concerns.

You see, most of the grilling in this country is performed by men, and men like fire. In fact, I suspect that the backyard cooking boom this country witnessed in the late 1940s and 50s was really about playing with lighter fluid. It's not our fault, of course. I trust that someday the lab-coaters will have identified a gene, unique to the Y chromosome, that will be dubbed the "firestarter gene."

Whether it's for the love of fire or food, grilling is more popular today than ever before[7] despite the rise in concerns over potentially cancer-causing compounds in the smoke created when animal fats burn.

FUEL MATTERS

The average hardwood log contains around 39 percent cellulose, 35 percent hemicellulose, 19.5 percent lignin, and 3 percent extractives and such. When you burn it—well, I shouldn't say "burn," because wood doesn't actually burn—it undergoes a kind of thermal degradation known as pyrolysis.[8] During this process, the wood beaks down into a slew of volatile substances (carbon monoxide and dioxide, hydrocarbons, hydrogen, aldehydes, ketones, alcohols, tar, phenols, that sort of thing) and a solid carbon mass. When you see flames and smoke, that's the volatiles burning. When those are exhausted, what's left of the wood glows. These are called coals, and they burn much hotter and much cleaner than

[7] Almost 85 percent of American families own a grill.

[8] If wood actually burned, there wouldn't be anything left after combustion—which there is.

the stuff that fueled the flames. They are also the stuff of which all good grill sessions are made.

Charcoal is nothing more than wood that has had its volatile components removed. Although it's a lot more complicated than it sounds, commercial charcoal is made by heating wood (or in the case of briquettes, wood chips) to about 1000° F in an airless environment. Natural lump charcoal is fired with grain alcohol; most briquette makers opt for petroleum. This cooking removes those volatile components while leaving the carbonaceous mass intact. After cooling, the lump charcoal is bagged and shipped. Chips get mixed up with lime, cornstarch, and other binders and are compressed into briquettes. This is not to say that all briquettes are bad. "Natural" briquettes still contain binders like cornstarch but they lack the nitrates and petroleum, and the non-burning filler (sand) you find in standard briquettes. Natural briquettes burn longer than lump or chunk charcoal, which lights faster and burns a good deal hotter. Consider using a mixture of the two fuels in certain situations. If you're interested in smoking foods, remember that chunk charcoal and charcoal briquettes are processed products that burn to produce hot coals but do not alone have the ability to transport flavor via smoke. Adding wood chips or chunks is necessary to produce the smoke that flavors food.

LIGHT MY FIRE

Although natural charcoal fires up far easier than briquettes, charcoal is still just lumps of carbon, and lumps of carbon aren't exactly fireworks. Clever hairless monkeys that we are, we've come up with a wide range of devices designed to speed lighting. Only one of these am I wholeheartedly opposed to: fast-lighting briquettes. I'm not naming names, but you know what I'm talking about. It's not that I'm afraid that one of these chemical-laden lumps is going to just go off in my hand, it's just that no matter how far I burn them down before I put the food on the grill, I can swear I taste something … funny. That's all I'm going to say … funny.

A BARBECUE BY ANY OTHER NAME

Folks like to argue about what defines great barbecue. What they really should be arguing about is what the word actually means. It is just about the only word that out-connotes roast. You could, for instance, say, I fired up my barbecue and barbecued a mess of barbecue for the church barbecue. (Try that out on a French cook someday—it'll crack him like an *oeuf*.)

The origins of the word are traceable. When Columbus landed on Hispañola, he found the natives smoking meat and fish on green wood lattices built over smoldering bone coals. The natives called this way of cooking *boucan*. The Spaniards, being good colonialists, decided to change it to *barbacoa*. On his next journey from Spain, Columbus brought pigs to Hispañola. A few of them got away, and soon there was more *boucan* than you could shake a flaming femur at. As word got around that the gettin' was good on Hispañola, bandits, pirates, escaped prisoners, and runaway slaves made for the island and lived high on *boucan* three times a day. The French, witty as they are, called these individuals *boucaneers*.

So, the folks in Tampa have a football team whose name means "those who cook over sticks."

As far as modern usage goes, barbecue the noun refers to slow-cooked pork or beef. Barbecued chicken is grilled chicken served with barbecue sauce. Barbecuing is the act of making barbecue; cooking directly over coals is grilling.

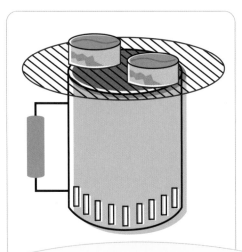

YOU WANT CHAR? I'LL SHOW YOU CHAR

When you want serious firepower, place a small grate (the cooking grate from a Smokey Joe is perfect) directly on your chimney. This is like cooking over an upturned F–16. It's not suitable for everything, but I'll sometimes do little hunks of prime tuna as a stand-around-the-grill appetizer.

Lighter fluid may be the perennial pyro-preference, but there are other firestarter options. My favorites are electric coil starters and chimney starters. The first requires 110 volts of power and a safe place to set it down once you've removed it from the grill, but it does the job quickly and effectively. A chimney starter is also fast and it allows you to have lit coals standing by at all times. A chimney does, however, require a safe place to live. I keep mine on a cinder block (but never on gravel—see page 15).

During a multiday grilling binge last summer I padded out to my extremely carbonaceous carport to fire up one of the three grills that always seem to be there. I loaded a chimney with chunks and reached for some newspaper to stick in the bottom. But the only paper I could scrounge was a big wad of paper towel I'd used to wipe down grill number two the night before. So I used it. Fifteen minutes later the paper towel was still burning. Of course: I'd rubbed grill number two down with a bit of vegetable oil, essentially making the wick for an oil lamp. I was delighted with this discovery despite the fact that the rest of mankind had figured it out a few hundred thousand years ago.

To make a long story short, now I lay a sheet of newspaper on the ground, mist it with vegetable oil, wad it up, and stick it under my grill's charcoal grate. I pile on the charcoal, then light the paper through one of the air vents with my pocket torch. It never, ever fails—or at least it hasn't yet.

I still keep a couple of chimney starters around for those times I need to have some charcoal lit before adding it to the fire or have a filet or hunk of tuna to sear (see illustration, left). Other than that, I've gone to the oil-on-paper method, which is a lot cleaner and a lot less dangerous.[9]

[9] I'm not trying to imply that chimney starters are dangerous, but I think that any time you're holding, moving, and pouring something that's glowing red, there's a potential for trouble.

The Grill

I have to preface this section with a set of simple admissions: I do not own a gas grill. I have never owned a gas grill, nor do I foresee a time in the near future when I will own a gas grill. It is not that I have anything against natural gas as a fuel (even if it does burn a little wet), it's just that the only gas grills I've seen that are worth a darn cost more than my first three cars put together and I cannot in clear conscience justify spending that kind of money even if I could manage to scrounge it together. Besides, if you ask me, gas grilling is really just upside-down broiling. The only advantage that this kind of cooking would have over oven broiling (assuming, of course, that you have a gas broiler) is that the grill will produce nice grill marks—but if you use the right pan under the broiler you can do that, too (see How to Make People Think You Grilled When You Didn't, page 62). If you only have an electric broiler, a gas grill makes some sense.

A WORD ON COUNTER-TOP GRILLS

A certain retired boxer has made approximately a gazillion dollars by marketing an electric counter-top grill. I know plenty of folks who like them, but I've never been able to get any real lasting heat out of one. And without real heat there will be little if any sear. And, of course, with the top down there's going to be steam. Don't get me wrong, it's a valid method of cooking—it's just not grilling, and you should adjust your expectations accordingly.

I am very much at home with charcoal. I love charcoal. I can reach a Zen-like oneness with the coals. A couple of summers ago I constructed a 4-by-8-foot fire pit in my backyard and had special grates made to fit it. I cooked whole pigs over hickory fires, then harvested the leftover charcoal to use in my three grills. I am a freak, but I can live with that.

By the way, even truly fine gas grills cannot generate the heat of natural chunk charcoal. That's because a glowing coal simply has so much of the light spectrum going for it. Don't believe me? Go into a darkened hangar with a gas grill and a charcoal grill. Fire them both up and observe them through your infrared goggles. See what I mean?

Up until the late nineteenth century, rural communities would get together to build a charcoal kiln, a giant "teepee" of wood with an airshaft down the middle. The structure was covered with a kind of adobe made by mixing ash with mud and water. Once this covering had dried, a fire was set in the center shaft and the mouth sealed. Holes were opened at the base of the kiln so that the fire would have just enough air to cook the volatile elements out of the wood, leaving a carbonaceous mass behind. After a few weeks the kiln was torn down and voilà: charcoal for everyone in the family.

CHARCOAL LORE

Henry Ford was really into camping. The Ford archives are lined with photos of the godfather of the assembly line lined up with his cronies, all sitting around smoldering campfires in suits and morning coats and ascots and spats and things. (I'd love to spend more time camping but I just don't have the right cufflinks.) One is always struck by how puny the fire looks compared to the assemblage and their mansion-tents. Turns out that campfire starting and management was always an issue among the gents, who no doubt resented snagging their watch chains on kindling.

Now it just so happens that during this time Ford's company was manufacturing an automobile called the Model A, and it was a ragtop. When engaged, the fabric top was held in place by wooden staves. The factory that made these staves had a lot of leftover wood chips to get rid of. One of Henry's buddies started thinking about the chip problem and the campfire problem and in a true flash of genius conceived the charcoal briquette. The fellow's name was Kingsford. Up until the 1950s, you could only buy Kingsford charcoal (boxed not bagged) from Ford dealerships. To this day, Kingsford charcoal controls 50 percent of the country's charcoal market.

Grilling

When Brillat-Savarin made his famous remark "We can learn to cook but must be born to roast," he was actually talking about the process we know as grilling, the cooking of foods (especially meats) via the radiant energy and convection heat generated by glowing coals or an actual fire. B-Savarin was right inasmuch as grilling cannot be taught; it can, however, be learned through experience. In other words, the only way to learn to grill is to grill.

Many people do not want to hear this. They want a recipe to follow, which is why there are so many books about grilling published each year. The problem, of course, is that besides the usual considerations that go into the cooking of a given food, there are many other factors unique to grilling. Among them:

- The size, shape, and style of the grill
- The type of charcoal
- How much charcoal is involved
- How that charcoal is positioned in relation to the target food
- The outside temperature
- The outside humidity
- Available airflow

All of these factors are concerned with the management of heat. Many fine grill teachers have wrestled with this issue, and one prevailing method has emerged: It is to hold one's hand a certain distance from the fire and count how many seconds you can stand to hold it there.

This is a fine method for the experienced griller who has learned how to interpret the information his hand/sensor gathers, but for the novice it is a buggy system at best. (See illustrations, opposite.)

The other popular method is to use charcoal volume as a guide. You often see references to "a chimney starter's worth of charcoal" or "about a quart." This is not a bad point of reference if you're using something standard like briquettes, but for lump it's a little dicey. Besides, the volume system doesn't take arrangement and distribution into account, and that's probably the biggest factor in grilling.

The heat you feel when your hand is held 8 inches over a bed of coals includes not only the radiant heat but the convection heat being carried by rising air. This feels a great deal hotter than...

... holding your hand 8 inches from the coals on an angle. All radiant heat here. No convection.

And who can tell 8 inches that accurately? You'd have to use a ruler to get it exact and the ruler would probably either melt or catch fire.

Then there are those who are either lousy judges of distance, are impervious to pain, or, like Gary Busey in Lethal Weapon, just plain crazy.

MORE LORE

Until 1951 all grills were "table" grills. Since the food had to be cooked directly over the coals, the only way to control the heat was to move coals around by reaching though the grates and pushing them. Such devices were extremely limited in scope—not to mention incredibly unsafe due to their high centers of gravity.

Then, along came a genius. Like the rest of postwar America, George Stephen enjoyed backyard cooking. But George chaffed at the lack of control he had over the grills of the day. He lived in Illinois, where the wind would whip in from the prairie and blow out his fire.

George worked at the Weber Brothers Metal Works, a company known for its darned fine marine buoys. Legend has it that one day George was fastening the bottom to the top of a buoy when, like the monkey picking up the bone in *2001: A Space Odyssey*, the potential gradually dawned on him. He took home some scrapped parts and created the first kettle grill. Friends and coworkers were shocked and surprised by both the quality and consistency of his creation. George headed up the new barbecue division of Weber Brothers and things must have worked out, because in 1965 the company became Weber-Stephen and has been ever since. Today George occupies a rightful place next to Prometheus on the high throne of fire.

PRE-1951 GRILL

Bright red paint job can't camouflage medieval design. Charcoal goes in the bottom, food goes on the grate. Okay for cooking a thin steak but outside of that, not great.

POST 1951

Brave new grill. George Stephen's grill was the Volkswagen Beetle of the cooking world—it changed everything. The lid, spherical shape, and air vents made it possible to control heat levels by controlling air flow. Since heat could convect throughout the vessel, indirect heat grilling suddenly became possible. Lacking vision, the Nobel Committee failed to acknowledge Stephen.

piece of tail pipe from auto store

electric hairdryer

AB WEBER MODIFICATION V1.0

No one at Weber knows I've done this and I'm confident that if they knew they wouldn't like it. I removed the rotating cover plate from one of the bottom air vents and fitted it with a length of tail pipe and a hair dryer. Essentially, I've turned the grill into a blast furnace capable of generating enough heat to please the average blacksmith. I got the idea after seeing a chef in Italy cook steaks over a fireplace grate after whipping the fire into a frenzy with a hair dryer. Why does it work? Remember, combustion is really a chemical reaction in which the carbon in the charcoal (or any coals for that matter) has a thermal fling with air. More air, more combustion, more heat available for radiating to a target food. I'm contemplating a new version utilizing the motor out of an old vacuum. Oh and by the way, if you do this and burn the house down, you're on your own.

SMOKEY JOE TRASH CAN SMOKER (FUN FOR THE WHOLE FAMILY)

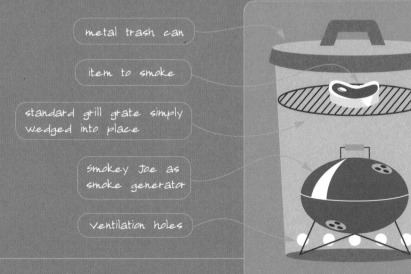

metal trash can

item to smoke

standard grill grate simply wedged into place

Smokey Joe as smoke generator

ventilation holes

MY GRILLS

First there's my hulking Bar-B-Chef, manufactured by Barbecues Galore, an Australian company. This very stout piece of ordnance has an actual coal elevator inside that allows you to crank the coal grate up and down in relation to the food, which sits on heavy, wide, cast-iron grates above. It's wonderful for direct-heat grilling and for rotisserie work. For all indirect cooking (what I call grill roasting), I have a 22 ½-inch-diameter Weber 1-Touch Gold (meaning it has an integrated ash catcher). It's bright orange and I love just about everything about it. Of course, I've made some modifications (see illustration, above) that I'm not sure the folks at Weber-Stephen would endorse, but hey, what they don't know won't hurt 'em, right? I've also got a couple of Smokey Joes, which look like the 1-Touch's spawn. They're great travel grills and capable of some lovely tricks of their own (see illustration, left).

CLEAN YOUR MACHINE WHERE IT COUNTS

It may look like a beat-up '74 Gremlin on the outside, but your grill grate had better be squeaky clean or food will absolutely, positively stick, especially high-protein items like meat. Not only will sticking badly damage the food, it removes those groovy (literally) grill marks. Now, I'm not a very neat person, but here's my plan: I never clean the grate after I use it; I clean it before I use it.

GRILL TOOLS

Essential

- fire extinguisher
- spring-loaded tongs (long)
- stem-style analog thermometer
- stable table or other work surface
- grill rag: a tied towel for rubbing down grill (see illustration, right)
- clean platter for retrieving cooked food
- for fish or burgers, a grill spatula
- pumice stone for heavy crud (and light rust) removal
- wire brush for general cleaning (the bristles need to be closely clustered and short; otherwise they'll simply wave to either side of the grate)
- spray bottle or squirt gun for putting out flare-ups
- digital timer

Awfully Nice But Not Essential

- grill light for night maneuvers
- metal skewers
- sauté basket (looks like a giant square metal ashtray with lots of holes drilled in it)
- portable hairdryer (for churning up the fire)
- ash bucket
- small metal trash can with lid for charcoal storage
- fire stick for lighting fires
- fireproof mat for underneath grills on decks or wooden structures

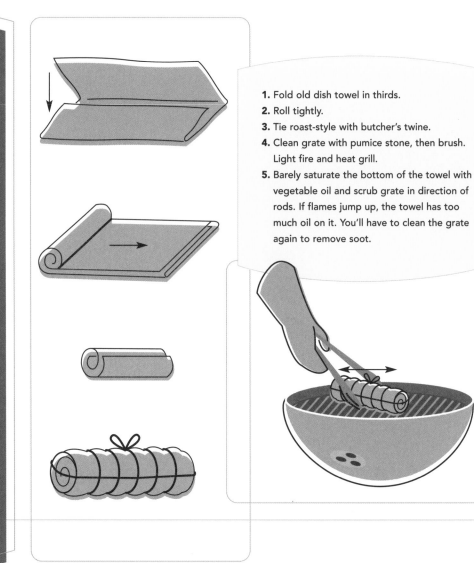

1. Fold old dish towel in thirds.
2. Roll tightly.
3. Tie roast-style with butcher's twine.
4. Clean grate with pumice stone, then brush. Light fire and heat grill.
5. Barely saturate the bottom of the towel with vegetable oil and scrub grate in direction of rods. If flames jump up, the towel has too much oil on it. You'll have to clean the grate again to remove soot.

HOW TO GRILL BY DIRECT HEAT

Despite its mystique, I wasn't quite ready to buy into the grilling as a snatch-the-pebble-from-my-hand Zen thing. I asked a bunch of cook friends what factor they thought most important in grilling, say, a perfect steak. All five of them said the same thing: heat control. Then I asked them how they knew they had it right. They all said: experience. Having recently seen the film *Memento*, I decided to give myself a problem: what if a person couldn't make memories and had no way to accumulate experience? Could he or she still grill a New York strip? Perhaps you could load the equation in this person's favor by identifying a set of controllable factors (time, mass, heat), then provide the tools for their control.

Time was the easy one, so a timer would definitely be part of the kit. I thought too of weighing the steak, but figured that in direct-heat cooking, what really matters is how far the heat is going to travel, so thickness matters more than any other single factor. So I bought a strip and cut myself nine 1½-inch thick steaks. Next, the big one: heat.

Many a grill aficionado judges the heat of the grill with a thermometer mounted in the dome of the grill cover. (Although the thermometer that Weber builds into the handle of their nicer kettle grills seems relatively accurate, I always back it up with another stem thermometer inserted in the top vent.)

That thermometer can only tell me what the cumulative air temperature is inside the dome. That's great info to have if I'm planning to grill-roast with the cover on. But if I'm planning to grill a couple of steaks, it's useless. For that I need intelligence from the front lines, so to speak. I need to know what's going on at the grate. And I'm not going to put my hand anywhere near it, thank you.

I figured that measuring out the charcoal was a good idea, even if it only got us into the ballpark, so I settled on a single chimney's worth (about one quart of lump charcoal). I fired it up, and once the coals were glowing, I dumped them onto the fire grate. Now what? I tried placing a coil-style oven thermometer right on the grate, but since it's designed to read air temperature, it got a little confused. Besides, I really needed to know not only the temperature of the radiant heat at grill level but the temperature of the grate itself.[10]

I was flummoxed. Standing there staring at the coals had warmed me up, so I went back to the Airstream to ponder the situation over an icy beverage.

Ice melts when its temperature rises above 32° F. That's a known factor, so one could say that ice is a good thermometer.

Since I knew that the thickness of the food mattered a heck of a lot more than its width or length, I decided to stretch my meat supply by cutting the steaks down to 4-by-4-inch squares that were 1½ inches thick. These I seasoned liberally with kosher salt and allowed to come up to room temperature.[11] I filled an ice bucket, grabbed a stopwatch, and divided my grill grates into four zones. My plan: select a cooking time and a desired doneness, then finesse the fire until it delivered my steak in that time and to that doneness. Then all I'd have to do is time how long that same fire took to melt a cube of ice and I'd have a measuring stick to steakhood.

I started the test by melting cubes in all four sectors. I used the standard cubes made in ice trays in some 90 percent of American household freezers, shaped like this:

The times were radically different, which I'd expected, given the fact that I hadn't really arranged the charcoal but let it fall where it may (see illustrations, opposite).

I laid a square steak on each sector of the cast-iron grill grate and hit the timer. I figured that 4 minutes per side was reasonable, so I left them for 2 minutes then rotated them 90 degrees and gave them another 2. At that point I turned over all four pieces (with

[10] Grate temp doesn't matter very much with a wire-style grate like those that come standard with Weber kettles. But I already knew that dense, heavy iron grates did a much better job of searing the meat, so I use an iron grate.
[11] I also took the opportunity to try another experiment at the same time. I had always thought that a thin sheen of oil on the meat was necessary for a good char and to ensure a stick-free grilling experience. But I was suspicious: If meat proteins brown so well, why not rely on them alone? By heavily salting the meat several minutes before cooking, water-soluble proteins had a chance to gather at the surface of the steak. As it turned out, they were all I needed to produce great color, nice grill marks, and no sticking. I won't be oiling my steaks anymore.

tongs of course) and let them cook again for 2 minutes, then rotated them for 2 minutes more. I removed them and let them rest for 5 minutes.

Both the steaks from the right side, those from zones A and B, with ice cube melt times of 24 and 35 seconds looked the best, and once sliced, the steaks were very close to perfect: the steak from zone A was on the medium-rare side of rare, and the steak from zone B was on the rare side of medium-rare. Both steaks were darned tasty. The steaks from the slower sectors were undercooked inside and out. I hypothesized from this that if an ice cube melted on the grate in 30 seconds, give or take a couple of seconds either way, you could produce a darned fine steak in 8 minutes, 4 on each

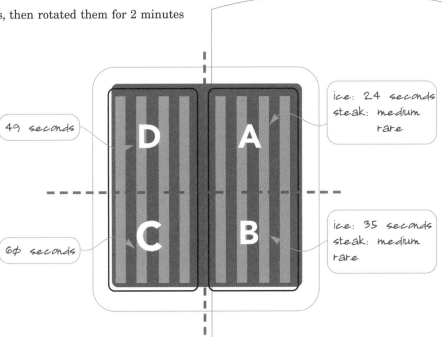

side with a twist after 2. Subsequent testings bore this out. At one point, the ice took over 50 seconds to melt so I stopped and added more charcoal; 15 minutes later we were back to 25 seconds and great steak.

Next I wanted to find out how much the grate material itself mattered, so I replaced the cast-iron grates with the standard-issue grate from my Weber and retested.

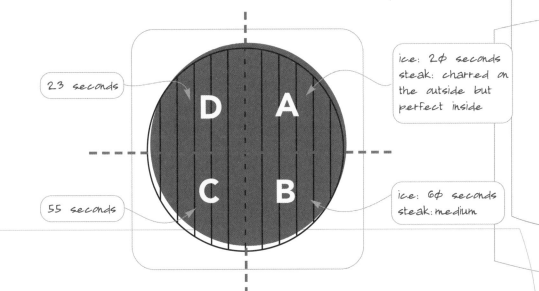

The melt times for the ice cubes were significantly longer—almost twice as long on the thin grate as for the same level of fire under the iron grates. That made sense. Conduction kicks butt when it comes to delivering heat, so the denser mass and greater surface area of the iron grates would deliver more heat to the ice quicker. To compensate for the lack of actual contact, I cranked the fire up physically and put on some more charcoal. Within another 15 minutes the fire was at its hottest.[12] I dropped my ice again and hit the timer.

Hoping to conserve steak, I decided not to split hairs and went with the zone with the highest contrast, zones A and B again. As soon as the meat hit, I knew I'd have to change plans, as the meat in the zone A started popping and blackening around the edges almost immediately. At the 1-minute mark I turned the steak, but held to the 2–2, 2–2 timing of the original test for the steak in zone B. After 2 minutes, I turned the steak in zone A, exposing a surface that I would have called just short of burned. I figured it was toast but went ahead and let it cook another minute, then turned it and let it cook a final minute. I let both steaks rest 5 minutes.

When I sliced the steak from zone A, it was beautiful. As terrible as it had looked sitting on the plate, once cut, it revealed a beautiful red, medium-rare interior that contrasted nicely with the charred edge. Flavor-wise, it was a great contrast of char bite and creamy meatiness. All the tasters proclaimed this as their favorite; the steak from zone B, at medium, came in second.

On a lark, I tossed on even more charcoal, then cut another steak crosswise into 1½-by-1½-by-4-inch rectangles. I mounted these on steel skewers, 2 per skewer, then salted them rather heavily and let them sit at room temp for 10 minutes. I grilled them on the near-nuclear fire for 1 minute on each side, slid them off the skewers while they were still hot, and rested them for 3 minutes. I sliced them into cubes (again: a great contrast between mahogany exterior and almost rare interior), sprinkled them with balsamic vinegar, ground on some pepper, and served.

---

[12] When a fully lit charcoal fire develops wisps of transparent flame, it's hot—really hot.

The tasters devoured these the fastest despite the fact that they had already gorged themselves on the earlier tests. Turns out that the added surface area allowed for more crust development. And that was a good thing.

SO WHAT WAS LEARNED?

Ice cubes can be used to gauge the heat at the grate level. Using widely spaced bars, arrange the charcoal so that a standard ice cube melts in 30 seconds; cook your meat for 2 minutes, then rotate 90 degrees and cook for another 2. Flip and repeat. Rest for 5 minutes, slice, and serve. If you like more char, consider the narrow bars and coals that will melt the ice in 20 seconds, then cook 1–1, 1–1. Or you can grab your own bucket of ice and figure out what you like. The next time you grill steaks for company they may chuckle when you start grilling ice, but with practice you'll be able to hit your desired doneness every time. Finally, all other things being equal, meat on widely spaced, dense grates will cook faster than on small, wiry grates.

Despite America's fascination with hunkin' hunks of meat, I no longer serve steaks in their whole state. And boy do I have reasons:

- Nine times out of ten, a 12- to 16-ounce steak is too darned much for one person. By slicing a grilled steak, you still get the illusion of "a lot" without plopping half a cow on your plate. Two people can suddenly feel full on what would normally feed one.

- Slices are easier to eat. By controlling the thickness of the slices, you prevent your guest from cutting off more than he or she can comfortably chew. The meat will also seem more tender, regardless of the temperature to which it was cooked.

- Don't be afraid to cut a steak before you cook it. The kabob experiment taught me that. Also, the 4-by-4-inch blocks used in the test were trimmed of most of their perimeter fat, and that prevented flare-ups.

HAMBURGER SUCCESS

There are six or seven ground meat options, not counting pork, lamb, and veal. Successful meat cookery depends on knowing the nature of the cut. Ground round and ground sirloin come from the round and sirloin primals, respectively. They're lean and, if cooked to recommended hamburger temperature, will be overcooked and dry. Chuck comes from the chuck primal. It has a bit of connective tissue and contains about 30 percent fat. When ground, chuck is exceptional for hamburger making. Hamburger or ground beef is made from leftover meat trimmings. That's likely to include filet and rib—good stuff. So when buying hamburger or ground beef, it's likely to be better than buying ground round.

- Keep seasonings to a minimum—a little kosher salt is all you need.
- Don't make mega-burgers, a 5-ounce patty works great.
- Make sure your grill is hot before adding the meat in order to get that great crust.
- Don't apply pressure to burgers when they're cooking. It only serves to push the juice out of the meat. Plus, using a spatula on the raw meat can lead to cross contamination.
- Flip burgers only once.
- For a burger that's medium-rare (130° F), cook 4 minutes per side. For a burger that's medium (150° F), cook 5 minutes per side. Anything beyond medium just ain't worth cooking.

HOW TO GRILL BY INDIRECT HEAT

On the surface, the use of indirect heat or grill-roasting would seem to be no more than an imitation of cooking in an oven. After all, we're talking hot air and an enclosed space—sounds like an oven to me. So why is it that grill-roasted foods taste so much better than anything that ever came out of an oven? Well, I'm here to tell you why: magic!

Okay, there's a little more to it, but we'll come back to magic later. Here are some unique characteristics of grill-roasting to consider:

- It's a truly dry method (as noted earlier, the burning of natural gas produces some water; electric coils do not).
- The heat source is mobile (so far, no one has come up with a home range or oven in which the heat source itself can be moved around).
- Smoke: Even if a great majority of the volatiles have been driven out of the charcoal there still are compounds being released. Add a few smoke-creating elements, and you're really onto something.

Indirect grilling is suitable for just about anything that will fit on the grates. No, you don't want to bake a pie here, but you should try a wide range of plant life from onions to bananas in the peel. Chiles are especially wonderful when their heat is tempered by smoke.

RED, WHITE, AND WHAT THEY CHEW

Somewhere along the line "red" meat got a bad reputation, while "white" meat was deemed healthful. But should we really judge an animal by the color of its flesh? What makes red meat red and white meat white? Grazing animals, like cattle, eat grass. Grass contains iron, which fuels myoglobin, which in turn tints red meat red. Non-grazing animals, such as pigs, don't eat grass; they primarily eat corn, and therefore their flesh is lighter in color.

Master Profile: Grilling

Heat type: dry

Mode of transmission: 100-percent radiation when food is below radiation source; 70:30 radiant to convection ratio when food is above radiation source; 50:50 radiant to convection ratio if food is above radiation source and cover is used

Rate of transmission: high

Common transmitters: Glowing coals, ceramic rocks, calrod, gas flame

Temperature range: medium to very high

Target food characteristics:

• Meats, fruits, vegetables, and doughs that profit from some degree of surface browning and/or smoke exposure

Non-culinary use: space heaters

WHAT YOU'LL NEED TO ADD TO THE GRILL FOR INDIRECT COOKING

• probe-style thermometer
• hinged cooking grate that allows coals to be added during cooking
• coffee can (for feeding in fresh charcoal)
• pocket timer
• various-size disposable aluminum pans to catch drips

Liz & Dick Rack of Lamb

Software:

Rack of lamb (2 pounds; I prefer
   domestic lamb)

Olive oil

Salt and freshly ground black pepper

6 red potatoes

Crushed rosemary sprigs

Hardware:

Cutting board

Heavy-duty aluminum foil

Chimney starter

Charcoal

Instant-read thermometer

Serving platter

Small cast-iron skillet

Elizabeth Taylor and Richard Burton were always on again/off again, so I call any dish that swings from direct to indirect heat "Liz & Dick." The goal is to develop a nicely charred crust and to cook the meat through without burning the outside. This method occupies the nether region between direct grilling and grill-roasting and could be applied to just about any food that has more mass than surface area.

Application: Grilling by direct and indirect heat

Hold the rack of lamb upright on a cutting board so that the ribs are straight up in the air. Cut in half by holding the center two ribs apart and slicing straight down between them. When you almost get to the board you'll have to shift your knife around the bone.

Lubricate the mini roasts with oil and season with salt and pepper. Fold a strip of heavy-duty aluminum foil around the exposed rib bones so that they won't burn.

Fill a chimney starter with charcoal and light. Arrange the coals on one side of the grill. (If you're working with a Weber kettle, open the bottom and top vents.) Let it burn for 5 minutes then execute an ice cube test directly over the fire. It should melt completely in 20 to 25 seconds.

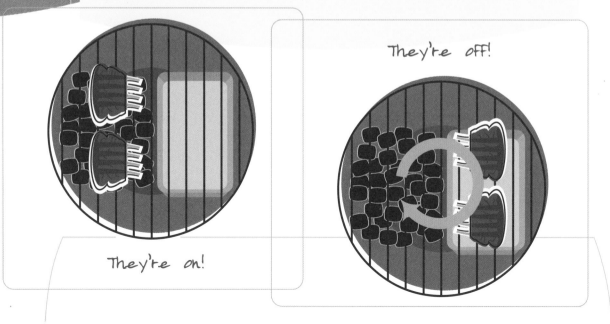

They're off!

They're on!

Place the lamb pieces on the grill, bone side up and pointing inward, and grill them for 5 minutes, or until brown. Flip bone side down and put the cover on the grill. Cook for 5 minutes, then lift the lid and rotate lamb off the heat. Replace the lid and cook for 8 minutes more or until the internal temperature reads 138° F on an instant-read thermometer. Transfer the lamb to a platter and allow the meat to rest.

By the way, there's a lot of room on that grill. So why not put something on the other side of the grate? Something that won't mind being directly over the heat while the lamb is off to the side. Say, a small iron skillet full of red potatoes, cut in half, tossed in oil, seasoned with salt, pepper, and crushed rosemary, and placed cut side down in the skillet. (Or you could make classic hobo packs by constructing a pouch from a triple layer of heavy aluminum foil and filling it with cubed root vegetables, herbs, and butter.) Go ahead, play: it would be a shame to waste all that good heat.

Yield: 2 servings

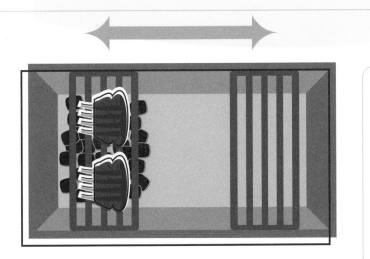

Over heat

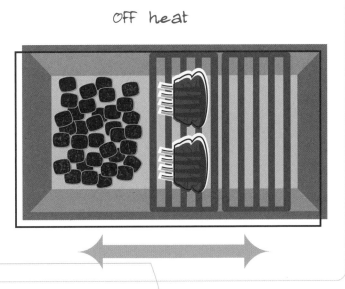

Off heat

Software:

1 side of farm-raised Atlantic
  salmon, cut from an 8- to 10-
  pound whole fish

2 to 3 tablespoons honey

3 tablespoons kosher salt

3 tablespoons sugar

Non-stick spray

2 tablespoons extra-virgin olive oil

Hardware:

Aluminum foil

Plastic wrap

Microwave-safe ramekin

Basting brush

3 sheet pans

Paper towels

Chimney starter

Charcoal

2 small disposable aluminum pans

One 16 x 36-inch piece of chicken wire

Wire cutters

Newspaper

Probe thermometer

2 wooden spoons or metal skewers

Serving platter

The Cure for Salmon

Application: Grilling by indirect heat

Crimp together 2 sheets of heavy-duty aluminum foil to form a sheet 1½ times longer and 3 to 4 times wider than the fish. Spread a single layer of plastic wrap over the foil. Pour the honey into the ramekin and microwave on high for 30 seconds or until it becomes thin. Brush the fish with the honey and set aside.

Combine the salt and the sugar. Spread ⅓ of this mixture down the center of the plastic wrap, roughly in the shape of the fish. Lay the fish on top and then spread the remainder of the mixture on top of the fish (see illustrations at far right). You should barely see the flesh through the rub. Finally, lightly wipe your hand from the fish tail to the head so the coverage will be lighter at the tail end than over the thicker meat of the flanks.

Pull the sides of the foil over the fish, then carefully crimp downward until you have a tight seal against the fish. Crimp the ends of the package in at least three turns. (Make the package as watertight as possible.)

Place the package on a sheet pan and cover with the second pan. Weight this down with a large, heavy book and place in the refrigerator. After 1 hour, turn the fish over, re-weight, and return to the refrigerator for 1 more hour.

Move the package to the sink and remove the fish from the package

To evacuate fish: run a wooden spoon or metal skewer through the fencing on either side of the fish. Repeat opposite end and lift.

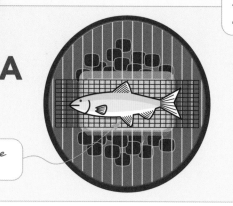

Place fish skin side down on the grill.

(be careful, there will be a lot of juice). Rinse the fish thoroughly to remove any remaining cure and dry the fish with paper towels.

Light a chimney starter full of lump charcoal. Line up two small disposable aluminum pans down the center of the coal grate. Distribute the lit charcoal evenly on either side of the pans. Divide another half chimney full of unlit charcoal between the two piles. Put the cooking grate on and then the lid. Let the cavity heat to 500° F.

Meanwhile, prepare the fish for the grill.

The most difficult thing about grilling a side of salmon is getting it off the grill in one piece once it's cooked. Good thing you went to the hardware store and bought about 16 inches of chicken wire that you cut down to the size of your grill top (see diagram A). Lay the chicken wire out on a few sheets of newspaper and coat it heavily with non-stick spray. Place the salmon, skin side down, on the chicken wire. Brush the fish liberally with extra-virgin olive oil. Insert the probe end of your thermometer into the thickest part of the fish, bring the corners of the wire together like a sling, and proudly carry your fish to the grill.

When the grill has reached a temperature of 500° F, carefully remove the lid and place the fish (chicken wire–side down) on the grate. Re-lid, being careful not to kink or crush the thermometer probe wire. Close the vents top and bottom, insert the probe wire connection into the thermometer base, then set the onboard alarm for 140° F. That's it.

When the alarm goes off, remove the lid, and use a pair of wooden spoons or metal skewers to pick up the chicken-wire sling (see diagram B).

Back in the kitchen, roll the fish off onto the back of a sheet pan. Place your serving platter upside down on top of the fish and then—holding the pan firmly in place—flip everything over. Now the fish should be right side up on the platter. (Be warned: there's going to be some juice and odds are good some of it's going to get on you.) Serve to a grateful and amazed assemblage.

Yield: 8 to 10 servings

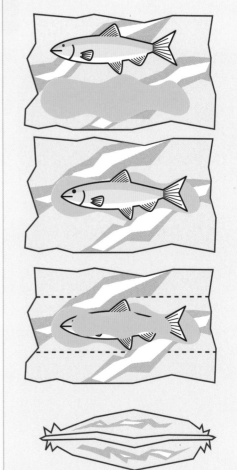

FISH CURE

Grilled Butterflied Chicken

This unusual method of grilling may produce the best-tasting chicken you've ever had. The spice rub may be altered to suit your individual taste.

Application: Grilling by direct heat

Prepare a medium-hot grill using about 3 quarts natural chunk charcoal.

Mix the salt and all the herb and spice ingredients together in a jar or other container with a perforated lid.

Wash the chicken, removing the giblets, and pat dry. Carefully remove the backbone from the chicken using poultry shears or a large boning knife. Remove the keel bone (or breast bone, if you prefer), and press the bird flat like a butterfly.

Liberally rub both sides of the chicken with canola oil, then sprinkle the spices to cover.

Place chicken, skin side down, directly over coals. Place a roasting pan flat on top of the chicken and weight it down with 2 bricks. Grill until brown and deeply marked, about 12 minutes. Turn the chicken over, re-weight, and allow to cook another 15 minutes or until chicken is just done. Let the chicken rest for at least 10 minutes, then bring to the table whole.

Yield: 2 to 4 servings

Note: This recipe makes enough rub for 2 whole chickens.

Software:

For the rub (see **Note**):

1 tablespoon kosher salt

2 teaspoons freshly ground black
   pepper

1 teaspoon whole cumin, toasted
   and ground

1 teaspoon whole coriander,
   toasted and ground

2 teaspoons garlic powder

¼ teaspoon cayenne pepper

1 teaspoon paprika

One whole broiler/fryer chicken

Canola oil

Hardware:

3 quarts natural charcoal

Glass jar or other lidded container

Poultry shears or a large boning
   knife

Roasting pan

2 bricks, wrapped with
   aluminum foil

Tropical Mash

This is my favorite grill-friendly side dish for jerk chicken, spicy pork roast, or any other spicy grill-worthy meat. Sure you have to crank up the fire an hour earlier, but it's worth it.

Application: Grilling by indirect heat

Just as you begin to fire up the grill, set the sweet potatoes on the grate, away from the heat. (You want to cook them indirectly or they'll be burned on the outside and raw in the middle.) Cook the potatoes for about 1 hour, turning them occasionally, until done; they should give to the pressure of your tongs. Cut a couple of small slits in the peel of the banana to allow steam to escape and grill it until the peel is black and the inside soft. In a small saucepan, heat the coconut milk and butter. Peel the skin from the potatoes and the banana and put them in a mixing bowl. Pour in some of the coconut milk mixture and mash with a potato masher, adding more liquid as needed. Season with salt and white pepper.

Yield: 4 servings

Software:

4 small sweet potatoes

1 banana

1 cup coconut milk

2 tablespoons butter

Kosher salt

Freshly ground white pepper

Hardware:

Tongs

Small saucepan

Mixing bowl

Potato masher

Grilled Romaine

Application: Grilling by direct heat

Heat up a charcoal grill. Quarter the romaine lengthwise so that the root keeps each piece together. Lightly coat with oil and season with salt and pepper. Mix together the capers, mustard, and vinegar. Lay the romaine on the grill, directly over the heat. Turn, with tongs, every few seconds until it begins to char and wilt (total grill time is about 1 minute). Remove to serving plates and spoon the vinegar mixture over each. Serve warm.

Yield: 4 servings

Software:

1 head romaine lettuce

Olive oil

Kosher salt and freshly ground
black pepper

1 tablespoon capers

1 tablespoon Dijon mustard

½ cup apple cider vinegar

Hardware:

Tongs

Mixing bowl

Broiling

In the United States, broiling is grilling inverted: fire up, food down. Broiling is hands-down my favorite cooking method. I broil asparagus, I broil just about every type of meat you can imagine. I broil shrimp. I've broiled marshmallows. I like this method because it gives you 75 percent of what you get from grilling. Since fat's not dripping down onto flame you don't have to fight flame-ups.   You also don't get some of the flavors that come from the gaseous portion of combustion—smoke for instance. You also don't get convection, so don't be surprised if broiling a piece of meat takes a little longer than grilling it. Then again, since broiling takes place in the oven, we have a lot less opportunity to pick at it, turn it prematurely and get in the way in general. Still it's way easier to broil asparagus than to grill it. (Gravity, you know.)

Marinated Flank Steak

Because of its shape and tissue structure, flank steak is, to my mind, the most marinatable hunk of beef there is. And the extra-virgin olive oil contains natural emulsifiers, which help pull the marinade into the meat.

Application: Broiling

Combine all ingredients except the steak in the bowl of a food processor and process until the onions are puréed. Pour into a large (1-gallon) zip-top freezer bag. Add the steak and carefully squeeze or suck as much of the air out as possible.

Place in a shallow tray (just in case the bag springs a leak) and refrigerate for 12 to 24 hours.

Remove the steak from the bag, pat it dry thoroughly, and let it come to room temperature. Preheat the broiler on High and place the rack and broiler pan so that the surface of the meat will be no less than 2 inches from the element or flame. Cook for 3 minutes per side for rare, 4 minutes per side for medium.

Let the steak rest on a resting rig for 5 minutes, then thinly slice it on an angle, the grain across.

Yield: 6 servings

Software:

1 cup chopped yellow onion

4 cloves minced garlic

⅓ cup white wine

¼ cup soy sauce

1 tablespoon honey

1 tablespoon extra-virgin olive oil

1 teaspoon Worcestershire sauce

½ teaspoon fresh minced ginger or ¼ teaspoon ground

¼ teaspoon freshly ground black pepper

1 flank steak (see Critter Map, page 240)

Hardware:

Food processor

Large zip-top freezer bag

Shallow tray or baking dish

Broiler pan

Resting rack

Broiled Chicken Salad

It's a good idea to occasionally leave home to cook in other people's kitchens. It's kind of like culinary Outward Bound: it forces you to focus, to improvise, to think. I recently found myself in just such a predicament.

I was working with an associate at her house one day when hunger struck. Take out didn't ring true so, fancying myself a cook, I headed into the kitchen to "whip something up."

First I surveyed the refrigerated edibles and found the following:

1 whole chicken
1 toy[13] box cherry and yellow pear tomatoes
scallions (they're in every refrigerator, including yours, right now)
1 bunch arugula (my friend often picks up farmstand items, which she then allows to rot in the refrigerator; luckily this bunch was perfect)
1 (6-ounce) package Montrachet cheese

Next I checked out the hardware and what I found frightened me badly. It was as if one aluminum pie tin had been melted down and cast into 15 different pots and pans, each of which had then been adorned with a rotting balsa-wood handle.

Despite the fact that it had been built in the mid-1950s, the oven still had its broiler pan. Rock-solid and gleaming clean, I had found my port in a storm.

Next I perused the pantry. Here's what I found:

A bottle of very nice garlic-flavored olive oil
A jar of mixed whole olives (black and green, in brine)
Half a loaf of good sourdough, stale, but not rocklike
An old but viable-looking bottle of champagne vinegar

And on the counter:

A peppermill

I heated the broiler. I found the biggest knife in the joint and butterflied the chicken by placing the bird spine down on a large cutting board, inserting the knife in the cavity and cutting straight down, first on one side of the spine then the other. Flipping the bird over I opened it up so that I could see the connective tissue over the keel (breast) bone. I made a shallow slit running from the junction of the wishbone down to the end of the breast, then folded the bird open so that the incision popped open revealing the bone beneath. This I levered out with my fingers on either side. The effect of all this is that I was left with a chicken as flat as a book with a broken binding. I moved the bird, breast up, to the broiling pan, lubed it with garlic oil, and seasoned it liberally with pepper and kosher salt (I always travel with a small supply).

The bird went under the broiler, second slot from the top.

[13] Industry word for the little plastic boxes that berries are often packaged in for sale in the produce department.

After washing every item the raw meat so much as even looked at, I pitted a couple handfuls of olives (lay them on the counter, apply palm pressure, pop), sliced the tomatoes in half (about 1½ cups total), and snipped 3 scallions to bits with a dull pair of scissors. All of which went into a bowl.

I checked on the chicken. Browning nicely but not burning—good.

Next I tore the bread into bite-sized chunks.

Once the chicken was about as brown as it could stand to be (15 minutes), I flipped it over and let it finish cooking inside-up (another 10 minutes). I removed the pan from the oven and flipped the bird breast up again so that any juices that had pooled under the skin would run out and into the bottom pan. I covered the bird with foil and left it to give up the goods.

Washed the arugula (always sandy, like spinach) and wrapped it in paper towels to dry.

Removed bird and grate from the pan, revealing the drippings below. Tossed the bread hunks in the drippings, then put the pan back under the broiler. Every couple of minutes I checked on the frying nuggets, turning them until golden brown and delicious.[14] Then they got tossed with a couple ounces of Montrachet, which the residual heat melted nicely.

While the broiler pan was still hot, I tossed in the olives, tomatoes, and scallions, seasoned the lot with salt and pepper, and sent it back under the broiler until the tomatoes started to take on a little color (10 minutes tops).

Meanwhile, I cut the chicken into 8 pieces: 2 legs, 2 thighs, 2 split breast halves.

I removed the pan from the oven and dumped the arugula (3 cups, I'd say) right on top. Tossed this with tongs (if she hadn't had those I'd have been in trouble) until the arugula barely started to wilt. Cooled it down with a few splashes of the vinegar, then tossed in the cheesy croutons. Plated the salad and served with the chicken chunks on top.

Mighty tasty indeed. And I'd never have done it at home.

---

[14] These nuggets were indeed broiling but since the chicken fat was acting as the heat conduit, the end product was more fried than anything else.

Get Breakfast

I learned to love broiling in college, when I lived in an apartment with an oven that wouldn't do anything else. Here is a breakfast I developed there (and please cut me a little slack, will you? I was in college and worked at a pizza place).

Application: Broiling

Remove hash browns from freezer to a sink full of water to thaw. Go back to bed. Get up half an hour later and drain the potatoes. (I didn't have a salad spinner back then so I wrapped them in paper towels to dry.)

Turn on the broiler and heat the skillet. (Since I used to keep the skillet under the broiler, this was a no-brainer. Also, the oven only had one shelf and it was stuck in the slot next to the top. No wonder I broiled a lot.)

In a mixing bowl, beat 2 of the eggs. Add the hash browns along with the spinach. Toss with plenty of kosher salt.

Using fireproof gloves, retrieve the hot skillet, coat it with oil, and spoon in the potato mixture. Pack it down into the corners and spoon the salsa on top. Slide the skillet back under the broiler, and cook for 12 to 15 minutes or until the tomatoes just start to brown.

Retrieve the skillet, sprinkle with a handful of cheese, and crack the remaining 4 eggs on top. Sprinkle with more salt and drizzle with some oil. Place the pan back under the broiler and remove it as soon as the egg whites set, about 4 to 5 minutes.

Place in middle of kitchen table. Shake on the chile flakes, hand a fork to whoever's there, eat and wash it down with the flat beer. (You can leave this step out, but that's the way it happened.)

Yield: 4 servings

Software:

1 pound 12 ounce package frozen Ore-Ida hash browns

6 eggs

½ (14-ounce) box frozen spinach, thawed

Kosher salt

Olive oil (stolen from pizza place)

Salsa (leftovers)

½ cup shredded mozzarella cheese (okay, I stole that, too)

Chile flakes (ditto)

½ bottle flat beer

Hardware:

10- to 12-inch cast-iron skillet

Mixing bowl

Fireproof gloves

Tres Amigos

This is a very cool dish, not only because it tastes good, but because it scares the heck out of people. On the plate, it looks like it was very difficult to make, which—of course—it's not.

Application: Broiling

Lay the fish on a cutting board and very carefully slice down the length of the filets into 8 thin strips of salmon and 8 strips of halibut. Preheat the broiler. Season the fish and scallops with salt and pepper. Lay one strip of salmon on the board and overlap it with halibut about halfway down. Beginning at the top of the salmon strip, wrap the scallop with the fish strips, forming a bi-colored "rose" of fish with a scallop in the center. Using tongs, gently place the wrapped scallops on a broiler pan and top each with a slice of the compound butter. Cook 4 inches below the broiler for 7 minutes. The fish will be perfectly cooked through and the scallop will be just underdone (which is perfect for this type of seafood).

Yield: 8 appetizer portions

Software:

½ pound salmon filet

½ pound halibut filet

8 sea scallops (21- to 25-per-pound is a great size for this recipe, but you can go with U-10s if you like really big scallops; see Shrimp Smarts, page 69)

Kosher salt and freshly ground black pepper

Herbed Compound Butter (page 211)

Hardware:

Sharp thin knife (such as a filet knife or slicer)

Broiler pan

Tongs

Chicksicles

Software:

1 tablespoon coriander seeds

2 teaspoons cumin seeds

½ teaspoon curry powder

¼ teaspoon cinnamon

1 teaspoon salt

2 teaspoons sugar

½ cup peanuts (or more to taste)

2 tablespoons sesame oil

2 tablespoons neutral vegetable oil

2 pounds chicken breast, cut into
    1-inch cubes or ½-inch slices

Hardware:

Heavy-bottom skillet

Mortar wth pestle or coffee grinder

Small bowl

Food processor

Metal or bamboo skewers (see **Note**)

Broiler and broiler pan or gas or
    charcoal grill

Kebob makers tend to squeeze their food-on-a-stick piece too tightly together. This does nothing but slow the cooking process. It's okay for these pieces to touch, but just barely.

Application: Broiling or Grilling

Place coriander and cumin in a heavy dry skillet and toast, tossing occasionally, over high heat. When the seeds just start to smoke, remove from the heat and pour onto a plate to cool. Then grind in a mortar with a pestle or an electric coffee grinder. Combine the cumin and coriander with other spices and sugar in a small bowl.

Chop the peanuts in a food processor until they're the size of small crumbs. Add the spices to the processor. While pulsing, add the oils and process to form a paste.

Rub the paste on the chicken pieces. Cover and refrigerate overnight.

Thread the chicken pieces onto skewers.

Heat the broiler and move the rack into position so that the chicken will be within 4 inches of the burner. Or fire up a grill or hibachi. Lay the skewers directly over the heat and cook, turning often until paste is dark and chicken cooked through.

Yield: 4 to 8 kebobs, depending on the size of the skewers

Note: Metal skewers are best because, unlike bamboo, they don't have the nasty habit of catching on fire. That said, bamboo brings a certain authenticity to the party. So, to prevent forest fires, you can do one of two things:

- Hit the hibachi. Most hibachi-style grills have grates that stand above the side of the grill. This makes it possible for the meat to lay flat on the grate while the skewers stick straight out to the side.
- Soak the skewers. This is a fine idea as long as you're going to cook right away, but if you plan on skewering and refrigerating, odds are good the woodworks will again be flammable by the time bird meets burner.

Scampi V1.0

Application: Broiling

Heat the broiler and position the rack to about 5 inches below the heat source. Arrange the shrimp in the broiler pan so there is no overlapping. Drizzle the oil and scatter the garlic over the shrimp and season with salt, pepper, and Old Bay. Put the pan under the broiler for 2 minutes, until the shrimp begin to turn pink. Sir in the lemon juice, add the panko and parsley, and toss to coat the shrimp evenly. Return to the broiler and cook until the bread crumbs are evenly brown. Serve immediately.

(Alternatively, sauté the shrimp in the oil and garlic and, when they are almost finished, season with salt, pepper, and Old Bay and deglaze the pan with the lemon juice and toss in the panko and parsley. Cook just until the shrimp are done. In my experience, this is the way you'll find the dish prepared in most restaurants, but broiling is the classic method and gives a much better flavor and texture.)

Yield: 2 entrée servings or 4 appetizer servings

Software:

1 pound peeled and deveined large shrimp

2 tablespoons olive oil

1 tablespoon minced garlic

Kosher salt

Freshly ground black pepper

Old Bay seasoning

4 tablespoons freshly squeezed lemon juice

¼ cup panko (Japanese bread crumbs)

2 tablespoons chopped parsley

Hardware:

Broiler pan

Shallow glass baking dish or an ovenproof sauté pan

SHRIMP SMARTS

When shopping for shrimp, focus on numbers, not labels. Shrimp are sized and sorted into count weights. The higher the number, the smaller the shrimp: 50/60 means 50 to 60 tails per pound. The largest shrimp have a "U" before the number, signifying that there are fewer than that number per pound: U/12 means that there are 12 or fewer shrimp per pound. Though they serve as rough guidelines, labels like "jumbo" or "medium" aren't very telling, as they're not standardized.

If dry cooking methods were the Beatles, roasting would be George Harrison. Quiet, but effective.

CHAPTER 3   Roasting

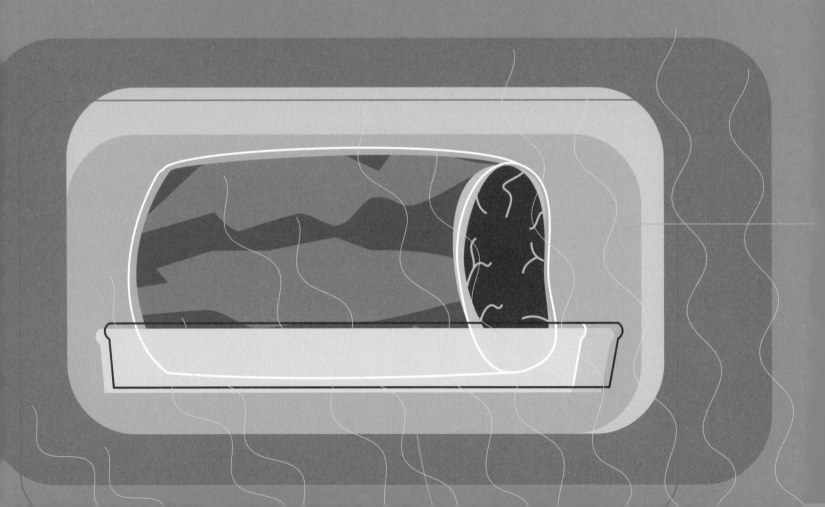

Roast Story

Had Pavlov gone to a few wedding receptions or hung out at a brunch buffet or two he might not have had to up measure spaniel spit. His theories regarding conditioning could easily have proven themselves at the carving station. I've worked the carving station and I don't care if it's a steamship round, a loin roast, a standing rib roast, or a charred buffalo head, flash some golden crust and a little rosy pink flesh and the culinary tractor beam engages. It's like a bug zapper for humans. I believe this auto-response has as much to do with ancient associations as it does flavor. Think about it: when do we roast turkeys? When do we roast standing ribs? What's at the end of the line at the wedding reception? That's right: roast beast. Where there is roast, there is a gathering. Done right, there is also a lot of satisfaction—not to mention enough leftovers for lots of lovely sandwiches.

So why don't we do the "Sunday" roasts anymore? Why are the grills of America stocked with burgers and chicken parts only? Why do our ovens echo with emptiness? Remember the previously quoted Brillat-Savarin remark, "We can learn to be cooks, but we must be born knowing how to roast." When he wrote this in the early years of the nineteenth century, roasting was still a medieval procedure involving iron spits and fiery pits (see Grilling, page 38). And in those days a cook who overcooked a "joint" of meat might be beaten with the charred appendage. (I had one thrown at me once, but that's a story for another time.)

Despite the advent of the modern oven, roasting remains a mystery to most. This may be due to the fact that modern cookery is about recipes, and you just can't learn roasting from a recipe any more than you can learn the tango from those cutout footprints they stick on the floor down at the Fred and Ginger Dance Academy.

For instance, a recipe can tell you to heat your oven to 350° F, to slather ingredients x, y, and z on a 4-pound beef eye round roast, and to cook it for 1½ hours. But what if your roast is a 5-pounder? What if the recipe was formulated in a Bob's oven and you own a Joe's oven? What if you don't have 1½ hours? What if all you can find is a pork loin roast? Are you out of luck? No, because B-Savarin was wrong. You can and should teach yourself to roast. It may take some time and attention, and you might even overcook a roast or two, but in the end you will be one of the few, the proud—the roasters.

By the way, the terms "roasting" and "baking" refer to the same method. The difference is the target food. If said food is a batter, or dough, or pastry, you're baking. If it's anything else, you're roasting. The only dish I know of that steps out of line is ham. You always hear about "baked" ham, never "roasted" ham. And yet you'd never say "baked" turkey any more than you'd say "roasted" brownies. Strange, isn't it?

THE SHAPE OF THINGS TO ROAST

Before the days of inexpensive, accurate digital thermometers, roasters relied on voodooesque charts that calculated cooking times based on the temperature of the vessel and the gross weight of the target food. This equation has stranded many a cook over the years because weight doesn't matter nearly as much as shape.

Master Profile: Roasting

Heat type: dry

Mode of transmission: 50:45:5 percent ratio of radiation to convection to conduction

Rate of transmission: very slow

Common transmitters: Air (convection), oven or container walls (radiation), container (conduction)

Temperature range: from your lowest oven setting to your highest oven setting

Target food characteristics:

- relatively tender cuts of meat including those from the loin and sirloin
- all poultry
- root vegetables and starch vegetables (potatoes)
- eggs
- a wide range of fruits including tomatoes and apples

Non-culinary application: curing pottery

AN ACCURATE OVEN TEMPERATURE

To tell the temperature of your oven, a coil style oven thermometer works best. The principle behind these bimetallic strip thermometers is based on the fact that different metals expand at different rates as they are heated. In this case, a coil sensor, made of two different types of metal bonded together, is connected to a pointer on a dial face. The two metals expand at different rates but because they are bonded together, work in unison to dictate the coil's change in length as the temperature changes. This in turn causes the pointer on the dial to rotate to indicate the temperature. I like this style for the oven because they're fairly accurate at oven temperatures and are easy to read through even dingy door glass.

SANDWICH-MAKING TIPS

- A good way to make a sandwich sturdy, besides toasting the bread is to use a layer of spreadable fat like butter or mayo to provide moisture, flavor, and a waterproof shield that prevents the bread from getting soggy.
- A good way to cut a sandwich made on a long baguette is to wrap the finished sandwich in parchment paper, place clean rubber bands every 5 inches, then cut.

A

B

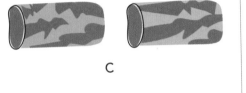

C

D

Case in point: pork tenderloin. If weight and oven temperature are the deciding factors, then *a*, *b*, and *c* should in fact be done at the same time, right?

Put these roasts in order from the first to be finished to the last.

The right answer is *c–a–b*, but what's interesting is that *a* and *c* are very close to one another in total cooking time. What's even more interesting is that even if you cooked only one piece of *c*, *a* still wouldn't be far behind. That's because the primary shape, not weight, is the deciding factor. Sure, one piece of *c* will cook quicker because its surface-to-mass ratio is a little higher than that of *a*, but the overall distance from the outside to the center is the same.

Despite an identical weight, *b* will take nearly twice as long to cook as *a* or *c* because its shape is different: its thickness has been doubled, so heat has to travel roughly twice as far into it.

Given that both pieces of *c* will cook a little faster than *a*, it stands to reason that cylindrical pieces of meat could be broken into several pieces to decrease cooking time. And since more surface area means more crust, you might consider breaking traditional roast shapes into single servings when appropriate (*d*). This might not work with a steamship round or even a prime rib, but various parts of the round, chuck, and loin do nicely (see Critter Map, page 240).

The greater the surface-to-mass ratio, the quicker the cooking. In other words, something the shape of your arm is going to cook faster than something the shape of your head.

HOW MUCH HEAT?

Roasting is a bit like deep-frying in that it's about even heating. The difference is that hot fat delivers heat via highly efficient conduction, while roasting depends on radiant heat and convection, both of which are relatively inefficient modes of heat transfer. That means that roasting is a relatively slow process, which is why it's better suited to large, dense items that require longer to cook through than thinner cuts.

Tortoiselike though it may generally be, there's still fast roasting and slow roasting. And which one you decide to use depends on the target food and your taste. Consider the

Roast Cutaways

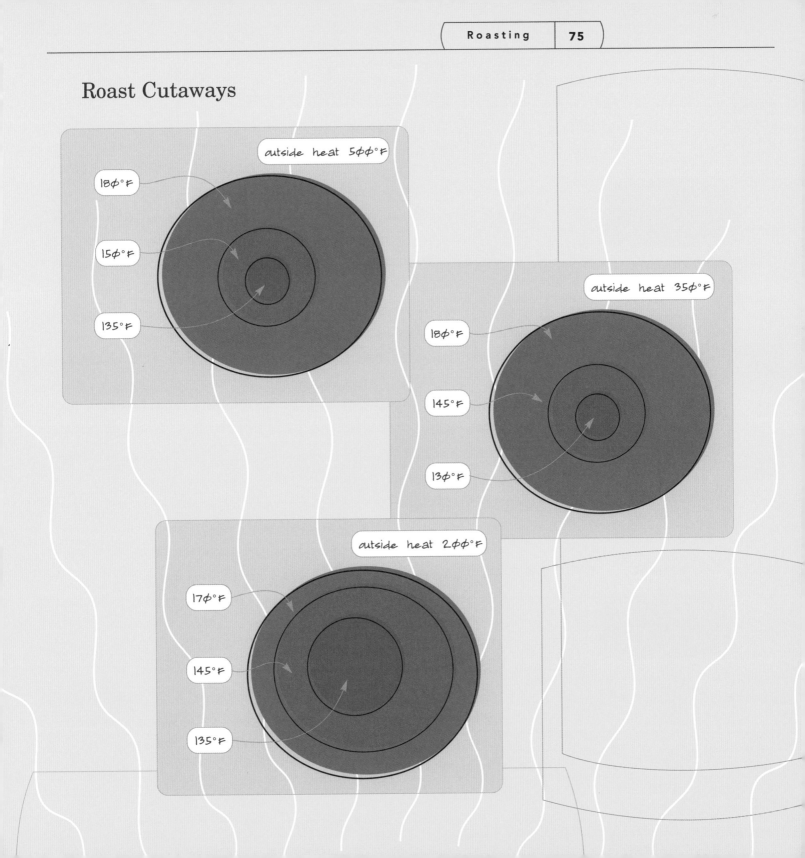

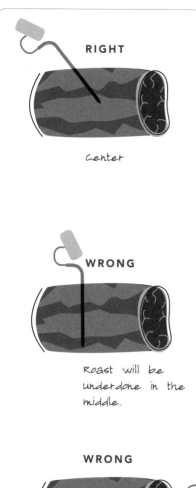

RIGHT

Center

WRONG

Roast will be underdone in the middle.

WRONG

Flat angle lets juice escape.

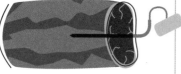

300° F is the minimum temp recommended by the USDA. I still stand by 200° for culinary reasons, but read Cleanliness is Next to... before you do.

cross section of your average hunk of beef—say, an eye of round roast—cooked in a 500° F oven (see illustrations, previous page). Like the growth rings of a tree, the roast shows us its thermal history. The outer crust, exposed for the longest time to the high heat has seared to a dark-brown and flavorful crust. As for the interior, we were hoping for medium-rare, and yet a great majority of the meat is well above that temperature; only the inner core is where we wanted it. We're understandably disappointed. To heck with this roasting business, we say.

But think about the heat for a minute. Cooking anything is a matter of bringing two environments into equilibrium with each other, right? And those outer layers of the meat are going to reach this equilibrium quicker than the inner portions, right? So if we want the majority of the inner mass to reach a certain temperature (medium-rare), we need to work with a lower temperature to begin with. If the oven temp is 200° F the roast will take longer to cook, but a higher percentage of the meat will be done to our liking. But if, like me, you're in it for the caramelized crust, this method will leave you cold. Oh sure, there will be some crustiness, but nothing to set you raging. To heck with this roasting business.

But wait: you can have your crust and pink meat too. Simply expose the roast to different temperatures at different stages of the cooking process. Here are two potential strategies for roasting beef and lamb.

Start the roast in a 500° F oven, and once a crust has formed, drop the temperature to 200° F and cook until done. This is a variation on the method most often seen in cookbooks. The instructions usually begin with "sear meat on all sides over high heat." As far as I'm concerned that's an added step that neither the cook nor the to-be-cooked needs. If the oven's hot enough, the sear will happen on its own. The only problem here is that meats that meet high heat right from the get-go tend to lose more moisture than those that heated up slowly, which leads us to:

Start the roast in a 200° F oven, and once the interior hits 10° below your target temperature, remove and cover lightly with foil. Crank the heat up, and when the oven reaches 500° F place the roast back in the oven and cook until a golden brown, delicious crust has formed.

Roasts don't care about time. They're not trying to catch a train. So forget the clock and use your thermometer. Traditional meat thermometers are hard to read, and their spikelike probes are better suited to pitching tents. Get yourself a digital thermometer with a probe that attaches with a length of wire. Stick this into the roast (see illustration, opposite) and set the thermometer's alarm to go off at the target temperature. No mysteries, no weight/time calculations.

MY SEARCH FOR A PERFECT PLACE TO ROAST

Let me get something off my chest: you can't roast in a grill. You can cook a roast (noun) in a grill via indirect heat, but I still don't consider it roasting because roasting requires even heat from all directions, which no grill can do. The real problem is that most home ovens can't do it either.

Figure **A** is your average home oven. The heat is generated from a gas burner array safely hidden under a metal plate in the floor of the oven. You turn the oven on and set the thermostat and this burner fires. The metal in the floor heats, creating convection currents

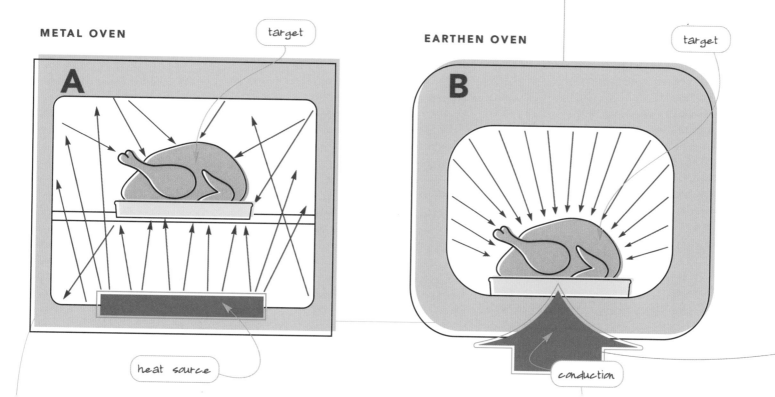

METAL OVEN

A

target

heat source

EARTHEN OVEN

B

target

conduction

ROASTING: THE SHORT FORM

1. **Bring target food (meat or otherwise) to room temperature before cooking. (See page 30.)**

2. **If the target is a beef roast, consider dry-aging it for a couple of days in the bottom of your refrigerator.**

3. **Lightly oil the meat. How light is light? Enough to make the entire surface of the meat glisten but not enough to leave a puddle on the plate.**

4. **Season the meat. Kosher salt and freshly ground pepper are all the seasoning you need. Most folks go too easy on them. Don't be shy.**

5. **Choose the right meat: broiler/fryer chickens and smaller, tender cuts of beef, pork, and lamb.**

6. **Roast at different temperatures. Either start low and finish high or, in the case of pork and chicken, vice versa.**

7. **If possible, build an oven (with firebricks or flower pots). The even heat will reward you.**

8. **Buy big: small roast—no leftovers; big roast—lots of leftovers (see Sandwich Making Tips, page 73).**

9. **When purchasing beef look for "choice" grades. The marbling in these cuts will help to keep them lubricated throughout cooking.**

10. **If you plan to make a *jus*, sauce, or gravy, consider doing your roasting on a bed of vegetables (carrots, onions, herbs, potatoes, and so on).**

in the air that rise and fall through the cavity. Then there's radiant energy, which rises up from the floor and bounces around like zillions of ricocheting bullets. (In electric ovens, a coil inside the cavity heats air and walls via radiant—both visible and infrared—energy.) If we place a piece of food in the oven, some of the careening waves will indeed strike and penetrate that food. These random hits, along with the convection air currents, are what roast it.

When a thermostat in the oven senses that the air in the cavity has reached the desired temperature, the burner turns off. When the thermostat senses a drop in temperature, it reignites the burner. How much of a drop is necessary to prompt the firing depends on the manufacturer.

All of this is fine and good, except for the fact that it's almost impossible to get all this heat into the food evenly. Some ovens are better at it than others, but I've never seen a metal oven that roasts as well as a pile of dirt (be it in the form of clay, ceramic tile, or what have you).

Earthen ovens have made a big comeback in the last twenty years. Restaurants are building them into their kitchens and home enthusiasts are erecting them in their backyards. I, for one, am happy about this de-evolution of culinary technology because several of the best meals I've ever eaten (or cooked, for that matter) have come out of such ovens. Why?

Consider figure **A** in comparison to figure **B** (previous page). **A** is your oven (and mine). **B** is an earthen oven. Oven **A** may be easy to use, easy to heat, clean and so forth, but under normal usage it cannot generate heat beyond 500° F, nor can its walls *conduct* and store heat; rather, they reflect it, which is not the same thing. The earthen oven can be cranked well beyond the 500s, and once heated it will radiate that heat evenly, which is why foods roasted in such ovens look and taste so darned good.

Let's say that you have no intention whatsoever of building a clay or adobe oven in your backyard. You can get the same effect by building another oven either inside your existing oven or inside your grill.

Few residential ovens heat beyond 500° F unless they're in self-clean mode, in which case temperatures of up to 800° F are not uncommon. Take firebricks and build a box in the oven just big enough to hold the smallest metal roasting or baking pan that can possibly hold the target food. Turn the oven to its self-clean mode. Wait one hour, then turn the oven off. Although I haven't been able to find a single manufacturer to condone the practice, it's my oven so I do it anyway.[15]

Place the thermometer probe into the room-temperature roast, then load the roast into the brick box. Close up with bricks and let the roasting begin. Do not turn the oven back on. What we're counting on here is thermal decay: the roast is going to sear quickly but as the bricks cool down the heat pushing into the meat will slow so that you get the benefits of bilevel cooking without having to pay any attention to oven temperature whatsoever.

The cool thing about using the grill instead of the oven is that once the bricks are hot you can take them out and quickly assemble yourself an oven right there in the carport. Then you can use the grill for other things.

Arrange a stack of fireplace bricks (available from your local home supply store) on the floor of your oven in such a way that it forms a box just big enough to hold a 9-inch square baking pan (see illustration, upper right). Like a cast-iron skillet, these bricks are dense and can absorb a great deal of heat, then dole it out. In fact, if properly charged, the bricks will function like thermal capacitors. Light a chimney starter's worth of charcoal and when the coals are good and hot (gray ash over all and lots of little dancing flames) dump them into the box and lid with bricks. The bricks will take an hour to charge, during which time you can prep the target food.

Sometimes in summer I heat my bricks in my large grill to 700° F or so, then, using fireproof gloves, assemble them in an oven shape right in my carport and bake bread in it. I've generally found that on a hot summer's day the bricks will remain hot enough to cook as many as three pizzas.

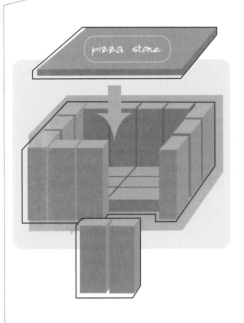

pizza stone

[15] The only problem I've encountered is that my oven (like most) has an automatic door lock that won't let me in while the oven's in this mode even if I turn the oven off. So since my oven's usually a mess anyway, I add the bricks and run the shortest clean cycle possible, three hours. When the lock disengages, the bricks are still as hot as a space shuttle belly during reentry.

A WORD ABOUT MOMENTUM

Find yourself a Lincoln Continental from the mid-1960s. Get on an empty stretch of road and get that bad boy up to say 70 or 80 miles per hour. Now stop as fast as you can without losing control. Takes time, doesn't it? That's because that big hunk of auto has a lot of mass, and mass + motion = inertia. Well, a roast in the oven has inertia too. Pull an 8-pound rump roast out of a 500° F oven at the moment it hits your final desired temperature, and it's all over. That Lincoln is going to cruise right past 135° to 140°, 150°, maybe 155° before stopping. If you go with a method in which you cook at a lower temperature, then boost the heat for a quick sear, you won't have as much momentum so you'll be able to pull the roast out of the oven maybe 10° from your final destination. If you choose to cook at a low temperature, then leave the roast out and let it rest while the oven's reaching searing temperature, this way you'll have even less momentum to deal with. No matter what you do, though, there's always going to be what I call "thermal coasting" and the more mass you're dealing with, the more coasting there's going to be. Then, of course, there's the resting.

THE SPUTNIK PARADIGM

When contemplating whether or not to roast a piece of meat, look at the shape. Does it remind you of: a. log; b. doormat; or c. Sputnik?

Okay, any of the above can be roasted, but should they be?

Because of its uniform surface shape and consistent surface-to-mass ratio, the log could be turned on a rotisserie over a grill, or simply rolled across the grill grate. If it's a tender piece of meat it could be cut into medallions and grilled, broiled, or seared. Still, it's a fine roast shape.

The doormat presents all of its surface area in two opposing planes, a physical fact that makes me think sear, grill, or broil—not roast. Flank steaks and flounder filets are rarely roasted.

Sputniks include any food whose shape is irregular and has a low surface-to-mass ratio compared to the log or the doormat. A chicken is a Sputnik, so is a sweet potato or a pork butt (which is actually a shoulder). These foods scream "roast" for no other reason than you can't really get a thermal grip on them any other way unless you drop them in a deep fryer, which isn't a bad idea except that most of us don't have Fry-o-laters built into our counter-tops (hey, we can't all be Emeril).

FOR THE BIRDS

As much as I dig the even heat of the stack-o'-bricks oven, I came to realize that even a freak like me doesn't want to stack bricks every time a chicken crosses the kitchen. And if I didn't mind the masonry, there was still the preheat time to be reckoned with: more than an hour depending on the available firepower.

What I needed was brick oven "lite," an easy-to-handle vessel that would absorb and evenly distribute heat to the bird. Clearly, it was time for a visit to the gardener's supply store.

I landed a 10-inch-wide heavy-duty Italian terra-cotta pot with a flared mouth; when inverted it looked like an earthen cloche. I also picked up a saucer of the same make, large enough so that the mouth of the pot fit neatly inside it. I put these into a cold oven and cranked the heat to full throttle: 550° F. I figured that oven and pot would both be at full heat within 20 minutes.[16] I removed a broiler/fryer chicken (2½ to 3½ pounds) from the fridge and countered it on a clean plate.[17]

When I knew the oven and the pot within had reached their thermal potential, I

rubbed the chicken down with a bit of canola oil and sprinkled it with lots of kosher salt and freshly ground black pepper.[18] I very carefully placed the dressed chicken onto the very hot saucer and covered it with the equally hot pot. I chucked this back in the oven and, assuming that there was enough heat stored in the terra-cotta to do the job, turned the oven off and left everything alone for 45 minutes. (See illustration.)

When I removed my inner oven, it was still two-towel hot, but when I stuck a toweled finger into the drain hole (how convenient) and withdrew the dome I found myself facing a fragrant and deliciously done yet pallid piece of poultry. Hmm. Obviously a kilo of terra-cotta wouldn't hold as much heat as ten kilos of firebricks. The next time, I left the oven at 550° F for the first 20 minutes of cooking, then killed it until my probe thermometer (I ran the probe wire through the drain hole) chimed 170° F. Perfect. Brown and crusty all over, juicy and flavorful inside. Decidedly superior to a standard oven-roasted bird.

You're in an airplane that's just landed. The flight's over, and yet there's that voice on the PA telling you that the FAA requires that you remain in your seat with your seat belt fastened until the aircraft has come to a complete stop at the gate. You may be on the ground, but technically the flight is not over. Same thing with a roast. Just because it's out of the oven doesn't mean that the cooking's over—it isn't. The roast has to coast to its final temperature. Besides, you cut into that hunk now, and juice is going to fly everywhere. Resting gives the heat and pressure inside the meat time to subside, and that allows the juices locked inside to be absorbed back into the meat tissues. So unless your roast has spent half an hour on the counter in heavy-duty foil, leave your seat belt on. (If you like your meats well done, you don't really need to rest them. The muscle fibers are toast and can't possibly hold any moisture at all. It's ruined.)

[16] I don't quite trust my oven, so when it beeps at me to say that it's heated, I always give it at least 5 minutes more.
[17] Yes, holding chicken in the zone can promote bacterial growth, but if you cook the chicken properly you'll nuke every one of the little nasties. This doesn't mean it's okay to leave raw meat lying around the house, but it does mean you can take the time to do what's right for the food, as long as you keep it isolated from any work surfaces and/or other raw or cooked foods.
[18] Whenever I work with poultry, I keep a latex glove on one hand for handling the bird and a clean hand free for messing with salt and the like.

Software:

For the brine:

1½ cups kosher salt

½ cup dark brown sugar

One 6-ounce container of frozen
orange juice concentrate

1 gallon water

One 16- to 18-pound turkey

1 gallon of ice cubes

Canola oil

Hardware:

1 large pot

1 large cooler with lid

Paper towels

Roasting rack

2 disposable aluminum roasting pans

Heavy-duty aluminum foil

Probe thermometer

TURKEY RULES

Stuffing is evil. Traditional stuffings soak up meat juices, meaning a potential for the presence of salmonella unless the temperature of the stuffing reaches 165° F. That increases the cooking time of the turkey, which means dry meat. If you cannot live without stuffing, cook it in a casserole dish then spoon it into the cavity prior to serving. (If you want the exposed portion of stuffing to have that "roasted" look, hit it with a blowtorch.)

Basting is evil. Skin is waterproof, so flavor and moisture will not soak through it. Besides, you have to open the door to baste, which lets heat out of the oven. That increases the cooking time of the turkey, which means dry meat—so don't do it.

Roast Turkey

Why start with a higher temperature? Poultry skin turns brown because it sautés in the thin layer of fat beneath it. If you start the bird at a low temperature, a lot of this fat will simply melt and run away. Starting with high heat gives you a deep brown bird, while the lower finish delivers moist, evenly cooked meat.

Application: Roasting

To brine the turkey: dissolve the salt, sugar, and juice concentrate in 1 quart of hot water. Cool the solution with 3 quarts of cold water. Remove the giblets (and any other foreign matter) from the turkey interior and place in the cooler. Pour in the brine mixture to cover. If the bird is not completely submerged, add more liquid. (Since I don't want to weaken the solution, I use canned chicken broth.)

Cover with ice, close the lid, and soak the turkey for 6 to 8 hours. (Exact soak times will vary per your taste. Start with 6 hours and make changes to subsequent birds.)

When the bird has ½ hour left to soak, move the oven rack to the lowest level and preheat the oven to 500° F.

Remove the turkey from the brine and pat dry with paper towels. Rub the turkey liberally with canola oil. (Be sure to get all the nooks and crannies around the wings.) Discard the brine and thoroughly wash the cooler.

Place the turkey on a roasting rack inside 2 disposable aluminum roasting pans.

Roast at 500° F for ½ hour. Remove the bird from the oven and reduce the oven temperature to 350° F.

Cover the turkey breast with a double layer of heavy-duty aluminum foil folded into a triangle. Insert a probe thermometer into the thickest part of the breast (push it right through the foil) and set the thermometer to 161° F. A 16- to 18-pound bird should arrive at the target temperature in 2 to 2½ hours.

Remove the turkey from the oven, cover the bird and the pan loosely with aluminum foil, and allow to rest for 15 minutes before carving.

Yield: 10 to 12 servings

Dry-Aged Standing Rib Roast

Application: Roasting

To dry-age the roast: Place a refrigerator thermometer at the back of the bottom shelf of your refrigerator. Reduce the temperature to just below 38° F. Cover the bottom of a roasting pan with several layers of paper towels. Place the roast, bone side down, on the towels, and store—uncovered—at the back of the bottom shelf of your refrigerator. Allow the meat to age for 3 to 5 days, checking the refrigerator temperature often.

When you're ready to roast, let the meat sit out of the refrigerator for 1 hour until it reaches room temperature.

Preheat the oven to 250° F for ½ hour. If you're planing to roast in an unglazed terra-cotta vessel, place it in the oven while it's still cold and heat at 250° F for 45 minutes to 1 hour.

Rub the roast with just enough canola oil to make it shine, then rub with the salt and pepper. Place the meat in a shallow roasting pan, bone side down (to prevent the meat from sitting in liquid). Insert the probe of your thermometer into the center of the roast and set for 118° F. Place the roast in the oven and reduce the temperature to 200° F.

When the meat has reached 118° F (about 4 hours), remove the roast and cover lightly with foil. Raise the oven temperature to 500° F. When the oven reaches 500° F, let it heat for another 15 minutes, then return the roast to the oven until the desired degree of crust is achieved, about 10 to 15 minutes. Transfer the roast to a cutting board and cover with foil until ready to serve.

Place the roasting pan with its accumulated juices on the cook-top over medium heat and deglaze the pan with 1 cup of water. Allow the liquid to come to a boil, scraping occasionally until any bits stuck to the pan are freed. Add the wine and then transfer the liquid to a gravy separator. Allow five minutes for separation of fat from juice and then pour the liquid (but not the fat) back into the pan. Add the leek and return to a simmer. Stir in the garlic butter and serve over lovely, red slabs of goodness.

Yield: 10 servings

Software:

One 4-bone-in standing rib roast, preferably from the loin end (for its higher meat-to-bone ratio)

Canola oil

2 tablespoons kosher salt

1 tablespoon coarsely ground black pepper

1 cup water

1 cup red wine

¼ cup thinly sliced leek

1 to 2 tablespoons garlic butter or unsalted butter

Hardware:

Refrigerator thermometer

Roasting pan or unglazed terra-cotta vessel with lid

Paper towels

Probe thermometer

Heavy-duty aluminum foil

Gravy separator

A Perfect Baked Potato

This application provides a crisp crust and a tender interior. If you feel the need for speed, you can start the potato in the microwave. Let it cook on high for 9 to 12 minutes, but then finish it in the oven.

Application: Roasting

Preheat oven to 350° F.

Wash the potato with a vegetable brush and dry with paper towels. With the fork, poke holes all over the potato surface. This will allow steam inside the potato to release as it heats, which will result in a great fluffy texture. Pour a small amount of canola oil into a bowl, add the potato and turn until the entire surface is lightly coated with the oil. This not only makes for a slightly crunchy skin, because the oil can get so much hotter than the water inside the potato, it will regulate the moisture. Sprinkle the potato skin with the kosher salt.

Place the potato directly on the rack in the center of the oven. A medium-size russet should be fully cooked in about 1 hour. To check for doneness, give the potato a squeeze (wearing fireproof gloves). If the skin feels kind of crunchy but the meat inside is soft, it's time to eat.

Yield: 1 perfect baked potato

Software:

1 medium-size high-starch potato
  (russet or Idaho)

Canola oil

Kosher salt

Hardware:

Vegetable brush

Paper towels

Fork

Small bowl

Fireproof gloves

Meatloaf

There are a million ways to make meatloaf (another roasted dish that we call "baked"), and I'm not about to say that this is the only way. You can play around with the seasonings all day, you can even trade off some chuck for round. However, I do strongly suggest that you pick out a nice roast at your market, take it to the meat counter, and ask the butcher to grind it for you.

Application: Roasting

Preheat oven to 350° F.

In a large mixing bowl, beat the eggs together. Using your hands, combine the rest of the ingredients and blend together. Now is the time to taste your food so you can adjust the seasonings if necessary. So, heat up a small pan and make a tiny patty of the mixture and cook it. If it tastes good, put the uncooked meat mixture into a 9 x 5-inch loaf pan and bake on a rack over a sheet pan. (If the cooked patty doesn't taste good, adjust the seasonings, cook, and taste again). Cook for 1 hour and 15 minutes. Once out of the oven allow the meatloaf to rest in the pan on a rack for an additional 10 to 15 minutes. Remove the meatloaf from the pan and discard the rendered fat. Think about your mom, slice and serve.

Yield: 1 to 8 servings, depending on how hungry you are

Note: I always sweat the onions before adding them to a mixture such as this—the taste will be sweeter. To sweat onion (or any aromatic vegetable), heat a small amount of fat (oil or butter) in a small sauté pan. Add the diced onion and stir to coat with the oil, cover, and cook slowly over low heat until transparent but not browned.

Software:

2 large eggs

2 pounds ground beef chuck

1½ cups diced onion

1 tablespoon minced garlic

2 slices white sandwich bread, diced

3 tablespoons ketchup

½ teaspoon paprika

3 tablespoons red wine vinegar

1 tablespoon Worcestershire sauce

1½ teaspoons kosher salt

½ teaspoon freshly ground black pepper

2 tablespoons chopped parsley

Hardware:

Large mixing bowl

Small sauté pan

Loaf pan

Rack

Sheet pan

Roasted Beet and Broccoli Slaw

Software:

2 large yellow beets (red beets are
     fine, but the whole slaw will be
     a deep red)

2 stems from broccoli, peeled (eat
     the florets some other time)

¼ cup olive oil

3 tablespoons apple cider vinegar

1 teaspoon sugar

Kosher salt

Freshly ground white pepper

½ cup red onions, sliced thinly

Hardware:

Aluminum foil

Paring knife

Box grater

Mixing bowl

Roasting has the uncanny ability to highlight complex flavors that are often washed away by wet cooking methods. The intense flavor of the beets in this slaw is always a surprise and delight.

Application: Roasting

Preheat the oven to 425° F. Wrap the beets in aluminum foil and roast for about 1½ hours, until they are tender but still firm when pierced with a paring knife. When the beets are cool enough to handle, peel with a paring knife and shred through the large holes of a box grater. Shred the broccoli stems. In a mixing bowl, stir together the oil, vinegar, and sugar. Season the vinaigrette with salt and white pepper. Add the beets, broccoli stems, and onions and toss with the vinaigrette; place in the refrigerator to marinate for at least 1 hour, or preferably overnight.

Yield: 4 side servings

Slow-Roast Tomatoes

Roasting doesn't have to be performed at high temperatures. In fact you're only limited by how low your oven will go.

Ever wondered what to do with a bounty of summer tomatoes? These homemade "sun-dried" tomatoes beat anything you could buy. Try them warm right out of the oven on toasted country bread with basil and extra extra-virgin olive oil. Add them to salads, soups, risotto, pizza or yes—spaghetti sauce. Bagged and tagged, they'll keep a month in the refrigerator, or you can freeze them for a century or two.

Application: Roasting

Preheat the oven to 170° F (or the lowest temperature setting on your oven).

Place tomato halves closely together, cut side up, on 2 half sheet pans. Drizzle the tomatoes with the oil, and then sprinkle the sugar over the tops, followed by the herb mixture, and finish with the salt and pepper.

Roast in the oven for a minimum of 10 hours. (Start right after dinner and leave the tomatoes in the oven overnight. When your alarm clock goes off the next morning, you'll think you're in Provence.)

Yield: 40 tomatoes

Software:

20 ripe tomatoes, halved crosswise

½ cup extra-virgin olive oil

3 tablespoons sugar

2 tablespoons mixed fresh herbs
including thyme, rosemary, and
sage, minced

1 tablespoon kosher salt

1 tablespoon freshly ground black
pepper (a coarse grind is best)

Hardware:

2 half sheet pans with racks if
possible. (I haven't been able
to find racks that I like for my
half sheet pans so I bought
a heavy-duty full sheet pan
model at my favorite restaurant supply shop and cut the
thing in half with a hack saw.)

Americans adore fried foods and yet we're willing to entrust the process to tenth graders wearing polyester smocks and funny hats...strange.

CHAPTER 4   Frying

I Fry

YOU: *What the heck's so great about frying?*

ME: *Remember the mean Terminator in* Terminator 2?

YOU: *The guy that was made out of that liquid metal stuff?*

ME: *Imagine having a pan made out of that stuff. That's what frying's like.*

YOU: *How's that?*

ME: *Because you fry in fat, and fat's dry.*

YOU: *But it's a liquid.*

ME: *Just because it's a liquid doesn't mean it's wet. Mercury's a liquid.*

YOU: *Well, it doesn't matter. Fried food's greasy.*

ME: *Not if you do it right.*

Fat is one of the three substances that act as both ingredient and cooking medium, and yet it brings something to the party that neither of the others can. Sure water can add flavor to simmered foods (especially to foods that must be hydrated, such as pasta and rice) and air can also carry flavor in the form of that wondrous vapor, smoke. But in both of these instances additives are required. Frying adds flavor simply through the interaction of the fat with the target food.

Fact: American home cooks have turned their backs on frying. They say that it's unhealthy—that it will make them fat and plug their hearts and give them cancer and God knows what else.

Fact: American per capita consumption of frozen potato products is thirty pounds a year, almost all in the form of fast-food fries. This of course doesn't include all those orders of fried calamari—and hush puppies and fried fish planks down at Admiral D's. Obviously, something's going on here.

In practical terms, here's how my fry world breaks down.

Pan-Frying uses enough oil to come one-third to halfway up the side of the food. Unlike sautéing, the food is not moved around during cooking. Unlike deep-frying, the food is not immersed in the cooking medium. Pan-frying is most commonly the first step of a hybrid cooking method, and is followed by pan-braising. In this method the food is dredged, fried in very little fat until a crust forms, then liquid is added and the pan is covered. The food finishes cooking via stewing, and the flour that hasn't already gelled into a crust becomes available for thickening the liquid into a sauce.

Immersion-Frying (a.k.a. Deep-Fat Frying): food is completely immersed in the medium. Unless the food is very high in both water content and starch content (such as potatoes or sweet potatoes), the food needs to be protected from the intense heat and turbulence by either a batter or dredge.

Sautéing: in sautéing, there is barely enough oil to cover the bottom of a wide, shallow, heavy and hot pan. The target foods are ideally small and uniformly cut. (A sauté is often erroneously called a stir-fry, which is actually performed at even higher temperatures and is not included here because most of us can't consistently produce that much heat at home.)

Pan- and Immersion-Frying

What makes pan-frying different from immersion-frying? For one thing the food is touching the pan bottom as well as the fat. This provides for darker browning and thus a more intense flavor. Also, the food is not immersed; that is, one half of the food is always exposed to the air. This is especially important when the food first enters the pan and the top side is raw. Unlike with foods that are immersed, heat is pushing into pan-fried food from one side only. (See illustration, above.)

Pan-fry: oil comes ⅓ to ½ up side of food. Food still has contact with bottom of pan.

Immersion-frying is like a siege. The hot oil surrounds the food and looks for ways in. The water at the surface of the food defends its home by turning to vapor and pushing out in all directions (why most foods seem to boil furiously at the beginning of the process), which is a good reason not to over-fill the vessel.

As the water vapor exits the food, it is replaced by moisture moving up from the food's interior. The same thing happens to the moisture in a baking potato, which explains why the center of a properly cooked french fry tastes pretty much like a baked potato.

Fried food cooks so fast that it's actually tough to determine whether it does so via conduction or internal steam; at the very least it's a combination of the two. (See illustrations on the following pages.)

SECRETS TO MAKING GREAT FRIES

1. Start with high-starch potatoes (like russets) for fries that are crunchy on the outside and fluffy on the inside.

2. Cut potatoes in uniform pieces with a V-slicer for even cooking.

3. Soak cut potatoes in water to get rid of the excess starch on their surface. This will prevent the fries from turning dark and enable the moisture to escape via steam so that the fries aren't gummy.

4. Fry twice. This is essential for great fries. During the first fry (at a lower temperature of 300°), fries will go floppy and turn pale gold. During the second fry (at a higher temperature of 350°), they'll crisp and darken a little. Result: crispy golden outside and tender inside.

5. Now you've got great fries, but you're not done yet. Fried foods have to drain properly or they'll become greasy. Don't use paper towels or brown paper bags; they'll just hold the grease right up against the food. Use a draining rig instead (see illustration, page 117).

6. Last but not least, season fries while they're hot. Why? Because salt and pepper will stick to the thin film of hot oil that remains on the surface. If you wait too long, this oil will either drip off or soak in and your seasoning will have nothing to hold on to.

Anatomy of a French Fry

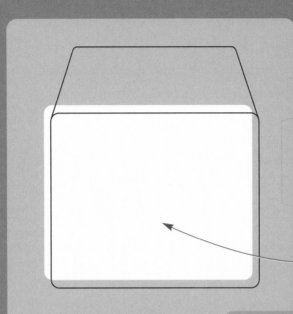

Cross section of a freshly cut shoestring fry. It is smooth and almost waxy. The relatively high moisture content is homogenized throughout.

Once the fry hits hot oil, the internal temperature rises very quickly forcing the moisture inside the potato to turn to vapor. The expanding gas has to find a way out, so it digs its way out creating a vast network of micro tunnels. As long as the pressure of exiting vapor exceeds that of the intruding oil, the oil will not be able to penetrate the narrow tunnels and will simply crisp the now-textured surface of the fry, producing a delicious crust. The inner fry however will remain, high, dry, and fluffy—but especially dry.

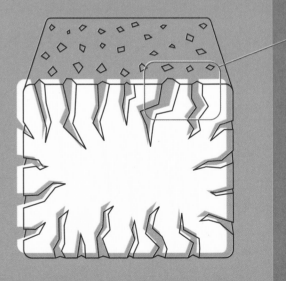

oil droplet   air bubble

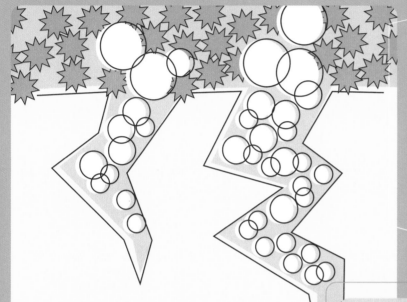

THE SIEGE

Hot oil conducts heat to the surface of the food. Water held within the food cells heats very quickly, converting to vapor. In order to exit, these micro-bubbles carve escape tunnels through the food. As long as the oil supplies enough heat (325–350° is ideal) and the moisture inside the food is sufficient to produce plenty of bubbles, the outside gets crispy (as well as the opening of the crevices) while the inside cooks without becoming greasy (it does in fact steam).

THE SIEGE LOST

Once there's no longer enough moisture to fuel bubble production, the invading oil moves in. Your food will now be greasy and, if the heat remains high enough, burned.

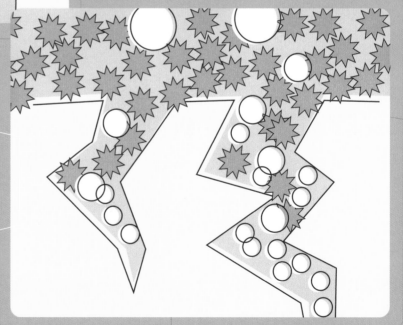

Why New Fat Doesn't Brown Well

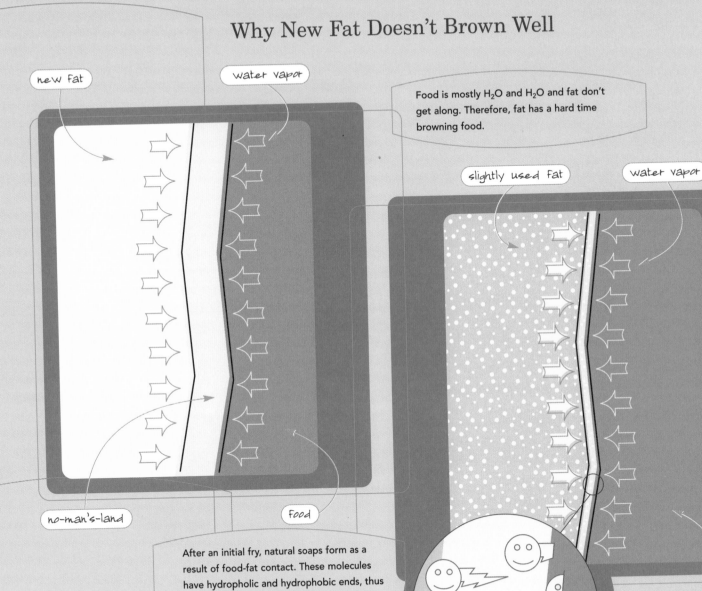

new fat

water vapor

Food is mostly H₂O and H₂O and fat don't get along. Therefore, fat has a hard time browning food.

slightly used fat

water vapor

no-man's-land

food

After an initial fry, natural soaps form as a result of food-fat contact. These molecules have hydropholic and hydrophobic ends, thus forming bonding points where fat and H₂O can come into closer contact. This is why experienced fry cooks always keep a little of the old fat when changing the oil in fryers.

food

Making Oil Last

Fine mesh strainer

4-fold cheesecloth

metal canning funnel

dark green wine bottle

rubber band shows proper re-fill level

A lot of respected cooking authorities will tell you that you should use oil once, then toss it. Fine, but where? You can't pour it in that ditch behind the house, and pouring it down the drain would do a lot of damage to your pipes. The EPA suggests saving it, along with bacon drippings and the like, in a resealable can which you can tape up and throw away when it gets full. Great: so every time I deep fry I've got to find a quart can, and seal it, and store it like so much toxic waste. If I followed this line I would never fry again. Luckily, most great fry cooks agree that oil can be reused several times, as long as it's cleaned and stored properly and cut with new oil each time it's used.

After I deep-fry, I let the oil cool down to a manageable temperature then filter it through the oil rig pictured here. A strainer catches the big pieces, while the cheesecloth between the strainer and the funnel works as a fine filter (If the oil is still warm, a cone-shaped coffee filter can be used.) I use a clean green wine bottle because, like red wine, oil doesn't like light. The tall, narrow shape of the wine bottle helps keep most of the oil away from the other thing it doesn't like: air. After the filtering, I add new oil up to a line, marked by a heavy rubber band, which tells me I've got enough to reach the "fill" line on the fryer. I cork the bottle tightly and store it away from the light. This doesn't mean I never get rid of the oil—it won't last forever—but if I start out with peanut or safflower oil, I find I get five or six sessions out of it, depending of course on the target food.

When it is time to ditch, I've still got a challenge because I don't generally have many coffee cans around. I do have some pretty stout freezer bags, though, which I hold on to after they seem to have picked up a few too many fragrances for my liking. So, I put the bag inside an empty paint can, fill it up, seal it (here comes the nerdy part), and use my cigar lighter to barely melt the edge, thus sealing it forever. I then seal this in yet another bag and after that the dog doesn't even try to get into it—you could drop it on the sidewalk and nothing would happen.

Why is frying in 350° F oil so fast and furious compared to cooking in a 500° F oven? Remember, from my rambling diatribe on conduction, that temperature is only one piece of the heat equation, just as voltage is only one part of an electrical equation.

Consider:
- Joe weighs more than some cattle and pummels people for a living.
- Clive weighs less than a heavy wind and punches a keyboard for a living, or at least he used to.
- Based solely on this information one might determine that Joe has more potential to do damage to you if he were to hit you.

But there are other factors to consider:
- Joe has been hit in the head many, many times. He is easily distracted by things like puppies, which he likes to pet. In other words, his ability to deliver on all that physical potential is limited.
- Clive, on the other hand, has years of rage stored in his wiry frame. He just got laid off, blames the world for his persistent acne, and is carrying a piece of lead pipe.
- Joe is a 500° F oven. Clive is 350° F oil.

FIRE!

The majority of home fires start—you guessed it—in the kitchen. Prevention, of course, is the best medicine, so keep recipe books, dishtowels, and the like away from heat sources, and be prepared if you do see flames. Don't automatically think bucket brigade. A grease fire needs to be starved of air; dousing it with water will make it worse. Small fires can be smothered using the lid to a pot or a couple of handfuls of baking soda. If that fails, reach for your trusty fire extinguisher. Yes, you should have a fire extinguisher nearby. There are three classes of fire extinguishers. Class A are for standard combustibles, paper, fabric, and wood, but should never be used on burning liquids or electrical fires. Class B are for flammable liquids, while class C don't conduct electricity and are the choice for "live" electrical fires. Every kitchen should have a BC-class or ABC-class extinguisher.

Joe vs. Clive

500° OVEN VS. 350° OIL
Which of these individuals would you rather be hit by

Clive, 130 lbs., Tanked up on black coffee, mad about being laid off from dot.com job, hiding what appears to be a lead pipe behind his back, and has a chip on his shoulder. Personal hero: Bernard Goetz

Joe, 320 lbs., ex-center for the Rams. Multiple injuries to shoulder and elbow, currently sleepy from beer consumption. Personal hero: Captain Kangaroo

BREADING, DREDGES, AND BATTERS, OH MY

Fried foods are unique in that they usually have some kind of starchy coating. This coat, which Brillat-Savarin referred to as the "surprise," can be as simple as a dusting of flour or as complex as a multilayered breading.

The purposes of such a coating are to:

• Create a great tasting crust that intensifies and highlights the flavor of the food.

• Protect the food from the thermal maelstrom of the hot oil.

How does the crust happen? Once the food hits the oil, the escaping moisture gets together with the oil and the starch to create a kind of gel, which hardens as it cooks.

Standard breading usually consists of:

• all-purpose flour

• beaten egg (or egg white)

• "crumb" coat (could be anything from bread crumbs to crushed corn flakes)

To really shine, the crumb layer needs to make very firm contact with the food and at least a little contact with the bottom of the pan. This accomplishes two things: it holds the breading on, and it creates spots of deeper browning where crumbs actually touch the bottom of the pan.

Target foods must be in thin slabs—tofu slices, eggplant slices, tomato slices, and meats like pork chops. Odd man out: fried chicken. The flour serves as a primer coat because egg doesn't like to stick to wet stuff. Cornstarch can also be used, but I find that flour works better with the egg. Don't try whole wheat flour by the way, you will be disappointed.

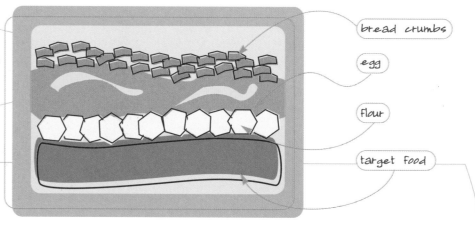

A successful standard breading. A very thin layer of starch acts as a primer for the egg layer, which then cements on the crumb layer. Ready to cook after a 30-minute rest.

bread crumbs

egg

flour

target food

Finally, wherever there are eggs there is potential complexity. Here we're talking a protein glue (which holds the outer crumb layer on), a browning agent (proteins), and a sealant (once set in the oil, the egg protein forms a pretty darned tight envelope). The fat in the egg attracts fat, making it possible for the cooking oil to get into the breading, which can be dangerous because if you let the fat temperature drop below 325° F the breading will go greasy.

The crumbs provide texture and insulation, further protecting the target food.

Some possible crumb layers include:

- homemade bread crumbs
- mixture of bread and cake crumbs
- panko bread crumbs (coarse Japanese bread crumbs shaped like little shards), my favorite for fried shrimp
- crushed cereal (corn flakes are especially nice, although I have a friend who uses Cap'n Crunch from time to time)
- coarsely crushed Ritz crackers: my personal favorite. I've been known to cut their buttery, salty goodness with gingersnaps.
- potato chips (salt and vinegar–flavored . . . yum)

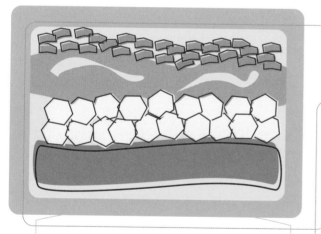

The number one reason breadings fail (fall off) is too much primer coat (flour). There is nothing to hold the layers together so they unzip from each other and your breading is floating free in the fryer, which is bad all around because all that particulate matter will only speed the degradation of the oil.

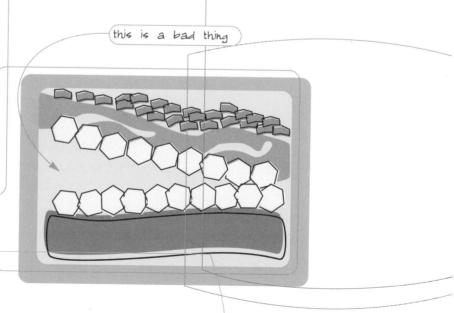

this is a bad thing

BREADING AND PAN-FRYING: THE BASIC STEPS

Manufacturing a standard breading requires that each piece of food move through a breading assembly line. If that sounds too structured for you, consider the consequences: a big mess, a hand that looks like something the Elephant Man might sport, and food that's darned spotty lookin'.

Note: Great fryers work with a wet hand and a dry hand; that is, one hand for the flour and crumbs and one hand for the egg. Once you start layering egg, flour, and crumbs on your hand, you will be a victim of club hand and your life will be miserable.

1. Set up a breading assembly line (see Stations of the Dredge, below). Season food with salt and pepper.
2. Dredge in flour (seasoned but not salted).
3. Shake off all excess (very, very important).
4. Coat in eggs that have been beaten together with 2 teaspoons water for every egg used.
5. Coat with crumbs.
6. Let rest for 20 to 30 minutes so that the egg has time to set. You'll be glad you

> try to wash it off in hot water and it'll be even worse because the outside layer of flour will gelatinize.

Stations of the Dredge

SALT & PEPPER   **FLOUR OR CORNSTARCH**   **EGGS & WATER**

Station 1: Season the dry food with salt and pepper if desired.

Station 2: Dry food is thoroughly dredged in flour or another starch. All excess is shaken off.

Station 3: Both sides of dredged foods are dipped in egg mixture. Again, all excess is allowed to run off before moving to the next station.

did. The coated food can be wrapped, frozen, and stored for up to a month (since flavor-absorbing fat is involved, airtight wrapping is required; I generally freeze everything on a flat tray then portion it into freezer bags).

7. Fry in fat no deeper than half the height of food.

Immersion-Frying: Dunk 'n' Dredge

This is my personal favorite breading method because it requires no mixing or measuring and generates a really great crust.

Target foods: seafood such as calamari and bay scallops. Also darned good on portobello mushrooms that have been cut into strips. This breading doesn't provide much in the way of insulation, so whatever food you choose needs to be relatively small and relatively moist. Squid is perfect, baby carrots not so perfect.

1. Dip seasoned food into buttermilk (low-fat but not skim).

2. Dredge in cornstarch (sifted if you have time).

3. Fry.

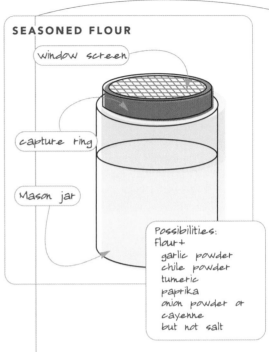

SEASONED FLOUR

window screen

capture ring

Mason jar

Possibilities:
Flour +
garlic powder
chile powder
tumeric
paprika
onion powder or
cayenne
but not salt

BREAD CRUMBS

Station 4: Make sure the bottom of the dish is covered with crumbs, and lay the food in. Rather than flipping the food, try gathering up enough crumbs to cover the top then press down so that the crumbs adhere completely top and bottom.

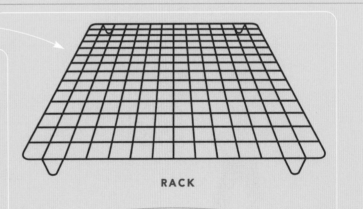

RACK

Station 5: Rest the food 20 to 30 minutes before introducing it to the fryer.

Why Hot Oil and Water Don't Mix

Oil and water don't mix—especially when the oil is hot and on top of your stove. When water meets with hot oil, it immediately (not to mention violently) vaporizes, aerosolizing a good bit of the already angry oil with it. Let a few molecules of this hit the heating coil and you will shortly find your kitchen in flames.

The entire effect is not unlike the cylinder in your car engine, but this time, you're the piston.

This is not meant to scare you from deep-frying; it's just to let you know that some things don't forgive you if you don't respect them. Vats of hot fat qualify. Avoiding such disasters means paying attention, that's all. Don't leave the room when you're frying. And remember, fats heat much faster than equal volumes of water, so don't try to guess the heat time—use a thermometer.

REAL SPARK PLUG AND PISTON

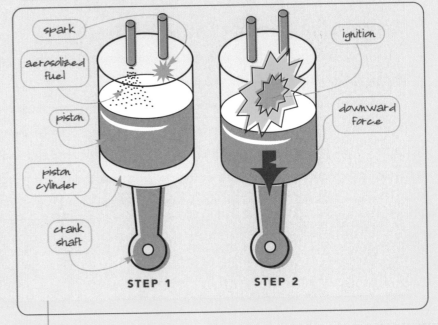

spark
aerosolized fuel
piston
piston cylinder
crank shaft
ignition
downward force

STEP 1 STEP 2

HUMAN SPARK PLUG AND PISTON

kitchen
aerosolized fat
open flame
ignition

Guess who the piston is now?

STEP 1 STEP 2

Master Profile: Frying

Heat type: dry

Mode of transmission: 90:10 percent ratio of conduction to convection

Rate of transmission: very high

Common transmitters: liquid fats, such as canola, peanut, and safflower oils

Temperature range: relatively narrow, between 250° and 375° F

Target food characteristics:

- small, uniform pieces of food containing high protein and/or starch content
- foods that can be dredged, breaded, or battered such as onion rings or fish strips
- firm vegetables

Non-culinary application: fast-food french fries

Batter Up

A batter is basically a liquid version of a standard breading, or at least the first two parts of it, liquid and starch. For my money, the best batters emulate the Portuguese-Japanese hybrid style of frying called tempura. Such batters create an almost impossibly thin and light coating that is like wrapping a present in tissue paper: you can literally see through it. This is my basic batter recipe, although I do also use a beer-based batter for fish and chips and occasionally chicken fingers (you know … for the kids).

Steer clear of the blender versions of this recipe, which produce thin, overworked batter. Also, since tempura is Asian, you'll probably serve it with some sort of salty soy or ponzu sauce, so you don't want to oversalt the batter.

Application: Immersion-Frying

Heat the oil to 350° F.

In a small bowl, sift together the salt, pepper, and cornstarch. In a medium bowl, whip the egg whites until soft peaks are formed. Continue whipping while gradually adding the cornstarch mixture.

Holding the target food at the end with tongs, quickly wave the food through the batter (this type of frying is best done one piece at a time), retrieve from the batter, let it drip for a few seconds, then put it into the oil.

Using the tongs, press the food down to keep it completely submerged in the oil (to prevent the food from flipping over—if an air bubble forms on the top between the food

Software:

2 quarts peanut or safflower oil (see **Notes**)

Salt

Freshly ground white pepper

¾ cup cornstarch

1 cup egg whites

Target food (see **Notes**)

Hardware:

Electric fryer or heavy Dutch oven fitted with a fat/candy thermometer

Small mixing bowl

Mesh strainer for sifting

Medium mixing bowl

Electric mixer

Tongs

Draining rig (see illustration, page 117)

and the batter, it will just keep rolling over). When the food has turned golden brown, approximately 3 to 5 minutes, remove the food to the draining rig. Repeat with remaining target food and serve immediately.

Notes: Previously used oil works better than fresh for this recipe. If you use fresh oil, the target food will be done before the batter has turned golden brown.

Possible target foods include: butterflied shrimp (split them down the middle, but not far enough to split them in half; you can also leave the tails on to allow an unbattered "handle"), and blanched vegetables, such as sliced sweet potatoes, broccoli, squash, and flat-leaf parsley. This recipe makes enough batter to coat about ½ pound of U21/25 shrimp, a medium-sized head of broccoli cut into florets, and one large sweet potato, thinly sliced.

PONZU

Ponzu sauce is Japanese and is typically made with lemon juice or rice vinegar, soy sauce, mirin or sake, seaweed, and dried bonito flakes. Bonito flakes, also called katsuobushi, are made of strongly flavored tuna.

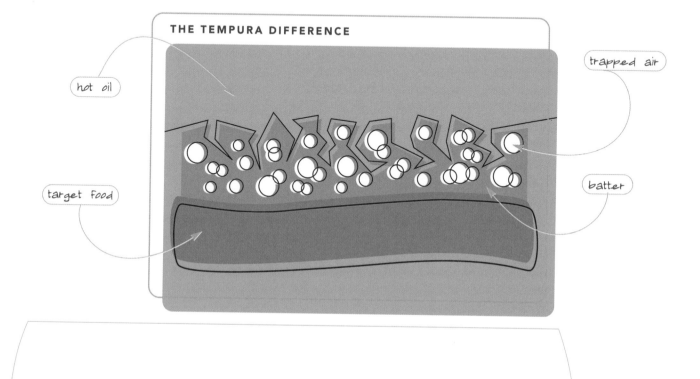

THE TEMPURA DIFFERENCE

trapped air

hot oil

batter

target food

FRY VESSELS

Until recently I did all my frying on the cook top in a big Dutch oven. I still fry french fries there because I use a two-pass method, which requires a pass at 300° F, then another at 350° F. That said, I recently came into possession of an electric fryer and I have to say, I like it.

I'm not talking about one of those fancy Italian numbers with the hinged lid and the "cool touch" chassis. This thing looks like a dark metal bucket with a cord coming out of the base. It's called a "Dual Daddy" and it's nice and wide but still deeper than wide, which is good. And get this: no thermostat. It shoots for about 380° F, then waits like a dog by the door. You put in the food, and unless you really overload it you'll never see the underside of 320° F. I've learned this with the help of a fat/candy thermometer, which comfortably fits on the side of the fryer. I never add food until the oil has reached its full 380° F and I never put in enough food to cause the oil to drop below 320° F.

Using this device, I have gotten the cost of cooking a large bag's worth of potato chips down to approximately 22 cents. The only craft to using this device is knowing how much food to put in at one time. This simple frying device comes with a big snap-on plastic lid; the implication is that you store your cooking oil in the device itself, but this is not a good idea since the more oil/air air contact you have the faster the oil will oxidize and go rancid.

Fats for Cooking

Fat is one of the body's basic nutrients. According to Harold McGee in his *On Food and Cooking*, fats account for about 10 percent of daily caloric intake in developing countries, while in affluent societies like our own the figure is more like 40 percent.

As consumers, we became saturated with fat talk years ago when doctors decided that fat was bad. Since Americans have been steadily plumping up for the last few decades, this wasn't a great leap of quantum thinking. But then somebody figured out that different fats elicit different responses in the body, depending on their saturation. Thus began the great dialogue and even greater confusion regarding the nature of saturated, monounsaturated, and polyunsaturated fats. As for cholesterol, well, let's just say that the amount of cholesterol in the foods we consume is not necessarily reflected in the amount of serum cholesterol in our bloodstream. But, just in case you've been buying one particular brand of vegetable oil simply because the container proudly proclaims it "cholesterol free," you can feel safe and secure in knowing that it's true. Of course, there's no such thing as a vegetable oil containing cholesterol. Only animal products, such as lard, contain cholesterol.

All culinary fats are called triglycerides. The term refers to the fats' molecular architecture, comprising three fatty acids that are esterified, or hitched, to a glycerine molecule. The structure of these fatty acids greatly determines how the fat is going to act when it gets into the culinary (and biological) food chain. Although there are a lot of different fatty acids (a whole lot actually), they all fall into one of three categories: saturated, monounsaturated, and polyunsaturated.

A fatty acid is basically a long chain of carbon atoms. Besides being anchored to the carbon in front as well as behind, each carbon has two chemical arms that can each hold a hydrogen atom. When all the carbons in a chain have their hands full of hydrogen, it is saturated, meaning that it can hold no more. Fats high in this kind of fat tend to be solid at room temperature, and they make cardiologists nervous.

If two adjoining carbons on a chain are lacking a hydrogen (this always happens in twos; there are never singles or threesomes), they join hands, creating a double bond.

If this occurs just once on a chain, the fatty acid is referred to as monounsaturated, meaning that there is a vacancy, but only one. If there are more vacancies along the chain, it is polyunsaturated.

All fats contain all three types of fatty acids. What decides how a fat is to be classified depends on how many of each kind there are (See illustrations, next page).

Folks in lab coats are still duking out whether mono- or polyunsaturates are better for us. Culinarily speaking, things are a little more cut and dry. But there are still choices and trade-offs.

> ## FRYING: THE WRAPAROUND PAN
>
> **Frying works so well because it conducts high heat to the entire surface of whatever it is you're cooking. It's as if you had a pan that could wrap itself around the food. And when done right, very little of the fat is actually absorbed into the food being fried. The trick is to choose your fat wisely.**

Fat Saturations

	Saturated (%)	Monounsaturated (%)	Polyunsaturated (%)
Canola or grapeseed	6	65	29
Walnut	9	28	63
Safflower	10	13	77
Sunflower	12	19	69
Corn	14	28	58
Soybean	15	24	61
Sesame	15	41	44
Olive	15	73	12
Peanut	18	49	33
Cottonseed	27	19	54
Palm	54	38	8
Coconut	92	6	2

Fats high in saturated fatty acids create wonderfully crisp fried foods, but saturated fats have relatively low smoke points (see page 111) so you don't get much use out of them and they're not very good for you. Saturated fats come from animal sources and can hold their shape at room temperature. The most commonly used saturated fats are butter, lard, and suet.

FAT FACTS

- All oils are fats, but not all fats are oils.
- If a fat comes from an animal, it's considered a fat. If it's a liquid at room temperature, it's considered an oil.
- All animal fats are solid at room temperature, which is why we say "chicken fat" rather than "chicken oil."
- All vegetable fats (except coconut and palm) are liquids and therefore oils.
- Since cooking fats degrade steadily once they cross about 140° F, I add the fat to a hot pan rather than heating it along with the pan.
- Shortening is great for frying. Since it's used as a baking ingredient, it's very refined. That results in a nice, golden-brown skin on chicken and, more important, no frying odor in the air.
- Lard is rendered or clarified pork fat, the quality of which depends on the area the fat came from and the method of rendering. Lard is richer than many other fats. When substituting lard for butter in baking, reduce the amount by 20 to 25 percent.
- Suet is a solid fat found around the kidneys and loins of beef, sheep, and other animals.
- The Belgians are even more into *pommes frites* than we are and they swear by horse fat. I've been to Belgium, I've had the frites, and my money's on Mr. Ed. Horse fat is, however, oddly absent from the American supermarket shelf.

Unsaturated fats don't fry up quite as nicely as oils high in saturated fats, but they have high smoke points so they can be used more than once (if you're careful with them). Unsaturated fats are primarily derived from plants and are usually in the form of an oil. Monounsaturated fats include olive oil and peanut oil. These fats are known to aid in the reduction of LDL cholesterol levels. Fats high in monounsaturates are ten times less shelf-stable than saturated fats and have low smoke points.

Polyunsaturated fats include safflower, sunflower, soybean, corn, and sesame oils. These fats are also better for your health but because their carbon chains have empty hands on them, nasty molecules (oxygen, for instance) can dock with the fat, making it go rancid quickly.

Just to make things a little more complicated, there are hydrogenated fats and trans fatty acids, both results of tinkering by the big, hairless monkey.

In order to make a polyunsaturated fat solid at room temperature or resistant to rancidity, hydrogen is pushed into the molecule so that those empty seats won't be taken up by undesirable substances. Fatty acids receiving this elemental transfusion straighten out physically, which makes it easier for the fat to lock up with its neighbor. The result is a fat that's solid at room temperature and opaque rather than clear. Vegetable shortening is a good example of this kind of fat. Unfortunately, any health advantage that might have been gained by the unsaturated nature of the fat is blown out of the water by the fact that the added hydrogen essentially saturates the fat. A trans fatty acid is simply a polyunsaturate that has been partially hydrogenated. Most nonbutter, buttery spreads employ trans fatty acids.

"Fat" here is a blanket term for triglycerides. Technically speaking any triglyceride that is solid at room temperature is called "fat." Any triglyceride that's liquid at room temperature is called an oil. There are two exceptions: palm oil and coconut oil, both of which are solid at room temperature but for some reason are still referred to as oils rather than fats.

Smoke Points

The smoke point is the temperature at which a heated fat starts to release smoke and acrid odors and lend an undesirable taste to food. When a fat reaches its smoke point, it is degrading very rapidly and certain compounds are escaping as vapor. This is why a thermometer should be used all the time, no matter what.

It seems pretty clear that if an oil's smoke point drops a few degrees (as much as 10° F) each time it's used, you're better off starting with an oil with a very high smoke point—either peanut, corn, soybean, or safflower.

Approximate Smoke Point Ranges for Common Fats

Butter	350° F
Lard	365°–400° F
Vegetable shortening	350°–370° F
Vegetable oils	440°–450° F
	peanut, soybean, safflower: 450° F
	canola, grapeseed: 435° F
	corn: 400° F
	sesame: 400° F
	sunflower: 390° F
Olive oil	375° F

Fried Green Tomatoes

Software:

3 green tomatoes, each about the
size of a baseball

½ cup flour

½ cup cornstarch

Kosher salt

Freshly ground black pepper

Pinch of cayenne pepper

3 eggs

2 cups fine Ritz cracker crumbs

Vegetable oil for frying

Hardware:

Paper towels

3 containers for dredging

10-inch cast-iron skillet or heavy-
bottom pan

Oil thermometer

Tongs

Rack

Okay—so I'm Southern.

Application: Pan-Frying

Slice the tomatoes into ¼-inch rounds and spread out on paper towels. Top with another layer of paper towels and allow to drain. (The key to successful fried tomatoes is that they must be as dry as possible prior to breading; otherwise the coating will peel off in sheets after cooking.) Meanwhile, mix the flour and cornstarch and season with salt, pepper, and cayenne. In a separate container, beat the eggs until slightly fluffy. Put the cracker crumbs in a third container. In a skillet, heat ½ inch of oil to 350° F. Season the dried tomato slices with salt and pepper, dredge in the flour mixture, then dip in the egg, and then press into the cracker crumbs to coat. With tongs, working in batches, gently lay them in the pan and cook until crisp and brown on one side, then flip and brown the other side. Transfer to a rack as they are done. I eat my 'maters with hot-pepper vinegar and a glass of sweet iced tea.

Yield: 4 side servings

Eggplant Parmesan

Cheese provides a perfect moisture barrier between the crisp coating and the tomato sauce. But sauce lightly; too much liquid will destroy the crispness you've worked so hard to create.

Application: Pan-Frying

Cut the eggplant into ¼-inch slices either crosswise (round slices) or lengthwise (long slices), depending on your preference. Liberally sprinkle the slices with kosher salt and lay out on a baking sheet lined with paper towels (stacking is fine as long as the stacks are equal in height). Top with another layer of paper towels, place a second baking sheet on top, and then weight it down. Allow to press for 30 minutes. Rinse away the salt and pat dry. Season the flour with ¼ teaspoon kosher salt and pepper, dredge the eggplant slices in the flour, then dip them in the egg mixture. Mix the panko and the Parmesan and coat the eggplant slices with the mixture.

In a heavy-bottom pot, heat ½ inch oil to 350° F. Fry the slices in batches until brown on the bottom, then turn and brown the other side, about 5 minutes total. Remove to a rack and hold in a warm (250° F) oven until all the slices are ready.

Meanwhile, heat the tomato sauce. Pull the rack of fried eggplant slices out of the oven and crank the heat up to 375° F.

To assemble, in a glass baking dish lay one eggplant slice and top with provolone, spread a very thin layer of sauce over the cheese, and repeat with two more layers, or until all the eggplant has been used. Sprinkle with Parmesan. Bake until the cheese is melted.

To serve, ladle a bit of sauce on the plate and place the hot stacks in it. (Or, you could build the stacks in small individual baking dishes and serve them right from the oven.)

Yield: 2 entrée or 4 side servings

Software:

1 medium to large firm eggplant, with tight, shiny skin

Kosher salt for pressing the eggplant, plus ¼ teaspoon

½ cup flour

¼ teaspoon freshly ground pepper

3 eggs and 3 ounces of water beaten together

½ cup panko (Japanese bread-crumbs)

¼ cup grated Parmesan, plus additional for the table

Canola oil for frying

1 cup tomato sauce

¼ cup shredded provolone cheese

Hardware:

2 baking sheets

Paper towels

3 containers for dredging

Heavy-bottom pot or cast-iron pan

Rack

Glass baking dish

A Pack of Wild Corn-Dogs

Software:

4 cups vegetable shortening

½ plus ⅓ cup all-purpose flour

½ cup yellow cornmeal

1 tablespoon salt

¼ teaspoon baking soda

1 teaspoon baking powder

½ teaspoon cayenne pepper

½ jalapeño chile, seeded and finely
minced

⅓ cup fresh corn kernels, pounded
slightly

¼ cup grated onion

1 cup buttermilk

½ cup water

4 franks or precooked sausages
(I'm partial to buffalo sausages)

Cornstarch for dredging

Hardware:

Electric skillet

3 containers

Draining rack

4 Popsicle sticks

I really resent the fact that adults are supposed to give certain foods up, especially those that remind them of fond childhood memories. I don't have any fond childhood memories involving fois gras or blowfish or caviar (other than as fishing bait). I do however have fond memories of corn dogs. When I was a kid the carnival came to town every year and each year I had to beg, and I mean beg, my dad to take me. He hated carnivals because he knew everything was a rip-off—the games, the shows, the rides, the food. But each year he'd eventually give in and each year I got a corn dog. They too were a rip-off, but I loved them anyway. Years later I came across a piece of Texas history that suggested that German sausage makers who settled in the San Antonio area came up with the idea of encasing their goods in cornbread batter. I don't know who added the stick, but I'm thankful. By the way, don't use skewers, they…oh just trust me.

Application: Pan-Frying

Heat the shortening in an electric skillet. Set the thermostat to 350° F. (Do not go beyond this temperature or the shortening will burn.)

Combine the flour, cornmeal, salt, baking soda, baking powder, and cayenne. In a separate container, combine the jalapeño, corn, onion, buttermilk, and ½ cup water. Pour this wet mixture into the dry ingredients, stirring just to thoroughly combine. Allow the batter to rest for 10 minutes.

Thoroughly pat the franks dry. Dredge the franks in cornstarch, being sure to shake off all the excess, then dip them in the batter. Immediately add to the hot fat. As soon as the batter is set on the bottom side, roll the corn dog over to cook the other side. Turn every minute until the outer skin is mahogany brown and crunchy, about 6 minutes total. Drain briefly on a draining rack. Grasp the corn dog firmly with a towel and push in a Popsicle stick for a handle. (Leaving the handles off until the cooking is over makes for a lot more room in the pan. Besides, there's no other way to keep the handle from getting greasy—and a greasy handle is the last thing you need when you're chompin' a corn dog.)

Yield: 4 corn dogs

Chip Chop

This is trash cuisine at its best.

Application: Pan-Frying

Preheat the oven 250° F. Put the chips in a zip-top freezer bag, seal, and roughly crush them. Don't go for a uniform meal, just beat them up: you want a contrast of size and shape. Transfer the chips to a pie pan. Beat the egg together with 2 teaspoons water and place the mixture in a second pie pan. Place the chop in a third pie pan and dredge with seasoned flour. Shake off any excess flour and coat the chop in the egg mixture. Drain briefly, then transfer the chop to the chip pan. Press on the pieces so that the chop is completely coated. Place on a rack and let the chop rest for 20 to 30 minutes.

In the meantime, in a skillet, heat enough shortening to come halfway up the side of the chop to 350° F (it's tough to take the temperature of such a small amount of oil, which is one reason I prefer to work in an electric skillet).

Cook the chop for 1 minute on each side, or until golden brown. Transfer to the rack and place the rack in the oven. Bake for 27 to 30 minutes or until the internal temperature hits 145° F..

Serve the chop with something else golden brown like mac and cheese and a side bowl of collard greens. Or, if you think your arteries are up to it, fried green tomatoes.

Yield: 1 serving, easily multiplied

Software:

1 (12-ounce) bag salt-and-vinegar potato chips (such as Lay's)

1 egg

2 teaspoons water

1 rib pork chop (1 to 1½-inch thick, bone on), at room temperature

Shake of seasoned flour

Shortening or canola oil

Hardware:

Large zip-top freezer bag

Rack set over baking sheet

3 pie pans or round cake pans

10- to 12-inch cast-iron skillet or electric skillet

Meat thermometer

Calamari Crunch

Software:

½ pound calamari

1 cup buttermilk

¼ cup water

1 cup cornstarch

1 cup all-purpose flour

1 cup Rice Krispies, ground fine in
a food processor

2 teaspoons table salt (kosher salt
will sink to the bottom of the
dredge)

1 tablespoon freshly ground white
pepper

2 quarts safflower or peanut oil

Hardware:

Small hand strainer

Mixing bowl just large enough to
hold the strainer

Sealable plastic container

Large, long-handled, wide-mesh
hand strainer (referred to in the
trade as a "spider")

Clean plastic placemat

Electric fryer or heavy Dutch
oven filled with a fat/candy
thermometer

Draining rig

Fried calamari may be the most popular restaurant appetizer in all of Christendom. I'm amazed that McSquid hasn't started popping out of drive-thrus worldwide. And yet we never make it at home. I asked a calamari-crazed friend of mine recently why this was. He simply replied, "Man, that's strictly restaurant food."

That's silly. Calamari is a great home dish for snacking or entertaining. What's more, it plays well with others. Top a simple plate of spaghetti and tomato sauce with a handful of these golden rings and you've got…restaurant food. (By the way, feel free to replace the secret ingredient, Rice Krispies, with any brand of puffed rice cereal.)

Application: Immersion-Frying

Clean the calamari, removing the head and ink sac if necessary, and then the cartilage; rinse thoroughly. Cut the tubes of calamari into rings and make sure the beak has been removed from the tentacles. In a mixing bowl, combine the buttermilk and water, then place the small hand strainer inside the bowl. Add the calamari and toss to coat with the liquid.

Add only enough oil to fill the fryer half-full, then heat the oil to 350° F.

Meanwhile, in the plastic container combine the cornstarch, flour, cereal, salt, and pepper. Close the container and shake to combine.

When the oil is hot, use the strainer to lift the calamari from the liquid, let it drain, and then transfer to the dredge mixture, scattering the pieces so they do not clump. Reseal the container and shake until the calamari is evenly coated.

Using the spider and working over a plastic placemat, lift the calamari from the dredge, gently shake off any excess flour, and drop into the oil. Once the first burst of steam settles down, gently push down on the calamari with the spider to make sure that the rings don't fuse together.

Work in batches to avoid overcrowding the oil. Folding the placemat like a funnel, return any excess flour mixture to the container and add more as needed.

Allow the calamari to cook until it is just golden in color and floats to the surface of the oil, about 30 to 45 seconds. Remove one ring, cool it briefly, and give it a taste. If the crust has crunch and the calamari feels soft, you can remove the entire batch to the draining rig with a sweep of the spider. If you want a little more color, let it cook a little longer, but remember that calamari gets tough when overcooked. Repeat with the remaining calamari.

Yield: 2 servings

Note: If you're serving a crowd, fight the temptation to cook too large a batch. Move your draining rig to a warm oven and stockpile the calamari as it's cooked—it will keep for up to 30 minutes without becoming rubbery.

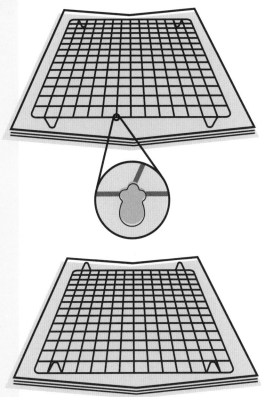

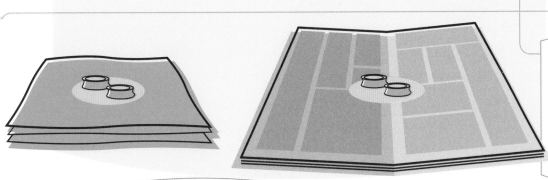

Racks are great except that fat (especially used fat) hangs in droplets under suspended bars and slowly soaks into food. What then must we do? The drainage answer: Turn the cooling rack over so that it's in direct contact with newspaper. That way oil runs off food over bars and onto paper. The food stays above the fray and no droplets accumulate on the rack.

Paper towels soak up oil but then the food has to sit in it. Newspaper also wicks oil well, but the food still sits in the grease. And, many inks are fat soluble, so you get a nice reversal of newsprint on the food. Yum.

Quick-Dip Potato Strips

Software:

2 quarts canola oil for frying

1 very large russet baking potato

Coarse salt

Coarsely cracked black pepper

Hardware:

Salad spinner

Electric fryer or heavy Dutch
    oven fitted with a fat/candy
    thermometer

Vegetable peeler

Splatter guard (optional)

Large slotted spoon

Draining rig

Once you taste your own you may never go back to store-bought chips again. I don't peel my potatoes here, but it won't matter if you do.

Application: Immersion-Frying

Place the drain basket of a salad spinner in its base (the bowl) and fill halfway with cold water.

Heat the oil. When it reaches 350° F, use a vegetable peeler to carefully carve long strips off the potato, moving straight from end to end. As the flat side becomes wider, rotate the potato a bit so that you don't end up with a surface wider than the cutting plane of the peeler. Repeat this so that you end up with three flat spots on the potato to peel from. This way most of your strips will be of uniform width—that is, as wide as the cutting area of the peeler, and about 4 inches long. Allow these strips to fall directly into the water in the salad spinner.

When you've cut about 15 strips, remove the basket from the bowl, drain the water, and spin the strips in the salad spinner to dry them; do not skip this step under pain of death.

Hold the strips in one hand just over the hot oil (its temperature should be between 360° and 380° F). Move your fingers back and forth so that the strips fall separately into the oil. Be ready with a splatter guard because the oil will bubble furiously for a few seconds. When the bubbles subside, use a slotted spoon to gently push down on the strips to keep them fully submerged and separate. Do not stir. As the strips dry and stiffen you'll be able to flip them over, which will help to ensure even doneness.

When the strips are pleasantly golden brown and the bubbles start to slow noticeably, spread the strips on a draining rack and immediately season with salt and pepper.

(If you use brand-new oil, the first batch of potato strips may be on the pale side. If this is going to bother you, make the first batch small and cook it a little past what you would consider done.)

Start peeling the next batch into the water, and repeat. The oil will be back up to temperature and ready to go by the time you are. While the new strips are in the oil, stack the finished strips in a serving dish.

You'll be shocked how many of these potato strips you can get out of one spud. You'll also be surprised by how great they look. Above all, you'll be surprised by the flavor.

Yield: A stack o' chips (which no matter how many you make, should be considered a single serving; if there's more than one person, there's going to be a fight).

Note: If your strips go a little stale on you after a day or two, lay them on paper towels and microwave on high for a minute or two to drive out the moisture.

Sauté: A Toss in the Pan

At the lighter end of the frying continuum there is the sauté. I say "the" sauté because it is both a method of cooking and a type of dish based on that method—"waiters" will say "a sauté of baby leeks," while a "server" will say "sautéed onions." Ah, nomenclature's a cruel mistress.

Literally translated, sauté means "to jump" in French. A chef (yes, a French one) said that when trying to dance your way from the bar to your beach blanket on a summer day on the Riviera, the hot pebbles of the beach make you "sauté."

So the logic here is flawed even if the method isn't. While it's true that food doesn't cook in the air, maybe that's the point. If it were to remain stationary on the bottom of the pan, the small pieces of food would probably reach a nice toastlike consistency while the inside was still raw.

What you need:

• high heat

• a heavy, wide pan with sloped sides

• a small amount of heat-friendly fat[19]

• food cut into uniform shape and size

• seasonings (from salt and pepper to dried and fresh herbs, flavorful liquids such as vinegars and juices, and flavorful oils such as sesame and chile)

• tongs for playing with your food

The Pan

Without the right pan you cannot sauté, which is not to say you have to have a sauté pan. As discussed in the section on searing, a dense pan is going to heat more evenly than a light one, especially if it's a metal sandwich of steel wrapped around a slice of aluminum or, even better (but more costly), copper. Since this pan needs to move during cooking, eschew cast iron unless you have anchor tattoos on each forearm and a girlfriend named Olive.

[19] Since the cooking fat is added to the pan immediately before the food, the issue here isn't the smoke point as much as flavor. Flavor-rich oils like extra-virgin olive oil and walnut oil lose most of their flavor when they reach high temperatures, so to use them for sautéing is a waste of money. I usually sauté in canola oil because its flavor is neutral. However, if you want to get some of the health benefits of olive oil, do your sautéing with "pure" olive oil rather than with extra virgin.

Since crowding the pan leads to stewing rather than sautéing, go for a wide-open plane of metal. I've got identical All-Clad sauté pans in both 10 and 12 inches. They cost a bundle but my grandkids will fight over them one day and darn it, that feels good.

Non-stick Sauté Pans

Yes, you can cook with amazingly small amounts of fat if you use the right non-stick pan, and that can be a good thing…maybe. The problem is, fat clings and conducts heat. Non-stick coatings (I'm a Teflon man myself) may conduct heat well but they do not cling. Therefore, there will be no flavorful browned bits on the bottom of the pan to deglaze and convert to sauce. And that's just a shame. That said, if a sauce is not in the offing, non-sticks do a fine job.

Fats for Sautés

You don't need a lot, but you do need some. A thin coating of fat brings out flavors and promotes caramelization. The trick is in using the right fats at the right time. Highly flavorful oils like extra-virgin olive oil, sesame oil, and nut oils provide an additional layer of flavor, but they burn easily. So do your cooking in a neutral oil like safflower and finish with a flavorful oil, or blend the two before adding them to the pan in the first place.

When picking an oil, consider the ingredients you're cooking. Asian ingredients will be complemented more by sesame oil than by olive oil, whereas foods with a Mediterranean slant will prefer the olive oil. French classics like green beans and shallots lean toward walnut oil. That's just the way things work.

The Toss

The airborne food antics of many TV chefs are just that: antics. Your food doesn't need "big air" to sauté properly, it only needs to move. Until you get the hang of it, concentrate on turning the food over itself by pushing the pan away from you, then snapping it gently back toward you. With a little practice you'll be able to turn everything in the pan over in a second or two without removing the pan from the heat.

Try this: Combine 1 cup of dry black beans and 10 individual white beans in your sauté pan. Practice your toss and watch where the white beans go—can you gather them all together and then move them over every inch of the pan?

Building the Perfect Sauté

1. Prepare all foods to be cooked: cut them into uniform, bite-size pieces. (Aromatics should be chopped smaller so that they release more flavor.)

2. Add the cooking oil only after the pan is hot.

3. Add the aromatics (onion, celery, garlic, ginger, and so on) and toss for 30 seconds or until fragrant. (If finely cut, aromatics can be added later in the process.)

4. Add firm vegetables or meats and toss until half-cooked, then add quick-cooking or high-moisture ingredients like zucchini or tomato and toss for another 30 seconds to 1 minute.

5. Add final flavors such as citrus juice or vinegar. If vegetables are still too firm, cover to steam briefly.

6. Toss a final time with salt and pepper, taste, adjust seasoning if necessary, and turn out into a bowl or platter.

7. Top with grated cheese, toasted nuts, bread crumbs, or additional herbs.

THE STORY OF TEFLON

The year was 1938, and DuPont chemist Dr. Roy Plunkett was at work on the creation of a new type of Freon refrigerant. Plunkett plopped some down and left them in his lab overnight. The next day, he found that something had happened. The gas had somehow polymerized into a waxy, slippery substance, which with further testing proved to be almost utterly inert, chemically speaking. He called it Poly-tetra-fluoro-ethylene or Teflon® for short. Some guys out at Los Alamos caught wind of the blunder/discovery and decided to order up some of DuPont's new goo. (Turns out they were working on something that required the containment of a uranium by-product that's highly corrosive—Teflon was the only material that would hold it.) Once its slipperiness became celebrated, Teflon was used to coat the nose cones of missiles carrying later generations of the Los Alamos spawn. Then, in the 1950s, a French fisherman came up with a method of applying Teflon to his fishing tackle, rendering it tangle-free. And when his wife got the idea of putting some on her pots and pans... well, the rest is non-stick history. Teflon is still considered the slickest solid on Earth.

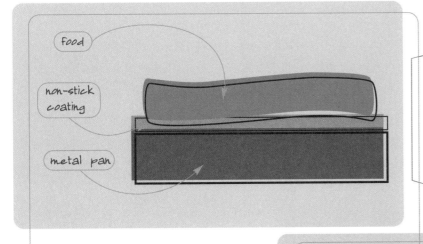

food

non-stick coating

metal pan

Early generation non-stick pans relied on a relatively thin and smooth application of the non-stick substance (almost always Teflon). The problem was that the substance wore off from use and metal utensils could literally tear the surface. The result: a pan with a very short lifespan. However, when they were new, they were slick.

Today many manufacturers have opted for a rockier terrain. The thought is that the less direct the contact between the pan and utensils, the longer the life of the pan. The surface still wears over time but even as the top wears, there's still plenty below.

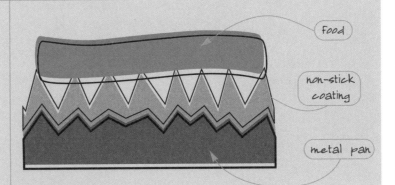

food

non-stick coating

metal pan

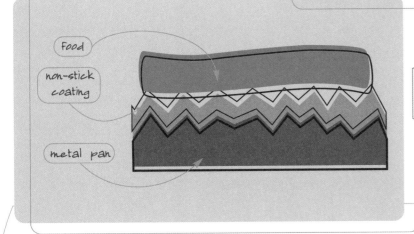

food

non-stick coating

metal pan

Theoretically, the surface on this pan will eventually erode flat, but I haven't seen this happen yet.

It is the fat most commonly called for in sautéing.

Butter

Butter is a flavoring agent, and a little in the sauté pan can go a long way. Because of its low smoke point, using butter in combination with a high smoke point oil can prevent burning. Butter is made by churning cream until it reaches a semi-solid state. By United States law, butter must be at least 80 percent milk fat. The other 20 percent is made up of water and milk solids. Many high-end butters contain up to 88 percent milk fat. The USDA grades butter based on flavor, body, texture, color, and salt content. These grades are: AA (or 93), A (or 92), and B (or 90); AA- and A-grade butters are what are commonly found in the grocery store.

Unsalted butter contains no salt. It's also referred to as "sweet butter," though it is not made with sweet cream (any butter made with sweet instead of sour cream is sweet butter). Since it has no salt, unsalted butter is more perishable than ordinary butter, which typically has a salt content of about 1.2 to 1.4 percent.

Whipped butter has had air beaten into it, thus increasing its volume and making for a more spreadable consistency. **Clarified butter**, also known as drawn butter, is butter minus its milk solids. To clarify butter, melt it slowly, thereby evaporating most of its water and separating the milk solids (they sink to the bottom) from the golden liquid on top. Skim off the foam and pour off the clear or clarified butter. Because the milk solids have been removed, clarified butter has a higher smoke point and won't go rancid as quickly as regular butter. The down side is that it loses some of its flavor along with the milk solids.

Traditionally, **buttermilk** was the liquid left after the butter was churned. Today, buttermilk is made by adding bacteria to low-fat or non-fat milk.

Margarine is a manufactured product made with vegetable oils; it was developed in the late 1800s as a butter substitute. It contains trans fatty acids, which result when hydrogen is added to a fat so that it will be solid at room temperature. Recent studies have linked trans fatty acids to health problems, including heart disease.

Chicken in Garlic and Shallots

This dish is an interesting hybrid. At first glance it appears to be a braise, but because it's cooked in fat, it's technically a fry. But nothing about the fragrant and amazingly flavorful results suggest frying. The oil itself comes out as the best garlic-herb oil you've ever tasted—perfect for sautéing greens or making garlic bread. Then there are the garlic cloves and shallots: soft, sweet, spreadable—stir them into mashed potatoes and prepare to amaze your friends and frighten your enemies.

I have to say that this dish sums up everything I love about cooking—in fact it is my favorite dish of all time to cook because it is amazingly easy, requires only one pan, can be made with any chunks of chicken (though I prefer the thighs), and it makes the house smell like I like to think the south of France smells.

Application: Slow-Frying

Preheat oven to 350° F.

Season chicken liberally with salt and pepper. Toss with 2 tablespoons olive oil and brown on both sides in wide frying pan or skillet over high heat. Remove from heat, add garlic, shallots, herbs, and remainder of the olive oil (there's no reason to chop the herbs, just distribute them around and in between the chicken chunks). Cover and bake for 1½ hours.

Yield: 6 servings

Software:

1 whole chicken (broiler/fryer) cut into 8 pieces or 10 chicken thighs

Salt

Freshly ground black pepper

½ cup plus 2 tablespoons olive oil

10 peeled cloves of garlic

10 shallots, peeled and split in half from stem to root

Several sprigs parsley, sage, and thyme (sorry, rosemary would put it over the edge)

Hardware:

Large ovenproof sauté pan with tight fitting lid (straight sides are needed. If you don't have such a pan you may need to brown the chicken in one pan then finish the dish in a casserole.)

Tongs for handling meat

Software

1 tablespoon peanut or safflower oil

2 cloves garlic, minced

2 teaspoons fresh ginger, minced

2 large carrots, cut into 2-inch sticks

1 large zucchini (unpeeled), cut
   into 2-inch sticks

1 tablespoon mint, cut into fine
   chiffonade

1 tablespoon rice wine vinegar

Salt

Freshly ground black pepper

2 teaspoons sesame seeds, toasted
   in a dry pan over high heat until
   you just begin to smell them

Hardware:

Sauté pan

Carrots and Zucchini with Garlic and Ginger

Application: Sautéing

Heat the sauté pan and, when hot, add the oil. Add the garlic and ginger to the pan and toss for 30 seconds. Add the carrots and toss until they are half-cooked, about 2 minutes. Add the zucchini and toss for 30 seconds to 1 minute more. Add the mint and the vinegar; if carrots are still too firm, cover and steam briefly. Sprinkle with salt and pepper, toss, and turn out onto a serving platter. Top with the sesame seeds.

Yield: 4 side servings

GARLIC

Garlic wasn't grown commercially in the United States until World War I, when some farmers in California started doing so in response to a government call for garlic to ship to troops overseas for use as an antiseptic. By 1920, Gilroy, California, in the San Joaquin Valley, established itself as the nation's garlic capital. Today, more than 1 million pounds of garlic are processed there each day, and the town is the proud host of an annual three-day garlic festival that regularly attracts more than 100,000 people. An old folk saying goes "Shallots are for babies, onions are for men, garlic is for heroes."

Scampi V2.0

Application: Sautéing

Chop the garlic together with the parsley until it almost reaches a paste-like consistency. (When salt is added, the French—yes, them again—call this mixture *persillade*.)

Heat the sauté pan and, when hot, add the oil. Add the shrimp and toss. When halfway cooked, about 1½ minutes, add the tomatoes and toss for 30 seconds to 1 minute more. Add the garlic and parsley mixture, the salt, pepper, butter, and lemon juice and toss one last time. Turn out onto a plate and serve.

Yield: 2 servings

Software:

2 cloves garlic

2 tablespoons finely chopped
   parsley

2 tablespoons olive oil

1 pound jumbo shrimp (headless)

2 ripe Roma tomatoes, seeded and
   diced

Salt

Freshly ground black pepper

1 tablespoon butter

Juice of half a lemon

Hardware:

Sauté pan

Hot Melon Salad

Software:

1½ tablespoons olive oil

1 red onion, sliced Lyonnaise-style

2 cups diced assorted melon such
   as cantaloupe and honeydew

1 tablespoon basil, cut into fine
   chiffonade

Splash of red wine vinegar

Freshly ground black pepper

Crumbled feta cheese

1 tablespoon pine nuts, toasted in
   a dry pan over high heat until
   just browned

Hardware:

Sauté pan

Application: Sautéing

Heat the sauté pan and, when hot, add the oil. Add the onion and toss for 30 seconds or until fragrant. Add the melon and toss until halfway cooked, about 2 minutes. Add the basil, vinegar, and pepper and toss for 30 seconds to 1 minute more. If the melon is still too hard, cover and let steam briefly. Remove the pan from the heat and immediately toss in the cheese. Turn out onto a serving platter and garnish with the pine nuts.

Yield: 4 side servings

Miller Thyme Trout

Somewhere between sauté and pan-fry is a method the French call *meunière*. The word means "miller's wife," who I'm betting could get her hands on just about all the flour she wanted. Unlike a sauté, we're talking a large piece of fish here, but the procedure for building flavors is closer to the sauté than to the pan-fry.

In the classic *meunière* style, food is seasoned, dusted with flour, and sautéed in butter, with a pan sauce created by the addition of lemon juice and parsley. In the bastardization that follows, dried thyme is ground and added to the flour, then the butter is turned into a light mustard cream sauce at the last possible minute. Why did I go to the trouble of changing something that was already perfect? So I could call the dish "Miller Thyme Trout," of course.

Application: Sautéing

Grind the thyme to a powder in a coffee grinder and mix it into the flour. Season the mixture with salt and pepper and dredge the fish in it. Heat a large sauté pan over medium-high heat and add the butter. When the butter begins to foam, carefully lay in the fish, flesh side down. Cook until lightly brown, about 3 minutes, and then flip and cook the skin side for another 3 minutes. Remove the fish to a serving plate. Stir the mustard and cream into the pan and bring to a simmer to thicken. Pour over the fish and serve.

Yield: 1 serving

Software:

1 tablespoon dried thyme

1 cup flour

Kosher salt

Freshly ground black pepper

1 whole butterflied trout (about 8 ounces)

2 tablespoons butter

2 teaspoons whole-grain mustard

¼ cup heavy cream or milk

Hardware:

Coffee grinder

Container for dredging

Large sauté pan

Bean and Garlic Sauté

Although the step known as "sautéing" is most often an opening gambit in a grander construction (how many recipes do you know of that *don't* begin with something like: "Sauté the onion in the oil?"), sautéing can also be the finishing touch, as in this simple bean recipe. Although butter is notorious for burning, no other common fat browns food as well or brings as much flavor to the party. Tempering it with a heat-friendly oil will keep the butter in line.

Application: Sautéing

Place the butter in a cold sauté pan and place over high heat. As soon as the butter melts and stops foaming, add the pecans and toss until they darken slightly.[20] Remove the nuts from the pan and set aside.

Add the oil to the pan and swirl to coat the bottom. Add the beans, season with salt, and toss until the beans start to brown in places, approximately 2 minutes.

Add the garlic and toss until fragrant.

Toss in the nuts, remove from the heat, and drizzle with the vinegar.[21]

Yield: 2 side servings

Software:

1 tablespoon butter

¼ cup pecan pieces

1 tablespoon peanut oil

½ pound slender green beans, blanched

Kosher salt

2 cloves garlic, minced

1 teaspoon sherry or red wine vinegar

Hardware:

10-inch sauté pan

---

[20] As long as the butter's foaming you know that it still has water in it, and as long as it has water in it it can't get hotter than 212° F.

[21] Why *off* the heat? Because if the pan is hot enough, when the water-based vinegar hits the pan a good bit of it is going to vaporize and exit the pan, taking microscopic droplets of the fat with it. If you're cooking over a gas flame, some of these droplets will ignite. Then, for a few seconds the whole pan will seem to be on fire. Such a sight can be exciting when viewed at one's favorite restaurant, but it can be a bit disconcerting when witnessed at home.

Sweet-and-Sour Tofu

I'm a huge sweet-and-sour fan and, oddly enough, I think this dish captures what a sweet and sour should be about: contrasts of flavor and texture. Why the tofu? Why not? It absorbs flavor better than meat and fries beautifully. And it's better for you than meat, too.

Applications: Marinating, Immersion-Frying, Sautéing

Drain the tofu, slice each "brick" lengthwise into 4 equal pieces, and set on a baking sheet lined with paper towels. Place a couple of paper towels on top, cover with a second baking sheet, and weight with cans of food. Set aside for at least 30 minutes, then cut into 2-inch cubes and place in a large mixing bowl. In a small mixing bowl, combine the soy sauce, garlic, 1 tablespoon of the ginger, ½ cup flour, and the cornstarch. Pour over the tofu and allow to marinate, refrigerated, overnight. Drain off any excess liquid (there won't be much; it gets pretty sticky), and dredge the tofu in flour seasoned with salt and pepper. In an electric fryer, heat the vegetable oil to 350° F and fry the tofu until golden brown on all sides. Work in batches, setting the fried tofu aside on a warm plate.

In another small bowl, combine the ketchup, sugar, vinegar, and honey, and mix to blend. Set the sauce aside.

In a small roasting pan over medium heat, heat the canola and sesame oils. Sauté the remaining ginger in the oil for 30 seconds, then add the vegetables and pineapple. Raise the heat to high; you should get a little caramelization without softening the vegetables too much. Work in batches if necessary. Add the tofu to the vegetables and pour in as much sauce as you like. Bring to a simmer and cook until the sauce is bubbling and has a nice shine. Remove to a platter and serve with any remaining sauce on the side.

Yield: 8 servings

Note: Firm tofu is sold in 1-pound bricks. It is important to slice lengthwise so the pan will weight equally on each piece and the pieces will be pressed evenly.

Software:
2 pounds firm tofu
1 cup soy sauce
2 tablespoons minced garlic
3 tablespoons minced ginger
½ cup flour, plus more for dredging
½ cup cornstarch
Kosher salt
Freshly ground black pepper
Vegetable oil for frying
3 cups ketchup
¾ cup sugar
2 cups red wine vinegar
¼ cup honey
2 tablespoons canola oil
1 tablespoon sesame oil
1 cup chopped Vidalia onion
1 cup chopped celery
1 cup carrots, sliced ¼ inch thick on a bias
1 cup chopped red bell pepper
1 cup chopped green bell pepper
2 cups cubed (1-inch pieces) fresh pineapple (canned is too sweet)

Hardware:
2 baking sheets
Paper towels
Cans of food for weight
2 small and 1 large mixing bowl
Electric fryer or heavy Dutch oven fitted with a fat/candy thermometer
Small roasting pan or large sauté pan
Wooden spoon
Large serving platter

Boiling... sure, you know it when you see it, but do you really know it?

CHAPTER 5

Boiling

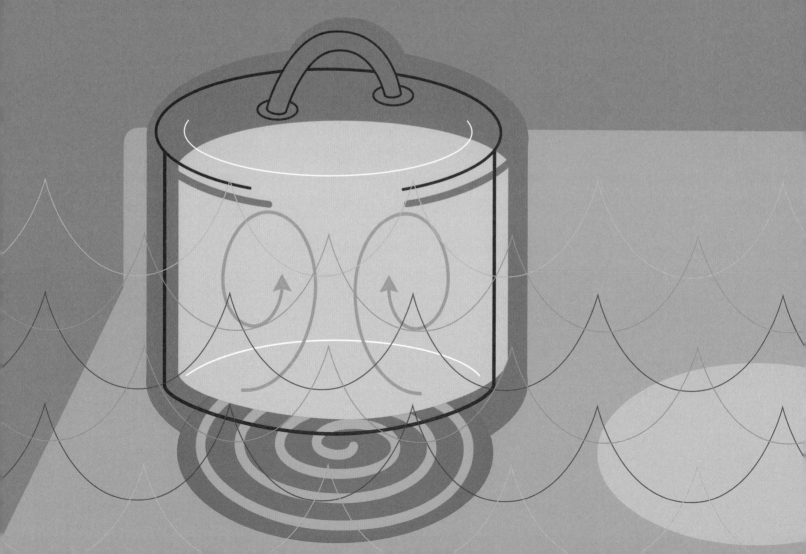

Water Works

Dictionaries may define cooking as the application of heat to food, but there have been plenty of food thinkers through the ages who have postulated that cooking has less to do with heat than it does with water management. After all, there is no food that doesn't contain water and the changes that take place in food during cooking can largely be quantified by what happens to the water in question. Water is not only our most common cooking environment, it is the only one that can act as a heat conduit and a solvent at the same time, which is especially important in the making of stock. The stuff is everywhere and yet science has yet to get a good grip on water. You, as a cook, must get your head into water before you can get it around cooking.

What Is This Stuff, Anyway?

Begin by putting on a Mickey Mouse hat. Now stand in front of a mirror and take a serious look at yourself. Yes, you do look silly but you also look like a molecule of water—your head representing an oxygen atom and each ear a hydrogen atom. Each of these elements has a long and interesting career (being flammable helps), but what makes them particularly interesting here is how they're joined.

The reason the hydrogen atoms are attached Mickey Mouse–style to the oxygen has to do with oxygen's attraction to hydrogen's electrons. It pulls on their orbits so strongly that the hydrogens list to one side, resulting in an asymmetrical and electrically polar molecule. If oxygen weren't so greedy for electrons, your hydrogen ears would connect at 180 degrees (think Princess Leia). Of course, if that were the case water would boil at about -150° F; you wouldn't need a hat, because you wouldn't exist—nor would any other living thing. In short, the curious triangular configuration of the water molecule makes life (and cooking) on Earth possible.

In its solid state, water's molecules are ordered and equally spaced, as if taking part in a very slow line dance. As it warms up, the bonds that hold it in this rigid but open pattern release, and you've got something like a disco on your hands. Now the molecules are packed tightly together and every atom on each molecule is free to hook up with other atoms on other molecules via hydrogen bonds. At any given time, dozens of water molecules can be loosely bound together in a molecular group hug. A food item placed in this environment is going to come in contact with a lot of water molecules and will conduct heat from them while getting physically tossed around a bit.

WATER CONVERSION

Because of water's fondness for hydrogen bonding, it can absorb a lot of energy (in the form of heat) without actually changing temperature. This explains why even twenty-first-century cars have radiators, elephants have big ears, and human beings sweat. In the case of the latter, moisture carries heat from the inner core of our bodies to the outside, where it evaporates. The conversion from liquid to vapor absorbs even more energy and we cool off. This also explains why a bottle of beer chills faster in a bucket of cold water than in the relatively dry air of the freezer.

Distilled water is pure H_2O. Everything else has been removed by either reverse osmosis or carbon filtering. Since no trace of anything else remains, distilled water tastes freakishly flat, but it is good for cleaning lab equipment and filling irons. Some water bottlers use it as an ingredient for "making" mineral water.

Natural sparkling water is naturally carbonated spring water or spring water that has gone flat and has been recarbonated to the exact level of carbonation it had before it wasn't flat . . . if that makes any sense.

Club soda, seltzer, and soda water are classified as soft drinks, not bottled waters, because they are essentially tap water that's been manipulated by man. In most cases sodium bicarbonate has been added along with other flavorings (quinine in the case of tonic water) and salts. Since it contains soda, these waters are often used in baking and in certain batters, such as tempura. If you have a recipe that calls for club soda or soda water, do not replace it with naturally sparkling mineral water or you'll be sorry.

Now, say you go into a store and pick up a bottle of water that bears a three-color graphic of crystal-clear water gushing from a pristine mountain crag. Looks good, right? Okay, now look for the words "purified water" or simply "drinking water." Find them? That water came from a municipal source—the tap—and has been purified and possibly fortified with minerals. So skip the pictures and go for the small type. "Glacial water" must by law come from a glacier. "Naturally sparkling" water must come straight from a spring, with bubbles.

As more heat is added, the action on the dance floor gets frantic. Add enough heat, and the water will eventually come to a boil. Hydrogen bonds break down, the atmospheric pressure holding the water in the pot will be overcome, and the liquid will begin to move into the vapor state we call steam. When that happens, the water expands radically, like disco dancers who suddenly decide to break into a Viennese waltz. Food placed in this environment may not bump into many molecules, but those that are encountered contain considerable energy. While this is bad news, for say, your hand, it's good news for delicate foods that would otherwise be torn to shreds in the boiling water discotheque.

Since most of us can open up a tap and take as much of the planet's water as we want, we tend to think of water as a constant rather than an ingredient. I've seen cooks spend all morning at the farmers' market, hand picking the finest designer-organic-heirloom vegetables, only to chuck them straight into a pot of tap water that smells like the kiddie pool at the Y. If your municipal *agua* leaves something to be desired, you should either filter it or give up and start from scratch. (If you're curious about what's coming out of your taps, request a water quality report from your local water company.)

Filter Your Water

I might be willing to pay three bucks for a latte every now and then, but I just can't bring myself to pay a buck for a pint of water. I don't care what glacier it dripped off of or

HARD AND SOFT WATER

Hard water happens when water absorbs CO_2 (thus becoming acidic like acid rain), then comes in contact with limestone or rocks or soil containing calcium, magnesium salts, bicarbonates, chlorides, and the like. Since it's a great solvent, the acidic water dissolves and absorbs large amounts of these solids. They remain in the solution until the water is either heated (in your hot water heater or tea kettle) or has its pressure rapidly reduced (your kitchen faucet or dishwasher sprayers). Then they become rocklike deposits that stick readily to things we don't want them to stick to. Hard water is also terrible at washing things. That's because it's already got its molecular mitts full of minerals and can't get a grip on soap or dirt.

Soft water is the opposite of hard water. It's relatively free of dissolved solids so it's a great solvent and soap's best friend. However, when it come to drinking or cooking water there is such a thing as too soft. Very soft water is flat tasting (like distilled water) and since it lacks minerals, not as good for you as harder water. Super-soft water also tends to brew lackluster coffee, tea, and beer.

ACTIVATED CHARCOAL

Activated charcoal is on my "top-ten coolest things in the world" list. Unlike the stuff that you burn in the grill, activated charcoal is a powder made up of tiny carbon sponges. These particles are amazingly porous and can absorb something like a zillion times their weight in organic compounds (including many poisons), as well as a host of nasty chemicals, such as chlorine, solvents, and even some pesticides. How do these tiny grains do the job? For one thing, they are 100 percent carbon, and so they act like Velcro, clinging to any substance containing carbon. More important, they possess an almost unbelievable amount of surface area—up to 160 acres per pound! Think about that a minute. That means that each gram of activated charcoal has in the neighborhood of 14,000 square feet of bonding space. Amazing though this is, all this space will eventually be taken, and the filter will need to be changed. Failing to change an exhausted filter is actually worse than having no filter at all, because the nooks and crannies of activated charcoal are like an ant farm for bacteria. If your water is chlorinated, pathogens shouldn't be a problem, but the longer that filter sits there, the more you're just asking for trouble.

what Alp it perked up out of, I still think it's a rip-off (see What's in Your Bottle, page 134). Luckily, we have water filters.

There are three types of water filtration systems, all of which utilize activated charcoal (see Activated Charcoal). Since my municipal water is safe and relatively good at cleaning things (see Hard and Soft Water) I don't feel I really need a high-volume system to scrutinize and scrub every milliliter that comes into the house or even through one particular tap. I'm not a fan of faucet-mounted models because they make every sink they meet look like a refinery and their size necessitates seemingly constant filter changing. I prefer the pitchers with pour-through filters that utilize drop-in filter cartridges. These devices are rather slow but they're effective and very affordable. Around my house we keep the filter pitcher on the counter and keep a gallon or so (tightly sealed) squirreled away for cooking those designer veggies we were talking about.

If you just can't bring yourself to spring for a filter (cheapskate), at least take these taste precautions. Let the water run while you count slowly to ten (for better oxygenation) before you fill any vessel. Then bring the water to a boil and keep it there for a solid minute, uncovered, before adding any food (this eliminates some of the chlorine).

Poaching

Poaching is defined as cooking food gently in liquid that has been heated until the surface just begins to quiver.

I personally have never seen water "quiver," but since no bubbles are mentioned I assume that we're talking about a temperature that's below a simmer. How much below? Who knows? Some cooks argue 180° F—others 185° F—either of which is nearly impossible to maintain on a standard home stove top. Then, of course, there's the food.

Fish, eggs, and chicken breasts are traditional poaching fodder because they profit from gentle (there's that word again) heat. The other side of the coin is that these foods get nasty soon after they exceed their relatively low ideal temps—140° F to 150° F in the case of fish and 165° F for chicken meat. So let's say you've got a flavorful liquid (see The

Liquid) and you bring it to 180° F and slide in a piece of sole. So far so good, you think, but how do you know when it's done? It's too thin to use a thermometer and it's impossible to time. You're left there to poke, ponder and pray that you'll recognize the moment when your dinner enters the narrow (10°) doneness zone, at which point you'll have to act quickly because the food will be well on its way to a state of thermal equilibrium with its surrounding environment, which is not a happy place for these kinds of foods to be. So, not only can't you tell when the food is done, it won't stay that way for long. No wonder nobody poaches anymore.

The solution?

As much as I'd love to claim this method as my own, I have to give credit to the patron saint of modern food scientists, Harold McGee, who wrote about this method in *The Curious Cook*.

1. Start with the liquid at a boil to kill any surface bacteria.

2. Drop the temperature of the liquid to the final desired temperature of the meat.

This way the food never overcooks. This doesn't mean you can leave the food in there all night, but—while its never a good idea to turn your back to a simmering pot—you could. Fruit, by the way, is often poached in syrup, but in that case the real goal is not to control the final internal temperature but to cook the fruit without blowing it to bits with the turbulence of boiling.

I like to poach in an electric skillet (see page 255), which I calibrate by filling with water, dropping in the probe of one of my many thermometers, and taking the thermostat for a ride. I found that the temperature range was way off, so I re-marked it with white tape and a pen. Then I went one geeky step further by wiring a dimmer into the cord so that I could maintain temperatures well below the "simmer" level. Of course, I'd never suggest you resort to such extreme measures for poaching, but hey, if you're handy with wiring, you can give it a try as long as you hold me and my publisher blameless for any potential damages.

The Liquid

I usually poach fish in either wine (I tend toward sweeter wines like Rieslings) or a mixture of wine and water with lemon juice and a pinch of salt. Adding herbs makes the room smell nice, but considering the relatively short cooking time I don't think it does much for the flavor of the fish—unless, of course, you're making sauce. One of the nicest things about poaching liquid is that as long as you have added the salt with a light hand, once the food comes out you can jack up the heat and reduce the liquid, mount it and serve it with the fish.

> To "mount" a sauce is to stir or whisk in a few bits of cold butter at the last minute.

Master Profile: Poaching

Heat type: wet

Mode of transmission: 90:10 percent ratio conduction to convection

Rate of transmission: slow

Common transmitters: any liquid

Temperature range: low and narrow 140–170° F (depending on who you ask)

Target food characteristics:

- tender proteins: fish, eggs, chicken and other poultry[22]

Non-culinary application: Jacuzzi on "stun"

---

[22] Typically, when these foods are added directly to boiling water the temperature immediately drops, giving the food time to catch up, temperature-wise. In steaming, the food rarely touches the boiling water below, so no reduction of heat occurs. For starchy foods such a thermal onslaught would immediately gelatinize the outer layer of the food, rendering it hopelessly gummy. Also, starchy foods need water to wash away excess starch—something steam just can't do.

Poached Chicken Methods

Combine the wine, stock, bay leaves, and peppercorns in a large heavy-bottomed pot, then proceed with one of the following methods.

Method 1

Place the probe end of thermometer in the liquid and place over medium-high heat to maintain a temperature of 185° F. Submerge the bird in the liquid and set the thermometer alarm for 190° F. If the alarm sounds, the water has gotten too hot, reduce the heat to maintain 185° F. This method takes about 1 hour and 10 minutes. Remove the chicken to a rack set on a baking sheet to drain.

Method 2

Cut the bird into serving-size pieces and submerge in cool liquid in an electric skillet set for 180° F. Use your thermometer in a leg or thigh, and when it reaches 180° F remove pieces to a rack set on a baking sheet to drain. This is probably the most foolproof method.

Now that you have all this poached chicken, what do you do with it? Well, you could simply eat it chilled atop a nice salad of mixed greens and fresh tomatoes with a boiled egg. Or eat it warm with Hollandaise Takes a Holiday (page 214), chop it into your favorite chicken salad recipe, or even simmer the pulled meat in your favorite barbecue sauce for delicious sandwiches. The possibilities are limitless.

Software:

1 quart white wine

Chicken stock (or water) to cover

2 bay leaves

½ tablespoon peppercorns

1 whole broiler-size chicken

Hardware:

Heavy-bottomed pot (or electric skillet) large enough to fit the whole chicken

Probe thermometer

Tongs

Rack

Baking sheet

Simmering

Master Profile: Simmering

Heat type: wet

Mode of transmission: 80:20 percent ratio of conduction to convection

Rate of transmission: moderate to high

Common transmitters: any liquid

Temperature range: narrow 175–200° F (depending on who you ask)

Target food characteristics:

- Dehydrated starches: rice, dry beans, oats, barley
- Hearty greens: collards
- Foods that can stand up to high heat and some physical convection

Non-culinary application: Jacuzzi on "kill"

Time and sub-boiling temperatures are the Lerner and Loewe of the kitchen world, a team capable of converting simple culinary notes into remarkable opuses (or is that opi?). Unfortunately, two factors conspire to prevent the cook from hearing the music: dropping below the visual benchmark boil is like flying on instruments; there's not much to see and what there is can rarely be trusted. Also, the sub-boil lexicon is a nomenclatural netherworld where terms like simmer, poach, braise, coddle, stew and scald create connotative chaos. Consider the most oft-mentioned cooking term in the English culinary lexicon: simmer. There are two common definitions:

1. To heat water (or a water-type liquid) to about 195° F or until tiny bubbles form on the bottom of the pan then travel to the surface.

2. To cook foods gently in a liquid held at the temperature mentioned above.

Already we've got problems. First there's this word "about." The reason so many cookbooks use "about" is that nobody seems to be able to pin simmering (or any sub-boil technique) down to a single temperature.

Then there's the trouble with bubbles. The temperature at which water will produce "tiny" bubbles depends a lot on the pot, the weather, even the water itself. (See Boiling in the Microwave, page 150) And what if there's more in the water than just water? Salt, starch, dissolved meat proteins (maybe oatmeal) can elevate the actual boiling point of the liquid. As stew liquid thickens, its sheer viscosity can impede bubble production. And yet how many stew recipes have you read that refer to those Don Ho bubbles?

Finally, there's the word "gentle." Since simmering liquid lacks the physical turbulence of boiling water, it is physically gentle. (Anyone who's canoed down a river knows that white water will beat you up a lot quicker than flat water.) But when it comes to heat, there are only a few degrees difference between a simmer and a full rolling boil. A "simmer" may not tear your fish to shreds, but it will squeeze the life out of it lickety-split, which is why you should never turn your back on a simmering pot.

So we've got all these cooking methods that depend on maintaining water or a watery liquid at relatively low temperatures, in some cases for a prolonged period of time. Now, where should the pot itself go? Well, I'll tell you where it shouldn't go: the cook top.

Most ranges, whether gas or electric, have

ON THE STOVE

not very hot

very hot indeed

large burners or eyes and a smaller "simmer" eye. The idea here is that since the burner is smaller it will generate less heat, which is true—sort of. The way I see it, natural gas burns at one temperature no matter how much of it there is. Place the tip of a thermometer into the flame of your oven's pilot light and it's going to read in the neighborhood of 3,200° F. Now crank your biggest burner and take its temp. They're the same, right? So what we're talking about here isn't so much a matter of the temperature of the heat but the rate at which it's being produced. That simmer eye, hot though it is, can't pump out enough heat to bring a large pot of water to a boil in less than a day or two. It can, however, maintain sub-boiling temperatures—but not effectively. That's because all the heat is being poured into a very small part of the pan (see figure **A**). Since the metal directly over the flame is very hot indeed, the water directly over it heats very quickly and moves upward, creating wicked-fast convection currents (see figure **B**). If it contains something thicker—oatmeal for instance—the water can't move quickly enough for the heat to convect, so the liquid boils and the oatmeal sticks to the bottom of the pan (see Clad Pans, page 144).

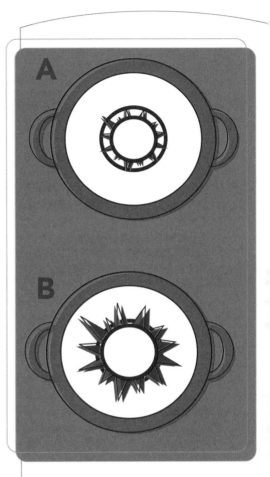

Such situations require constant management. We have to fiddle with the heat, which is a pain, and we have to stir to keep the heat distributed throughout the pot, which is also a pain because not all foods enjoy being smacked around by a big wooden spoon.

Those of us with high-end electric burners have it a little easier when it comes to sub-boiling because the coils generally have a wider diameter, which makes for more even heating. Still, I've yet to meet an electric eye I felt I could trust any more than the average rattlesnake.

So what's a cook to do? How are we to enjoy those soup beans, that beef stew, or that pilaf? Where can the heat be evenly applied and easily controlled?

The Oven

When it comes to sub-boil cookery, here's what I believe: Simmering (including the second act of braising and stewing) means cooking in a water-type liquid held just below the boil, and the best way to maintain that temperature is in an oven. With some exceptions, I do all my simmering in a 250° F oven for the first hour, and then 225° for the rest

CLAD PANS

Manufacturers of fine cookware are always trying to figure out how to construct pots and pans so that they evenly distribute the heat of a stove top to food. It's a tough nut to crack. As we discussed earlier, no one metal is ideal for cooking. Iron holds heat, and aluminum and copper conduct it, but all three are vulnerable to the kitchen environment. Stainless steel is tough and easy to care for, but it's a pretty lousy heat conductor. The answer: a metal sandwich. Take a sheet of aluminum or copper, wrap it in a protective layer of stainless steel, and you've got clad cookware. Some manufacturers are content to weld a clad disk onto the bottom of a nonclad, stainless-steel vessel, which does result in better (that is, more even) conduction across the bottom of the vessel, but not the sides. The very best clad vessels are actually formed from the clad metal. That means that everywhere there's pan, there's a core of highly conductive metal surrounded by stainless steel. Heat can therefore move easily up the sides of the pan, for more even heating throughout.

The downside of clad cookware is the cost. These are not cheap vessels to make, and you can easily shell out a hundred bucks for a sauce pan. All I can say is that you get what you pay for, and it really depends on how much control you want over your food. I fry my eggs in a twelve-dollar Teflon-coated aluminum pan from a restaurant supply store because I know what to expect from it, but I cook my soup beans (I really like soup beans, by the way) in a 150-dollar sauce pot because it makes a difference. Pick your battles. (See Appendix for more about pots and pans.)

of the cook time. The oven can maintain sub-boil temperatures for long periods of time (and I've got a thermometer to prove it). The heat moves into the vessel from all sides rather than through a small spot on the bottom, so the food inside cooks evenly, with little if any stirring.

Good simmering candidates include dried beans and other legumes, hearty greens, rice dishes, and meat stews and braises. Soup beans are the perfect example. Here's a very simple food that's darned good and good for you but that often comes out of the pot smushed to mush. Salt often takes the blame for cracked skin and spilled guts, but I'm not buying it.

With the exception of black beans and lentils, dried beans need to be soaked before cooking. Technically the step can be skipped, but the cooking process would take three times longer and the outside of the beans would be mush by the time the insides softened up. The argument for dumping the soaking liquid has to do with liquid gas—the kind that leads to unfortunate social mishaps. Legumes contain gigantic sugars called oligosaccharides. The human machine lacks an enzyme capable of breaking these megamolecules down into pieces small enough for the intestine to absorb. So they move downstream to the colon. Now, the colon is very different from the small intestine, it's rather densely populated with bacterial clans, all roaming around in search of a meal. When the oligosaccharides come floating by, the bacteria have themselves a feeding frenzy. One of the by-products of this frenzy is gas, which gathers uncomfortably, gurgles loudly, then, much to the delight of eight-year-old boys everywhere, seeks an exit.

While it's true that some of the oligosaccharides do leach into the water during soaking, so do a lot of nutrients and more than a little bean flavor. And I hate to see flavor go down the drain. So if you suffer from emission troubles, keep the bean water and pick up a bottle of Beano or one of the other commercial preparations containing alpha-galactosidase, the enzyme that breaks down oligosaccharides.

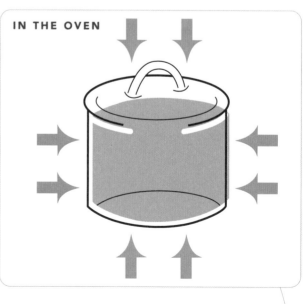

IN THE OVEN

Dried Beans Experiment

Application: Simmering

Do a quick inspection of the beans: remove beans that are discolored, cracked, or shriveled. Cooking will not improve a bad bean. Give the rest a thorough washing to remove dust and any other undesirables.

Soak the beans overnight in 6 cups of water. If dried beans don't soak overnight, they'll take at least twice as long to cook. The exceptions are lentils and split peas, which are fast-cooking to begin with, and black beans, which can squeak by with only a 3- or 4-hour soak. Be prepared: beans will double in volume during soaking, so make sure the soaking water covers them by an inch or two so they stay submerged.

Leave the soaking beans out on the kitchen counter, covered. Although you can refrigerate them, it is slower. Don't soak for more than 12 hours or you'll get mushy, flavorless beans. In a rush? You can do a speed soak by bringing the beans and water to a boil, removing from the heat, and letting them soak for about 4 hours.

Drain the beans and season with salt. Put the beans and chicken stock in the pot over medium-high flame and bring to a boil. Meanwhile, in the sauté pan, heat the oil and add the garlic, letting it toast until nice and brown. Add the rosemary for just a few seconds to release its oils, then add the garlic and rosemary to the bean pot. To the pot add the carrots, onion, celery, 2 teaspoons of kosher salt, and a couple of grinds of fresh pepper. Put the lid on the pot and place in a 250° F oven for 1½ hours.

When the beans are done, check the seasoning, correct if necessary, and serve them with style.

Yield: 2 quarts of delicious beans

Software:

1 pound of dried beans

Kosher salt

4 cups chicken stock

Olive oil

2 tablespoons garlic, sliced

2 sprigs rosemary

½ cup diced carrots

¾ cup diced onion

½ cup diced celery

Freshly ground black pepper

Hardware:

5-quart ovenproof pot with lid

Collander

Small sauté pan

Wooden spoon

Alabama Alchemy

Software:

2 pounds collard greens, stemmed
and cut into 2-inch strips

2 smoked ham hocks

3 cups water

⅓ cup vinegar of your choice (I
like a combination of cider and
rice wine vinegars)

Hardware:

The biggest covered pot you have
that'll fit in your oven

Heavy-duty aluminum foil

Another covered pot about
half as big

Being Southern, I like collard greens. Though there's a trend toward picking them young and cooking them fast, I still prefer mature greens cooked long and low in a flavorful liquid. In this case, time, liquid, and low heat collaborate to soften the cement that holds the leaf tissues together without turning them to mush. At the same time, the connective tissue of the ham hocks breaks down into gelatin. That gelatin mingles with the collard broth to produce a powerful liquid those who live below the M-D line call "potlikker."

Could you make this dish without the smoked ham hocks? You could, but no hocks, no alchemy.

Application: Simmering

Preheat the oven to 250° F.

Place the cut collards in a big sink of cold water and wash thoroughly. Using your hands, gently remove the collards from the sink to the large pot. Do not shake off the clinging water. Add the ham hocks, the water, and the vinegar and seal the pot with foil before putting the lid on.

Move the pot to the oven and cook for 2 to 3 hours or until the collards reduce to ¼ of their original mass. (How long this takes depends on the collards; mature plants are heartier and more time will be needed to break down the cell walls.) Move the collards and the hocks, with cooking liquid, to the smaller pot to keep the hocks submerged. Continue cooking for another 2 to 3 hours longer, or until the collards reach the consistency of your choice.

Although collards are often a side dish, I like to serve them in soup bowls, topped with the chopped hock meat, and cornbread on the side.

Yield: A mess o' greens

Pilaf

The word "pilaf" does refer to an actual dish, but more often than not it refers to a procedure, a way of cooking rice or other grains that includes a quick sauté in fat before any moisture is added. The result is far more flavorful than any boiled or steamed rice can muster. So why cook rice any other way? I honestly can't say.

Application: Simmering

Preheat the oven to 350° F (see **Note**). Add the salt to the liquid and bring to a boil in the kettle.

Heat the sauce pot over medium-high heat, then add the butter. As soon as the foaming subsides, add the onion and garlic. Stir with the wooden spoon until fragrant, about 1 to 2 minutes.

Add the rice and stir to coat. Stir off and on until the rice begins to smell slightly of nuts. Continue to stir, and pour in the boiling liquid (there will be some sputtering and steam). This will be the last time a spoon ever touches the rice until serving.

Cover the sauce pot tightly and place in the oven for 17 minutes. Remove the pot from the oven and remove the lid. Do not touch the rice in any way for one minute. Then fluff with the fork, and serve.

Yield: 4½ cups

Note: I simmer my pilaf at this higher temperature because of the amount of energy required to continuously convert the water involved into steam. The type of starch present in rice really needs that heat.

Software:

1 teaspoon kosher salt

4 cups liquid (water, stock, wine, or any combination thereof)

2 tablespoons unsalted butter

½ cup diced onion

2 tablespoons minced garlic

2 cups white rice

Hardware:

Kettle (I prefer electric ones)

Sauce pot with tight-fitting lid (if the fit is questionable, seal the pot opening with aluminum foil, then push on the lid)

Wooden spoon

Large fork

Boiling

OIL AND PASTA

I have received angry letters on this one from hardened pastaholics, but I can find zero science to back up the claim that adding oil to pasta cooking water keeps pasta from sticking. It's as simple as this: pasta is dehydrated, so it wants to be around water, especially hot water, which due to added molecular motion penetrates faster than cold. So you've got a lot of water and a lot of pasta, then you add a tablespoon or two of oil. Considering how oil and water feel about each other, I'd say that Butch and Sundance had a better chance of making it out of the Bolivian bank than that oil has of getting to first base with the pasta. What about during the draining, you say? By the time you get to the sink, most of the oil's back at the surface, so it's the first thing down the drain. If you want oily noodles, drain them thoroughly, then put oil on them.

Master Profile: Boiling

Heat type: wet

Mode of transmission: 70:30 percent ratio of conduction to convection

Rate of transmission: high

Common transmitters: any liquid

Temperature range: 212° F at sea level

Target food characteristics:

- Pasta
- Eggs in the shell
- British food
- Foods that can stand up to fierce convection currents (see Blanching, page 150)

Non-culinary application: sterilizing stuff

Boiling is also a position from which the cook retreats, as in "bring to a boil, then reduce to a simmer"

A temperature of 212° F at sea level is the point at which water converts to a vapor state, characterized by turbulence, bubbles, and steam production. No matter how heat is applied, once water reaches this point its temperature cannot increase. However, since it conducts heat so well, it can heat things very quickly—and heat is heat, regardless of whether it's wet or dry. Heat is also pressure and pressure squeezes juice out of meat via tissue contraction. To make matters worse, you can't look at a piece of meat in boiling water (or in steam, for that matter) and "see" that it's overcooking, because there's no browning. This can work to our advantage. Corned beef, for instance, is traditionally boiled, and most people would say that done properly it's not dried out. In reality, it's boiled to the point that the individual meat fibers break away from each other and thus become tender to the tooth—but they're still dry. Besides, corned beef has been corned, and that changes everything (see Have a Soak, page 181).

Once reached, the boiling point is constant, so it's a no-brainer to maintain. Because of its density, fluidity, and constancy of movement, boiling water delivers heat to food faster than any other method. It's also a great way to deliver salt into some foods. And in great enough volumes, boiling water can flush excess starch from foods like pasta.

A rolling boil matters when cooking pasta because it will wash away excess surface starches; heat and agitation are required for the rehydration and gelatinization of starch; and the convection keeps pasta in motion, which keeps it from sticking and helps speed cooking.

In all the cases of boiling, having a large pot and a large volume of freshly drawn, seasoned water is the key. No matter how few servings of pasta I'm cooking, I get out the big pot. It's one of the few aluminum pans I own, and I only use it for processing canning jars and cooking pasta. I need a big pot because I never cook fewer than four servings of pasta and I never cook it in anything less than a gallon of heavily salted water. Dry pasta gets cooked until done (I always pull mine just before I think it's perfect), then drained, and immediately sauced without rinsing. I do not add oil to the water—ever (see Oil and Pasta).

BOILING POINT

The "boiling point" is considered the North Star of the kitchen world, unwavering and loyal at 212° F. Sure, if you live within a thousand feet of sea level you can count on 212°, but as atmospheric pressure rises due to a high-pressure weather system or a physical drop in altitude, the boiling point rises to the tune of 2° F per 1000 feet. As the barometer goes down and/or the altitude increases, the boiling point drops 2° F per 1000 feet. This means it takes pasta twice as long to cook in Potosí, Bolivia, as it does in Kaliya, on the shores of the Dead Sea (13,290 feet above and 1,312 below sea level, respectively).

Blanching

Boiling water is at the heart of this technique, but since it's the most powerful tool we have in the war against mushy, olive-drab, nasty-tasting vegetables, blanching deserves its own section here. Blanching is the process by which foods (usually fruits and firm green vegetables) are par-boiled briefly in salted water then quickly moved to ice water to halt the cooking process. (Blanching is often followed by another quick-cooking method such as sautéing.) Why bother with all this? Because vegetables are merciless time bombs just waiting to go off and ruin dinner. Don't believe me? Grab a razor blade, a spear of asparagus, and a really big microscope.

Take a thin slice of the asparagus and look at it under the scope. It looks kind of like a box of Christmas ornaments. There are neat, enclosed cells containing various substances and mechanisms. Chlorophyll production here, food stores there, digestive enzymes in another, reproductive information in yet another. All kept safe and sound by cell walls, which are made out of a kind of plant cement, which is then reinforced with fibers (cellulose) just like concrete walls are reinforced with steel rods. The outer walls are encased in a waxy cuticle that keeps the whole thing air- and watertight. All is well, all is raw . . . all is unpalatable.

Now we drop the asparagus in rapidly boiling water. The temperature of the water drops quickly, but since we have a lot of water and leave the heat on high, the boil will recover soon. Almost immediately the cuticle and cement (pectins and whatnot) begin to soften from the heat and moisture. Within seconds the color begins to brighten because the oxygen and other gasses that were deflecting light away from the pigment in the chlorophyll dissipate out into the water. So do the acids that ordinarily would jump on those same pigments and turn them army green. Again, a lot of water will help flush those away as will a quick return to a boil, and an open pot (the gases have to be able to escape). If the target vegetable reaches satisfactory doneness before 6 or 7 minutes go by, you've got it made. The color, most of the nutrients, and the best of the flavor will be preserved. Pulling the food with a slotted strainer (good for working in batches) and moving it to ice water will immediately stop the destruction.

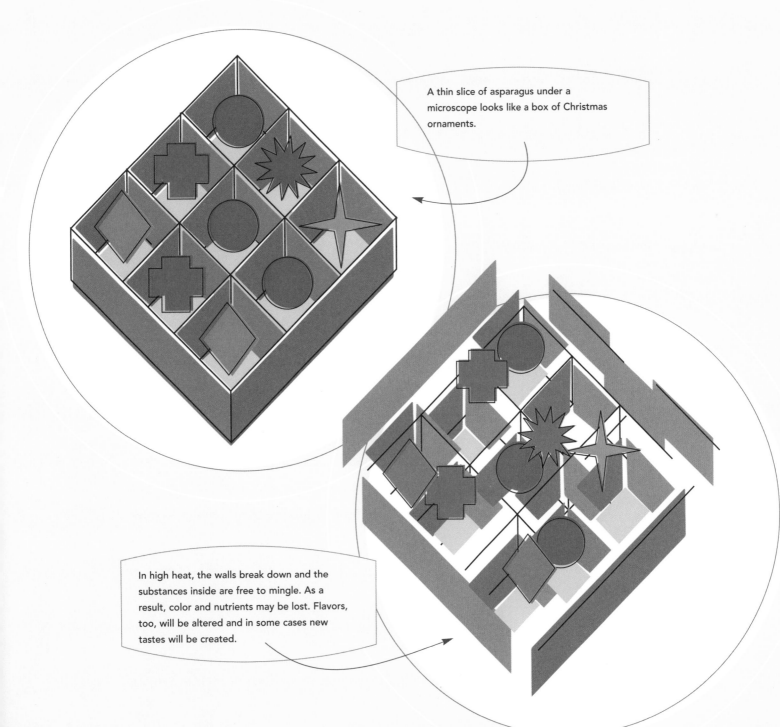

A thin slice of asparagus under a microscope looks like a box of Christmas ornaments.

In high heat, the walls break down and the substances inside are free to mingle. As a result, color and nutrients may be lost. Flavors, too, will be altered and in some cases new tastes will be created.

What happens if you forget to pull the vegetables out in time? Think of a botanical prison riot. You see, the stuff in those little cells doesn't necessarily get along, which is one of the reasons they're in cells to start with. If the walls break down enough, those substances will begin to chew on each other, acid on base, enzyme on protein . . . it's ugly. The gentle green pigments are the first to go, and the last are the fibers, the tough cellulose that so proudly held that little stem erect. And once the outer walls fail, those substances (including flavor and nutrients) will hightail it for the open sea. Now you're faced with a choice: serve your disgusting, mushy veggies, or try to make soup with them.

Even with perfectly timed cooking, blanched vegetables won't hold their color forever. Leave them sitting around in an acidic environment such as a salad dressing or a marinade and their color will be lost.

Blanching is also one of the easiest methods for peeling thin-skinned fruits such as peaches or tomatoes. That same cell breakdown that allows the color to brighten lets you remove the skin in a few quick peels, with no damage to the flesh underneath.

Steam

Through no fault of its own, steam has become the official cooking medium of the food inquisition, who use its power to inflict needless suffering on dieters who, thinking that if it's bland it's good for them, don't know to fight back. But if used only for good, steam is a powerful ally.

Vaporous H_2O is the result whenever heat produces enough molecular motion to break hydrogen bonds and enough internal pressure is generated to overcome atmospheric pressure.

Master Profile: Steam

Heat type: wet

Mode of transmission: 65:35 percent conduction to convection ratio

Rate of transmission: very high

Common transmitters: any liquid

Temperature range: 213° F and up (depending on atmospheric pressure)

Target food characteristics:

• Delicate meats and vegetables that would be destroyed by the convection of boiling

• Wide range of vegetables

Culinary advantages: steam doesn't extract and wash away food components the way immersion methods do

Non-culinary application: riverboat, locomotive, nuclear sub

I own two actual steaming devices. The first is a typical folding steamer basket (the kind that looks just like the laser-dealing satellite from *Diamonds Are Forever*, only without the diamonds). The second is an Asian-style bamboo steamer. Despite its ultra-low price tag I really, really dislike it. It's amazingly inefficient, makes everything taste like dry grass, and is impossible to clean. But when my daughter was an infant, we needed a way to steam lots of vegetables at once while keeping them separated from one another before puréeing them and we needed something that would stack. I later discovered a company that makes metal stacking steamers, but the kid's on to more solid fare, so I'll pass.

I employ four different steaming rigs depending on the food in question:

- The collapsible metal steamer basket, a rapid-response tool that I grab when I've absolutely, positively got to get a green vegetable cooked and on the table in five minutes. I also use it to roast chiles over a gas burner.
- A pair of dinner plates in a wide, low pan (see illustration **A**).
- A steel colander with its handles crushed inward so that it'll fit in a pot (**B**).
- Aluminum foil pouches (**C**).

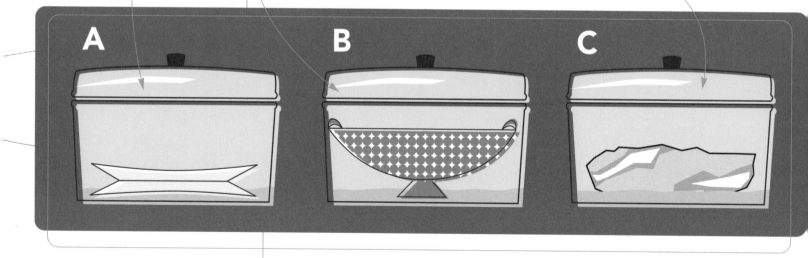

Steamed Whole Fish

Application: Steam

Have the fishmonger clean the fish, remove the gills, and scale it for you. Using a clean utility knife that can be set to a specific depth, score the fish on each side by making diagonal slashes in the flesh, about ⅛-inch deep, in a cross-hatch pattern, 5 or 6 slashes per side. Rinse the fish under cold water and season with salt and pepper. Rub half of the garlic and shallots into the slashes and lay the fish on a plate. Set another plate face-down into a braising pan and add enough water to come two-thirds of the way up the side of the plate. Place the plate with the fish on top of the bottom of the plate in the pan. Pour the vinegar on the top plate. Bring the water to a boil over high heat and cover the pan. Steam for about 10 minutes. Check the fish for doneness by gently lifting at the flesh with a fork. When it easily pulls away from the bone it is done. Carefully lift the fish to a serving plate and loosely cover with foil. Carefully pour the liquid that has accumulated on the top plate into a small sauce pan and heat the *jus* to a simmer. Heat a sauté pan and add the oil. When the oil is nice and hot, add the remaining garlic and shallots and sauté until brown. Add the chile flakes and basil and fry for a few seconds. Remove the foil from the fish and pour the hot oil over it. It will make a sizzling noise as the skin fries. Serve immediately, with a ramekin of the simmered *jus* on the side.

Yield: 1 whole fish for one person, easily doubled

Software:

1 (1-pound) whole round fish
   (Snapper, rockfish, or sea bass
   are good choices)

Kosher salt

Freshly ground black pepper

2 tablespoons thinly sliced garlic

2 tablespoons minced shallots

¼ cup herbed vinegar such as
   tarragon or basil

¼ cup olive oil

1 teaspoon chile flakes

1 tablespoon fresh basil, cut into
   fine chiffonade

Hardware:

Clean utility or matte knife

Braising pan with lid (or aluminum foil to cover)

2 steamproof plates large enough
   to hold the fish and fit into
   the pan

Small sauce pan

Sauté pan

Serving plate

Savory Savoy Wraps

Software:

8 large Savoy cabbage leaves

½ pound sweet Italian sausage, cooked and crumbled

1 cup peeled apple slices

1 teaspoon cinnamon

1 cup finely diced potatoes

Kosher salt

Freshly ground black pepper

Hardware:

Mixing bowl

Large pot

Steamer basket

These little gems are easy and delicious. You can make them as large as an egg roll or as small as a dolma depending on the size of the leaves.

Application: Steam

Lightly blanch the cabbage leaves so that they can be rolled without breaking (see **Note**). In a mixing bowl, combine all the ingredients except the cabbage leaves and season the filling with salt and pepper. Lay out a cabbage leaf, inside down (it's greener and prettier), and make a small pile of filling in the center. Roll into a tight package. Repeat with remaining leaves and filling, placing the rolls in a steamer basket, seam side down. Put enough water in a pot to come almost to the bottom of the steamer and bring to a boil. Put the lid on the pot slightly askew to allow steam to escape. Steam for 8 to 10 minutes.

Yield: 2 servings (or 4 appetizers)

Note: To blanch the leaves, simply immerse them in boiling salted water for 30 seconds and then immerse them in ice water to cool. Drain and pat dry with a towel.

Steamed Cauliflower and Broccoli

Sounds weird, looks a little odd, but boy is it delicious.

Application: Steaming

Place a collapsible steamer basket in a large pot. Add water almost to the bottom of the basket. Bring to a boil, then add the egg to the basket, cover with a tight-fitting lid, and steam for 6 minutes.

Add the vegetables to the basket and steam for another 6 minutes.

Using tongs, remove the egg to a bowl of ice water. With fireproof gloves, grab the center rod of the steamer basket (they all have one, though for the life of me I can't figure out why) and remove it to the counter with the vegetables still on board.

Peel the egg and shred it through the fine side of a box grater.

Heat the sauté pan over medium heat, then add 1 tablespoon of the butter. When the foaming subsides, toss in ⅓ of the bread crumbs and ⅓ of the grated egg then salt and pepper to taste. Stir until the crumbs begin to brown, then add ⅓ of the florets. Stir to coat, then transfer to a plate. Repeat with the remaining ingredients, making 2 more batches.

Why cook this in stages? Crowding the pan will mean more stirring, which can break the vegetables apart—and that would be bad.

Yield: 6 side servings

Software:

1 egg

½ head cauliflower, cut into florets

1 head broccoli, cut into florets

3 tablespoons butter

½ cup panko (Japanese bread crumbs)

Kosher salt

Freshly ground black pepper

Hardware:

Steamer basket

Large pot with lid

Tongs

Fireproof gloves

Box grater

Sauté pan

Sweet Onion Custard

For more about custards and eggs, see the Eggs-cetera section that starts on page 216.

Application: Steam

In a mixing bowl, whisk together the eggs, stock, and vinegar. Season with salt and white pepper. Divide the onions evenly among 4 ramekins and pour in the egg mixture to fill. Cover tightly with plastic wrap and then aluminum foil and set the ramekins in a steamer basket. Place steamer over a large pot of water at a low boil and gently steam for 12 to 15 minutes until custard is set but not firm. Serve hot.

Yield: 4 servings

Note: Onions will reduce by half as you caramelize them, so begin with 1 cup of thinly sliced onions. Place a pan over medium heat and add 1 tablespoon of butter per onion. When the butter has melted, toss the onions to coat. Cook, stirring occasionally, until they are brown and soft.

Software:

3 eggs

1¼ cups chicken stock

1 teaspoon balsamic vinegar

Kosher salt

Freshly ground white pepper

½ cup caramelized onions
(see **Note**)

Hardware:

Mixing bowl

Whisk

4 ramekins

Plastic wrap

Aluminum foil

Steamer basket

Large pot

Ramen Radiator

This is the coolest dish in the book, which is not to say that you shouldn't try the rest of the recipes. I just think this dish delivers huge dividends on a very meager investment.

Application: Steam

Preheat the oven to 400° F. Heat a sauté pan over high heat, add the oils, then add the mushrooms and toss; cook until caramelized, about 3 to 4 minutes. Transfer to a plate and set aside. Break the "loaf" of noodles into 2 equal parts. Season the fish with salt and white pepper, spread a little honey on each filet, and sprinkle with chile flakes. Line the serving bowls with aluminum foil, making sure there is a lot hanging over the edges. Lay one half-loaf of noodles in each bowl and top with the fish. Spread the shrimp, mushrooms, and onions around the bottom. Top with the scallions. Pull the foil up around the food and crimp it to seal, leaving one tiny opening in each pouch. Mix the liquids together and pour half into each pouch and then seal. Set the pouches on a baking sheet and place in the oven for 22 to 25 minutes. Set the pouches back in the bowls and open at the table. A delicious aroma will fill the air as the steam escapes. Serve with chopsticks and a spoon to eat the "soup."

Yield: 2 servings

Software:

1 teaspoon olive oil

1 teaspoon sesame oil

8 ounces brown mushrooms, sliced (preferably cremini or shiitake, but not button)

1 (3-ounce) package ramen noodles

2 (8-ounce) halibut or other mild white fish filets (salmon also works well)

Kosher salt

Freshly ground white pepper

1 tablespoon honey

Pinch of chile flakes

6 medium shrimp, peeled and deveined

½ Vidalia onion, sliced Lyonnaise-style

4 scallions, sliced on a bias

2 tablespoons soy sauce

¼ cup mirin (sweet rice wine)

2 cups miso or vegetable stock (if using miso, the measurement is 2 teaspoons miso paste for 2 cups water)

Hardware:

Sauté pan

2 large serving bowls

Aluminum foil

Baking sheet

Proof positive that dry and wet heat can get along in the same recipe.

CHAPTER 6   **Braising**

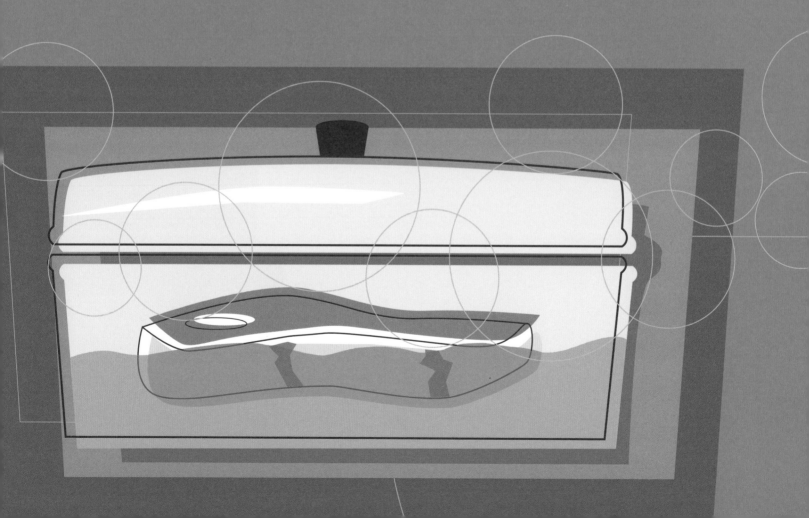

Amazing Braise

Braising and stewing are compound methods that begin with searing or pan-frying and finish with simmering, and as far as I'm concerned, braises and stews are the finest edibles on earth. They've got it all: caramelized crusts, tender interiors, and of course. . . sauce.

A braised dish typically contains either a large piece of meat or smaller pieces that are left whole. Pot roast is typically a braise, as is osso buco (braised veal or lamb shanks). The meat is seared in a hot pan to brown the exterior, then cold liquid is added (along with vegetables or other bits and pieces), the vessel is covered, and the dish is simmered for as long as it takes for the collagen in the meat to dissolve into gelatin. In a stew the meat is usually cut into bite-size chunks, which are sometimes dusted with flour, seared, then just covered with a flavorful liquid. A stew is as much about the liquid as the meat. (Besides beef stew, consider beef Stroganoff, veal blanquette, and chili.)

COLLAGEN AND GELATIN

Animal muscle is comprised of bunches of meat fibers held together by connective tissue. Cuts of meat from parts of animals that don't do much work don't have a lot of connective tissue, but cuts that either work a lot or have a lot of bone do. However, not all connective tissue is created equal. See, some of the tissues don't do much but shrink up and get chewy when they meet heat—we can refer to those as gristle. But others are coated in a protein collagen, and under the right circumstances collagen dissolves into gelatin, the stuff that brings body to homemade stocks and helps your family's favorite gelatin mold set.

Note that this transformation of collagen to gelatin takes time. In fact, to do it right it takes a lot of time. (That is, unless you swap hours on the clock for pressure; for more on pressure cookers see page 175.) How does this magical change happen, you ask? Gelatin is obtained by the hydrolysis of collagen, a process that is catalyzed by enzymes called collagenases. It all has to do with a slow, low, moist, covered cooking method. Taking the slow and low approach allows for increased conversion of collagen to gelatin and reduces the chance of overcoagulated muscle fibers. Upon cooling, the gelatinized protein partially resets, and can hold added moisture, resulting in a meat that is moist and flavorful.

The problem with most braising and stewing recipes is that they call for too much of a weak thing—liquid. Meat, like most living tissue, is mostly water, a good bit of which is wrung out of the meat during the long cooking necessary to render the meat tender. That liquid leaches out, and unless the liquid added by the cook is very concentrated, the result is a very weak sauce.[23] The key is to start with a flavorful liquid, reduce it, then let the meat liquids reconstitute it. Start with a quart of liquid, reduce it to a pint, and you'll have a quart of rich sauce at the end of cooking.

The braising of tough cuts of meat reminds me of an old saying that one hears quite a bit in the film business: You can have it fast, you can have it cheap, you can have it good. Choose any two.

The catch-22 of braising and stewing is that when it comes to tough cuts like chuck, brisket, ribs, and shanks, you can't have moist and tender. It's simply impossible. Here's why.

The metamorphosis of collagen to gelatin requires moisture, time, and heat. Since there's already a good bit of moisture in meat, the amount we need to add is relatively low. The heat required however (a minimum of 140° F, but most thoroughly at temperatures

[23] The way I see it, if the liquid is thickened by solids or stock, it's a sauce. If it's thickened by starch, it's gravy.

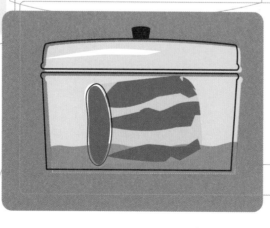

Despite the fact that there is very little liquid, the vessel is covered and the heat is low (we assume), this is not braising because too little of the food is in contact with the liquid.

Since more of the food is in contact with the liquid this could be considered braising, but since only half the food is in direct contact, it isn't very effective.

close to boiling), would certainly qualify as well done in anything other than the darkest meat of poultry. That's because as meat heats up, the individual muscle bundles tighten up like fists around wet sponges. The meat literally wrings itself out into the pan where it either waters down whatever flavorful liquid has been introduced or evaporates. That means that by the time the collagen conversion is just cranking up, a significant portion of the meat's juice is in motion. And since several hours can pass before the process is complete, we can only deduce that tender meat is dry meat. Sounds logical, but how is it that braises and stews are some of the most lip-smackin' foods known to man?

For one thing, if you cook most meats long enough in a wet environment, they will eventually relax, and just like a sponge, they'll reabsorb some liquid, but not nearly enough to feel moist in the mouth. The real trick is to capture two other liquids in the meat: melted fat and dissolved gelatin.

So we know what we're looking for: flavorful meat containing a good bit of connective tissue and a moderate level of fat. Take a beef round roast. It has moisture and some connective tissue, but very little fat, which is why it makes for a really crummy pot roast.

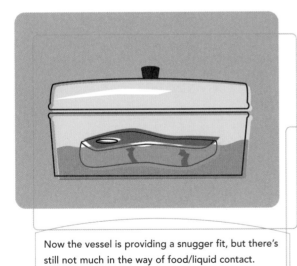

Now the vessel is providing a snugger fit, but there's still not much in the way of food/liquid contact.

meat and juices inside foil pouch

Because it's tightly sealed in foil, the meat is completely surrounded by the liquid (remember, the smaller the amount of concentrated liquid the better). The vessel is still necessary because no matter how good you are at metallurgical origami, the packet is going to leak.

Tenderloin and sirloin are even worse when cooked long, low, and wet. Besides, both are relatively tender, so are better suited to a dry method of cooking. Now consider beef short ribs. They've got it all: flavor, connective tissue, and enough fat to make up for the moisture lost during long cooking. They've also got bones, which bring flavor and even more connective tissue to the party. Short ribs are ideal for braising because they are durable enough to stand up to multiple-stage cooking.

Master Profile: Braising

Heat type: moist

Mode of transmission: 15:85 percent sear to sub-simmer ratio

Rate of transmission: One of the slowest methods around

Common transmitters: heavy pans (sear part) and flavorful liquids (simmer part)

Temperature range: 140° to 210° F

Target food characteristics: large cuts of meat that are high in connective tissue

Non-culinary use: tempering steel

Lamb "Pot Roast"

Pot roast is the poster child for braising. I know of no other dish that goes through such a spectacular metamorphosis during cooking, or that comforts so completely after. (I'm getting all teary-eyed just thinking about it.) Although I have nothing against beef pot roast, lamb brings more meat for less cash.

Application: Searing, then Braising

Preheat the oven to 300° F. Season the flour with salt and pepper. Lightly season the chops with salt and pepper and dredge them in the flour. Shake off any excess. Heat the braising pan over medium heat and add the oil. Sear the chops on all sides until browned; you may need to work in 2 batches to avoid overcrowding the pan (overcrowding eliminates the space needed for steam to escape—that sizzling noise you hear—and your food is then steamed and no crust forms). As the chops brown remove them to a plate. Add the garlic and shallots to the pan. Sauté until fragrant, then add the onions, carrots, celery, and fennel. Stir the vegetables around, then add the wine to deglaze the pan, scraping with a wooden spoon. All those browned pieces from the bottom of the pan will "leap" up and cling to the vegetables. Add the tomato paste, then pour in the stock and add the tomatoes and a few sprigs of rosemary (I leave it whole so I can remove it later; I don't like to eat the rosemary). Sprinkle an even layer of the dredging flour, about ⅛ cup, over the vegetables; this will help to thicken the sauce. Lay the chops on top, put the lid on the pan, and cook in the oven for 2 hours. Chill the meat, in the pan, overnight in the refrigerator, then cook for 1 hour in a 300° F oven. (Any collagen left will come leaping out.) Once finished, allow the chops to rest in the covered pan for 15 to 20 minutes. Remove the chops to a plate and loosely cover with foil. Use a ladle to de-fat the sauce; it should be thinner than gravy but thicker than *jus*. If you like a thicker sauce, purée it together with the vegetables.

Yield: 4 servings

Software:

2 cups flour

Kosher salt

Freshly ground black pepper

4 lamb shoulder chops

¼ cup olive oil

2 heaping tablespoons chopped garlic

¼ cup chopped shallots

2 cups diced onions

1 cup diced carrots

1 cup diced celery

1 cup diced fennel (optional, but it gives it a Mediterranean flavor)

1 cup red wine (remember: if you wouldn't drink it, why eat it?)

2 tablespoons tomato paste

3 cups beef stock

4 plum tomatoes, seeded and diced

Fresh rosemary sprigs

Hardware:

Large braising pan with lid

Wooden spoon

Tongs

Ladle

Stick blender if you want to purée the sauce

Software:

For the brine:

½ gallon dark beer, chilled (choose your favorite)

1 pound brown sugar

1 cup kosher salt plus enough to rub on the ribs

1 quart ice water

2 whole short ribs (about 5 pounds)

2 cups hickory wood chips, soaked in water

Canola oil

1¼ cup diced carrots

1⅔ cup diced onion

1¼ cup diced celery

½ cup red wine

2 quarts beef stock

Hardware:

2-gallon container

Heavy pot

Paper towels

Pie pan

Roasting pan

Wooden spoon

Aluminum foil

Strainer

Sauce pan

Smoked and Braised Beef Short Ribs

I start this cooking procedure with smoke. Since the connective tissue of the ribs doesn't really start dissolving until it reaches 120–130° F, there's no reason to cook these ribs in liquid the entire time. Short ribs are great simply seared and simmered, but the addition of smoke results in a dish that is far more than the sum of its parts.

Application: Braising

Make a brine. Bring three cups of the beer, the sugar, and the cup of salt to a boil in a heavy pot. Cook until all the solids are dissolved and then pour into the 2-gallon container. Add the remaining beer and the ice water to cool the brine below 40° F (this should be immediate if the beer and water were chilled). Liberally coat the ribs with salt and submerge them in the brine. Store, refrigerated, for at least 24 hours or up to 3 days.

Smoke the ribs. Remove the ribs from the brine, rinse thoroughly, and pat dry. Spread a handful of charcoal on the far side of your grill grate and light. When the coals are white and ashy, place the hickory chips in the pie pan and set this on top of the coals. Replace the cooking grate and place the ribs on the opposite side of the grill. Close the lid and allow the ribs to smoke for 20 to 30 minutes. Remove from grill and proceed to the braising.

Braise the ribs. Preheat the oven to 300° F. Set the roasting pan on the cook top over a medium high flame and add just enough oil to lightly coat the vegetables. Add the carrots, onion, and celery and allow them to caramelize. Deglaze the pan with the wine; using the wooden spoon to scrape up any delicious bits from the bottom of the pan. Set the ribs on top the vegetables and add enough stock to come three-quarters up the side of the roasting pan. Bring the liquid to a boil and very carefully seal the pan with foil. Place in the oven for 1 hour and 15 minutes.

Remove from the oven to the cook top and let rest, covered, for 30 minutes. Remove the foil and carefully pull the bones out of the meat—they are tapered, so just grab the wider end and gently pull. Trim away the tissue that used to surround the bones. Set the meat aside and strain the stock into a sauce pan; discard the vegetables. Bring the stock to a boil and let it reduce in volume by half. Taste and adjust seasoning with salt and pepper (it probably won't need salt due to the brine). Plate the beef and serve with the sauce.

Yield: 4 servings

No-Backyard Baby Back Ribs

Software:

1 full rack/slab baby back ribs

Kosher salt

Rub Number 9 (see **Note**)

½ cup orange juice (not fresh
   squeezed)

½ cup prepared Margarita mix

⅓ cup honey

⅓ cup ketchup

1 tablespoon Worcestershire sauce

1 teaspoon espresso powder or
   instant coffee (freeze-dried, not
   actual grounds)

⅛ teaspoon cayenne pepper

Hardware:

Paper towels

Extra-wide, heavy-duty aluminum
   foil

Shallow roasting pan

Saucier or small sauce pan

Kitchen shears

Broiler pan

I love baby back ribs because they deliver flavor and finger-lickin' goodness with little fuss and even less time. I have friends who smoke their 'back ribs for hours and hours and then wonder why they're tough. The reason is connective tissue, lots of it, and no amount of dry heat is going to dissolve that. If you can't imagine baby back ribs without smoke, however, go ahead and smoke them for an hour or so before the braising step (see Smoked and Braised Short Ribs, page 166). Personally I don't bother. I often wear rubber gloves at the table and eat these ribs over a large mixing bowl. It isn't pretty.

Application: Braising, then Broiling

Rinse the ribs and pat dry with paper towels. Place on a sheet of extra-wide, heavy-duty aluminum foil. (The foil should be 4 inches longer than the ribs on either end.) Season liberally on both sides with the salt and Rub Number 9.

Turn the ribs meat-side-down and tightly seal according to the illustrations at right.

Place the packet in the roasting pan and refrigerate for 6 to 12 hours, turning the sealed packet over once.

Preheat oven to 350° F.

Remove the packet from the refrigerator and unroll one end, shaping the foil upward like a funnel. Pour in the orange juice and the Margarita mix. Reseal the foil packet and see-saw it back and forth a couple of times to evenly distribute the liquid inside.

Return the packet to the pan and place the pan in the middle of the oven. After 1 hour, reduce temperature to 250° F and cook until tender, approximately 2 hours.

Remove the pan from the oven, unroll one end of the packet, carefully drain all juice into a *saucier* or small saucepan, and add the honey, ketchup, Worcestershire sauce, espresso powder, and cayenne.

Bring the mixture to a boil, whisking frequently until reduced to a glaze that coats a spoon. Remove the pan from heat.

Move oven rack to the next-to-the-top position and turn on the broiler (use the high setting if you have a choice).

Remove the slab from the foil packet and cut it into four equal sections (I use kitchen shears for this). Place ribs on the broiling pan, meat side up, brush with the glaze, and broil for 2 to 3 minutes. Reglaze and repeat until the ribs are a dark mahogany color. Flip the ribs bone side up, glaze, and broil a minute longer.

Remove and allow to cool a couple of minutes before serving, preferably with potato salad or copious amounts of coleslaw.

Yield: 1 to 3 servings, depending on who's doing the eating

Note: For one rack of ribs, ½ to ¾ cup of rub will be sufficient. The ratio of ingredients for Rub Number 9 is: 5 parts brown sugar, 3 parts chile powder, 1 part garlic powder, ½ part ground thyme, ¼ part cayenne, and ¼ part allspice. A part can be any amount—a tablespoon, for example—depending on how much is needed.

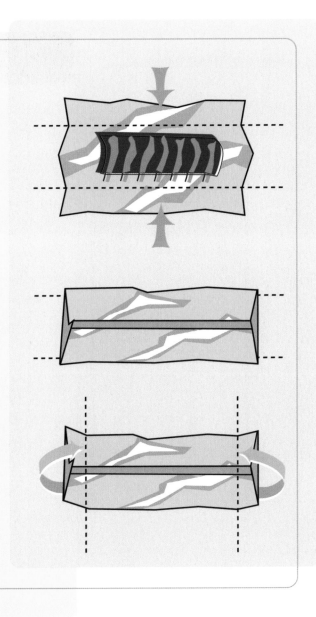

Chicken Piccata

Piccata is Italian for "sharp" and refers to the bright snappy flavor of this classic one-pan dish. Although there are thousands of ways to execute a "piccata," this recipe sets out some fair guidelines. Here, braising has less to do with tenderizing and more to do with sauce construction. The simmer stage accomplishes three things: it gently completes the cooking of the chicken, marries the flavors of the aromatics and the capers, and gelatinizes the starch in the flour, thus thickening the liquid so that it clings to the meat. Properly executed, there shouldn't be much sauce left in the pan.

Application: Pan-Braise

Place the chicken breasts, one at a time, on a sheet of plastic wrap; fold the wrap over to cover. Using the mallet, pound each breast to a uniform thickness of ¼ inch. Season the chicken liberally with the salt and pepper, dredge in the flour, shaking off any excess.

In a heavy skillet just big enough to hold all the chicken, heat the oil and 2 tablespoons of butter. When the oil and butter stop sizzling, add the chicken and cook, turning once, until just brown on both sides. Remove the chicken to a plate. Pour off any grease from the pan and add the remaining tablespoon of butter.

Add the onion to the skillet and sauté until translucent. Add the garlic and the scallions and sauté 1 more minute. Sprinkle 1 teaspoon of the flour over the vegetables and toss to combine.

Deglaze the pan with vermouth and the lemon juice. Add the capers and toss to combine. Return the chicken to the pan, cover, and reduce heat to low, simmering until chicken is cooked through, about 4 minutes. Correct the seasoning with salt and pepper if necessary, and serve on warm platter garnished with the parsley and lemon slices.

Yield: 2 servings

Software:

2 boneless chicken breasts, cut in half

Kosher salt

Freshly ground black pepper

Flour for dredging plus 1 teaspoon

2 tablespoons canola oil

3 tablespoons butter

½ yellow onion, chopped

3 cloves garlic, minced

6 scallions, chopped

⅓ to ½ cup sweet vermouth, sherry, or white wine

Juice of 1 large lemon

1 tablespoon capers, rinsed and lightly crushed

2 tablespoons chopped parsley

1 lemon, sliced thinly

Hardware:

Plastic wrap

Smooth mallet or heavy sauce pot

Container for dredging

Large skillet or electric skillet with lid

Tongs

Salisbury Steak

These steaks are browned in a combination of butter and oil. This will give you the flavor of butter while increasing the smoke point, allowing you to cook at a higher temperature than with butter alone.

Application: Pan-Braise

Preheat the oven to 275° F. Lightly season the steaks and the dredging flour with the salt and pepper, then dredge the steaks in the flour and shake off any excess.

Add 1 tablespoon each of the butter and oil to a hot sauté pan. Brown the steaks, two at a time, adding more butter and oil as needed, about 4 minutes per side. Remove the steaks to a plate.

Pour off any grease from the pan and add the remaining butter. Add the onion, garlic, and mushrooms to the pan and sauté until nicely caramelized, then deglaze the pan with the wine. Mix in the Worcestershire sauce, mustard, and stock, and stir to combine. Return the steaks to the pan, cover, and cook in the oven for 25 minutes.

Yield: 4 servings

Software:

4 (½ pound) beef cube steaks

Flour for dredging

Kosher salt

Freshly ground black pepper

3 tablespoons butter

2 tablespoons canola oil

½ medium onion, sliced Lyonnaise-style

2 tablespoons minced garlic

½ pound brown mushrooms, thinly sliced (an egg slicer works well)

¾ cup red wine

1 tablespoon Worcestershire sauce

½ tablespoon Dijon mustard

¾ cup chicken or beef stock

Hardware:

Dredge container

Ovenproof sauté pan with lid

Wooden spoon

Stewing

Classically, a braise involves a big hunk of meat, a very small amount of liquid, low heat, and a covered vessel. A stew involves lots of pieces of meat that are completely submerged in liquid, cooked over low heat in a covered vessel. The cooking goal is identical as far as the meat is concerned: slow, moist heat that will dissolve collagen.

However, the liquid part of a stew is as important as the meat and whatever other chunks of vegetable may be present. In other words, a stew is half a soup, so seasoning isn't just about the meat.

Also, just about every stew recipe out there is thickened by starch somewhere along the line. Either the meat is dredged before searing, or flour is sprinkled over the assembled ingredients before it heads off to the oven. There's a chili recipe coming up in a few pages that gets its starch from dissolved corn chips.

And just so we're clear, I don't consider dairy-thickened soups (bisques and chowders) to be true stews . . . but that's just me.

WHY STARCH THICKENS

When starch granules get hot and become saturated with liquid, they explode like popcorn. Then they get in the way of the liquid molecules, preventing them from pooling together. Voilà: thickness!

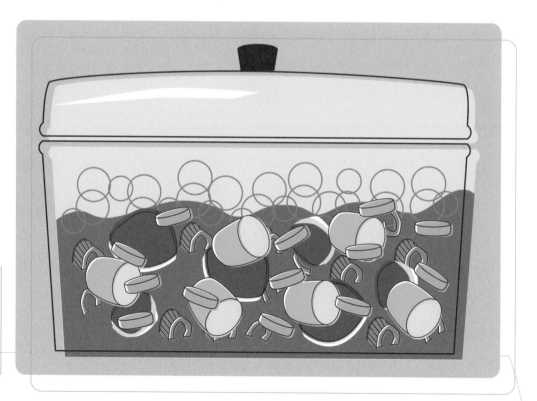

Beef Stroganoff

The components of this stew aren't that different from those of a pan braise, but the size of the pieces, the starch, and the extra liquid necessitates a new step here: stirring. That's why I reach for my electric skillet. It gives me heat control and quick access.

Application: Stewing

One hour before cooking, place the roast in the freezer. It will firm it up and make it easier to slice. Cut the meat into ½-inch strips. Season the meat and the flour liberally with the salt and pepper. Allow the meat to rest a few minutes so that the salt can pull a little moisture to the surface, then dredge in seasoned flour (see **Note**).

Heat the electric skillet to its hottest temperature. When the thermostat light goes out add 1 tablespoon each of the butter and the oil. When the butter begins to foam, add just enough of the meat to barely cover the bottom of the skillet. Do not crowd the pan. Turn the strips until they're brown on all sides, then remove to a rack resting over a pan. Continue browning the meat in batches, adding more butter and oil as needed.

When all of the meat has been browned, pour off any grease from the pan, add the remaining butter, then add the shallot, garlic, and mushrooms to the skillet and sauté until brown. Using a shaker or sifter, sprinkle a couple of teaspoons of the seasoned flour over the top of the vegetables and toss to coat. Deglaze the skillet with the wine, using a spatula to scrape up any stubborn bits.

Stir in the mustard and return the meat and any drippings to the skillet. Add enough beef stock to barely cover the meat. Drop the temperature to a simmer (between 180° and 200° F), and cover. Cook for 45 minutes, stirring occasionally. Stir in sour cream and serve over wide egg noodles or rice.

Yield: 4 servings

Note: Seasoned flour is typically a simple mixture of salt, pepper, and flour, but depending on the recipe, it may involve any number of different seasonings. What you're looking for when you taste—and you should get into the habit of tasting everything—is a subtle background of both salt and pepper.

Software:

2 pounds inexpensive beef roast, such as eye of round

Flour for dredging (see **Note**)

Kosher salt

Freshly ground black pepper

3 tablespoons butter

2 tablespoons canola oil

4 tablespoons minced shallot

1½ tablespoons minced garlic

½ pound brown mushrooms, thickly sliced (an egg slicer works well)

¾ cup red wine

½ tablespoon Dijon mustard, blended into 2 tablespoons beef stock (so it will incorporate easier)

2 beef bouillon cubes dissolved in 2 to 2½ cups beef stock

4 tablespoons sour cream

Hardware:

Container for dredging

Electric skillet

Rack and drip pan for resting

Shaker or sifter

Spatula

Wooden spoon

Software:

2 pounds chuck steak, cut into
   ½-inch cubes

Kosher salt

Freshly ground black pepper

1 teaspoon chile powder (see **Note**)

2 tablespoons olive oil

1½ cups finely diced onion

4 cloves garlic

2 ancho chiles, split, seeds
   removed, and roughly chopped

2 California chiles, split, seeds
   removed, and roughly chopped

2 roasted red bell peppers (see
   Note)

1 chipotle chile in adobo (one chile
   not one can)

4 ounces canned diced tomatoes

¾ cup beef stock

¾ cup delicious beer (I use
   Shiner Bock)

Hardware:

Sauté pan

Medium-sized heavy-bottom pot

Stick blender

Chili

For me, chili has to be all about the chiles. Once you come to grips with this seemingly obvious fact, you'll be the king of chili.

Application: Stewing

Season the beef with salt, pepper, and chile powder. Heat the sauté pan, add some of the oil, and brown the beef, working in batches if necessary and removing the browned beef to a plate. In a heavy-bottom pot, sweat the onions and garlic in some of the oil until tender, but not browned. Add the remaining ingredients (except the beef) and simmer for 10 minutes. With a stick blender, purée the mixture, then add the beef to the pot. Cook over low heat (below a simmer) for 45 minutes, stirring occasionally. Taste and season with salt and pepper if necessary.

This chili is really good as is, but if you cool it and store it for a day or two it's fantastic when reheated.

Yield: about 2 quarts

Note: As far as the chile powder is concerned, there are many types available on the market. I prefer ones that are a specific type of chile with nothing else added. Paul Prudhomme has a whole line of them. You can use a mild one or a hot one depending on what you like.

To roast a pepper: Cut in half from top to bottom. You'll leave behind the core, seeds, and stem. Now you can go several routes:

1. Lay them skin side up on a pan and broil until the skin is totally blackened.

2. Lay them skin side down on a hot grill until the skin is totally blackened.

3. Using tongs, set or hold them over the open flame of your range until the skin is completely blackened (the pepper is left whole while blackening for this option).

Once blackened (they'll look burnt), put them in a bowl and cover with plastic wrap to steam. Once cool enough to handle, peel away the black skin.

Working under Pressure

The first pressure cooker, called the "ingester," was designed in 1679 by French physicist Denis Papin. It consisted of a glass container to hold the food and liquid that was sealed before being placed inside a metal container. Water was then used to fill the gap between the glass container and the metal vessel, and a metal top was screwed on. The entire device was then heated on a fire. To ensure that the cooker didn't explode, Papin included a safety valve to let out excess steam once the desired pressure had been reached. By varying the weight used to keep the safety valve in place, the pressure could easily be regulated. Measuring temperature, on the other hand, was not so easy. Daniel Fahrenheit and Anders Celsius invented their temperature scales after Papin had died. So Papin created his own way to check temperature. He had a depression in the top of the pressure cooker, into which he would place a drop of water. He then used a 3-foot pendulum, which swings in a period of about 1 second, to time how long it took for the drop to evaporate. Unfortunately, the ingester blew up a year later.

In 1939, the first commercial pressure cooker (made by the National Pressure Cooker Company, known since 1953 as National Presto Industries) debuted in the United States at the New York World's Fair. The pressure cooker was put on the back burner during World War II, when many manufacturers had to turn their attention toward war efforts. But after the war ended, pressure cookers were a hot item.

Today's pressure cookers are both safe and efficient. The heat inside a pressure cooker creates steam, which expands, creating 15 pounds per square inch of pressure, which in turn raises the boiling point of liquid to 250° F. In this extreme heat, foods cook two-thirds faster than they would in boiling water.

All pressure cookers utilize a heavy pot or pan, a lid that locks, with an airtight seal and a pressure-control device. Noisy first-generation or jiggle-top cookers are reasonably priced but are problematic in that they lose a good deal of moisture via steam and require skillful handling. In modified first-generation cookers, instead of a weight there's a sophisticated spring-loaded valve, which means less moisture loss and a quieter ride. The second-generation cookers have a spring-loaded rod that maintains the pressure. They're quiet and work well, but are often expensive.

When you're out there shopping, look for a 6-quart cooker with double handles for safe moving. And pick it up—heavy is good. Remember that the first steam engine was based on a pressure cooker: it's a complex system, so be sure to read the manual.

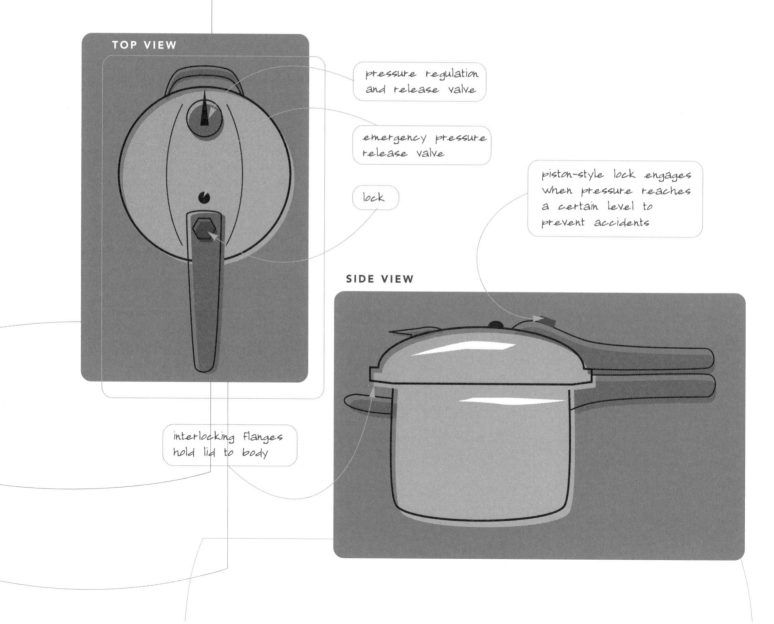

TOP VIEW

pressure regulation and release valve

emergency pressure release valve

lock

piston-style lock engages when pressure reaches a certain level to prevent accidents

SIDE VIEW

interlocking flanges hold lid to body

The Chili Bet

Folks fuss over chili. True "red"-heads spend hours coaxing buckets of pricey and sometimes exotic groceries into alchemaic stews, which they give names like "mouth of hell" and then enter into chili contests.

Some friends and I were sitting around a buddy's porch one afternoon bemoaning the silly seriousness of such endeavors and contemplating where it could lead (picture Texans on the set of *Iron Chef*, Colts drawn). Anyway, we sank into philosophy and came to the no-doubt accurate conclusion that the dish properly known as *chili con carne* is essentially a utilitarian field dish most likely concocted by chuck masters on the Chisolm Trail who needed to make use of really lousy cuts of beef. Another buddy put forth that if this were indeed the case, the criteria for judging a "true" chili would have to include grocery receipts, for economy would have to be a factor.

There was a moment's silence as we all considered what must be done. We had to hold a cheap-chili cook-off. I looked at my watch: 2:30 in the afternoon. We agreed to meet back on the very same porch at 7:00 P.M., which meant there wasn't a moment to lose.

3:00 P.M.

I ran home and checked the pantry and fridge. Not a shred of meat in the house that wasn't frozen into blocks—no time for even a speed thaw (you'd be surprised what you can do with a frozen chuck in the shower). I made sure that I had a small can of tomato paste, checked my supply of chili powder and ground cumin (my very most favoritest spice in the whole wide world) and headed to the market.[24]

3:17 P.M.

The cheapest stew meat I could find was $1.59 a pound. From the looks of the hunks, I'd guess it was chuck mixed with a little round, which was fine. There was also some lamb stew meat (unidentifiable, with lots of bone and connective tissue—shoulder, I'd bet) at $1.29 a pound. I bought 2 pounds of the first and 1 pound of the latter. (I could have gone

---

[24] Chili powder usually includes oregano, coriander, cloves, dried chiles, garlic powder, and cumin. Chile powder contains nothing but dried ground chiles. The two are not interchangeable so always check that final vowel.

with all beef, but why?) I wandered the market, pondering the next move and settled on a small can of chipotles in adobo sauce at $1.29.[25] Total so far: $5.76.

3:39 P.M.

On the way home I stopped by my favorite Mexican restaurant and ordered the cheapest beer they had, a tapped item called "Los . . . something." The beer came, along with a small basket of corn chips and a healthy bowl of hot salsa.

I poured the beer into my insulated coffee mug (hey, it was in the car) and the salsa into a zip-top bag that had previously housed an emergency supply of graham crackers for my daughter. Avoiding the suspicious gaze of the cantina keep, I made for home. Total spent: $1.00.

3:57 P.M.

Back at the house, I heavily seasoned the meaty cubes with kosher salt and placed my large cast-iron skillet over high heat. Two minutes later, I started adding the meat in small batches, turning the pieces every now and then with tongs to get as much surface browning as possible as quickly as possible.[26] As the meat browned, I set it into a bowl so that I could capture all the meat's juices.

When all of the meat had browned, I deglazed the bottom of the pan with ½ cup of the beer. It immediately came to a boil and I scraped the pan with a wooden spatula for a few moments until all of the stuck-on bits had dissolved. Everything left in the pan was added to the bowl holding the meat.

4:15 P.M.

Less than three hours to go. Most chili recipes require that long just to chop the ingredients. The actual cooking could take days, what with all that connective tissue to

---

[25] Chipotles are nothing more than smoked jalapeños. Pound for pound, they bring more flavor to the party than any other chiles. Adobo is like Mexican barbecue sauce: herbs and ground chiles with vinegar.

[26] As noted in Searing, zillions of recipes include this step. Why? Because browning via caramelization and the Mailliard reaction produces myriad flavors. So, if it's so darned good why doesn't someone simply manufacture this stuff and bottle it so we can pour it on everything? Darned good question. But personally, I'm glad there's still something you can't buy.

break down. Clearly, the pressure was on—heck, working under pressure had been the plan all along.

I broke out my heavy-duty 8-quart pressure cooker and poured in the salsa (16 ounces—I measured) and the rest of the beer (1 cup—again, I measured). Then I added the meat, along with all the juices that had accumulated at the bottom of the bowl. I stirred in a fat tablespoon of the tomato paste and then added 15 corn chips (did I mention these were the triangular kind?), which I broke to bits by pushing them down into the meaty melange with a wooden spoon.

4:18 P.M.

Lid on. I let the cooker come to full pressure over high heat, then backed off the heat until the steam dropped to a bare hiss and set the timer for 15 minutes.

4:33 P.M.

When the timer went off, I released the pressure valve and dumped the steam. (This always reminds of that scene at the end of *Alien* when Sigourney Weaver flushes the alien from its hiding spot on the shuttle.) I then added 1 tablespoon of chili powder, 1 teaspoon of ground cumin, 2 of the canned chipotles (chopped) along with 2 tablespoons of the accompanying adobo sauce. I stirred the whole thing, decided to add another handful of chips (the first load had disintegrated), lidded up, and brought the cooker back up to pressure for another 10 minutes. I then removed the cooker from the heat and allowed the pressure to abate on its own. When I removed the lid, the meat was fork tender and the sauce pleasantly spicy and thick.

7:00 P.M.

Back on my friend's porch, I served the chili with a dollop of sour cream and chopped green onions and won the bet. Total bill (including the tomato paste I already had): $7.74.[27]

---

[27] This does not mean I condone the thieving of chips and salsa from restaurants, but you get the point.

There are lots of ways to get flavor into food, but brining is the only way I know to season, enhance texture, and add weight to a piece of meat.

CHAPTER 7 | **Brining**

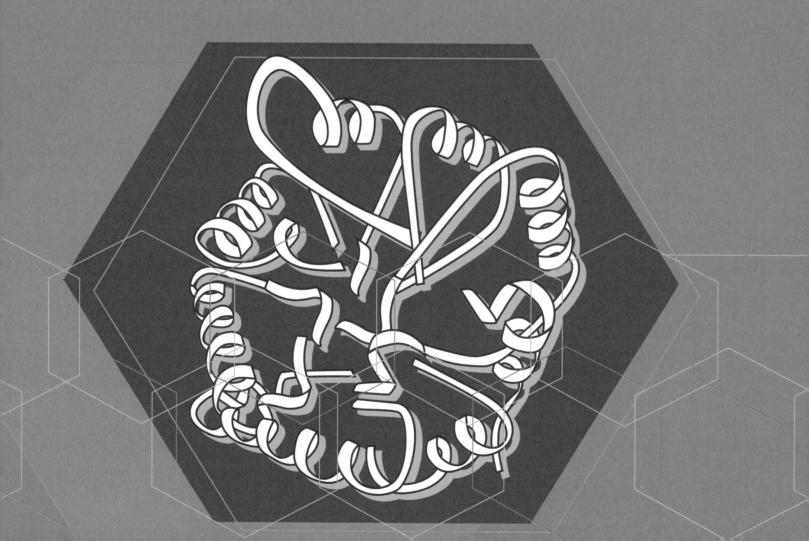

Have a Soak or Maybe a Rubdown

Like humans (or most of us), the words "marinade" and "brine" evolved from the sea: marinade's root is marine, and brine's—well, you know, briny deep and all that. Over time, marinade came to mean just about any flavorful liquid you soak a food in, and marinate came to mean the act of soaking a food in a flavorful liquid. Brine is both a noun and a verb: a salt solution and the act of soaking in said solution. It stands to reason, therefore, that while you can marinate a pork chop in a brine you can't necessarily brine a pork chop in a marinade—unless, of course, that marinade is a brine. Got it? If you haven't got time for a lengthy soak, try a quick rubdown—with spices, of course.

Marinades

Marinades have long been hailed as "tenderizers." They're not. Sure, acidic liquids (most if not all marinades contain an acid component such as vinegar, wine, or citrus juice) can dissolve proteins and even plant cellulose, but the effect is localized to the surface of the target food. Some food scientists even argue that the tenderizing effect doesn't kick in until the meat crosses 140° F, but that's not to say that marinating in the refrigerator is useless.

The reason that marinades *seem* to tenderize has more to do with flavor than any actual textural alterations. Most marinades contain salty, sweet, acidic, and spicy components. When these compounds are drawn into meat via capillary action,[28] they strongly season the meat. Then you cook it, slice it, and put it in your mouth. Immediately the salt and acid flavors divebomb your taste buds, which in turn tell your saliva glands to start pumping. By the time you're onto your third chew your food is thoroughly lubricated, and since saliva contains enzymes like amylase, the meat is already well on its way to becoming an easy-to-digest goo. Marinades may not actually do much in the way of tenderizing meat, but their use does help *us* to tenderize it.

Brine

A brine is nothing more than a solution of salt and sugar dissolved in water. Although brines may contain other substances (alkaline phosphates are often added to commercial brines because pH is a factor in brine absorption), all that's really required is salt and water.

Brines supercharge meats with flavor and moisture, and also can be used as a pickling agent for fruits and vegetables. Sauerkraut, for example, begins as little more than shredded cabbage and a weak brine that acts as a microbial bouncer, allowing the bacteria necessary for fermentation in, while keeping those that would spoil the party out.

[28] Remember when you were a kid and you went to the doctor and they pricked your finger and while you were bawling the nurse held a little tube to the drop of blood and all of a sudden it jumped up the tube, and that shut you up because it kinda seemed like magic? That was capillary action and that's the same thing that happens when you marinate a piece of meat.

Had Shakespeare chosen to reach for a culinary metaphor in his love sonnets, brining would have been the one. Brining is a wonderful thing because it's invisible. You brine a piece of meat, cook it, cut it, serve it, and everybody tastes it and exclaims in disbelief, "Man, this is great meat. You're a genius!" Learn to brine pork and poultry and soon you'll be clearing room on your mantel for that Nobel Prize in cooking. How can a simple concoction of salt and water make such a difference? Like most things, it's a matter of chemistry.

Meat is made up of cells. Cells are surrounded by membranes, which function like borders between countries: they are discriminating. Any substance that wants in or out of the cell must present its papers and pass a rigid inspection. The substance that moves across this border most often and most freely is water.

The micromilieu of meat is all about balance. Inside the cell there are dissolved solids—salts, potassium, calcium, and the like—and outside there's . . . well, it depends. Drop a pork chop in a bucket of distilled water and there's nothing but H_2O outside the border. In this case, the border officials are unhappy because there's a lot more salt inside the cell than outside, thus no balance. So the border temporarily opens, and the guards allow some water to move into the meat and some salt to move out into the water. Eventually the meat will lose a good bit of its native flavor to the water.

However, if there's salt in the water (even as little as a few hundred parts per million), the border guards—ever desirous of equilibrium—will throw open the borders and allow both salt and water to move across the membranes. Now this is where things get really interesting: after 8 to 24 hours there's more salt in the meat, and more water has to be retained to balance it—that's just the osmotic way. So now you've got cells that are perfectly seasoned with salt and nicely plump with water, which if you think about it is something of a paradox: salt pulls liquid out of meats, yet the right brine can pump water into meat.

But wait, there's more.

SALAD DRESSING'S SECRET

When you whisk up a vinaigrette, make extra to use as a marinade. I like to use dressings containing either soy or Worcestershire sauce as marinades because their high sodium content acts like a brine.

Extra-virgin olive oil and commercial emulsifiers like polysorbate 80 also can help meat tissues absorb flavors. I usually keep some commercial salad dressings around even if I don't use them on salads. The exception is French dressing, which I do keep around for salads. I can't make French dressing because I don't want to know what's in it . . . ever.

BRINING AND MARINATING: THE SHORT FORM

• Heavy zip-top freezer bags are great for marinating and brining because they allow for the most surface-to-marinade/brine contact. You can suck out the air before you seal the bag, and the bag itself provides the meat with an occasional massage, which helps the marinade or brine to be more quickly absorbed into the meat.

• PH matters: the more acidic the brine, the longer the journey into the meat. So if your brine is heavy on wine or vinegar, consider adding some baking soda to neutralize the acid.

• Temperature matters: meat proteins are more extractable around 34° F meaning that the tissues in question will hold on to more water if brined at refrigerator temperatures.

• Never wash off marinades or brines; simply pat the food dry before cooking.

• Although marinated foods can be fished from the drink and wrapped for several days prior to cooking, try to time your soak session so that the brined food can go straight from the liquid to the heat. All those cells are puffed up like blimps, and without the counterpressure of the brine, the shear weight of the food will begin to squeeze the brine out within minutes of leaving the bath.

• When brining large items like turkeys or multiple pork shoulders, I put them in a plastic cooler and replace about a third of the brine liquid with ice.

• Another good reason for brining and marinating at refrigerator temperature is, of course, sanitation. Most micro-bugs don't dig salty environs, but some don't mind a bit.

• A cure is simply a brine without the water. Since it's pretty darned strong, it's usually only used as part of a curing process, such as corning beef (the word cure is a reference to the size of the salt crystals used in the process) and making gravlax.

Like a molecular Trojan horse, the water can harbor other substances, specifically water-soluble flavors like brown sugar or various herbaceous elements whose flavors have been extracted via brewing. This means you can sneak various and sundry flavorings and seasonings into the meat.

And yet there's more. When salt gets into meat cells it runs into certain water-soluble proteins. They look like this (sort of):

That is, until they meet the salt. Then they look like this (sort of):

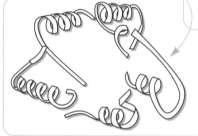

This is what denatured proteins look like. Notice that they've gone from tight little separate springy things to big loose coils that have managed to get all tangled up with each other. During the cooking process, this tangled-up structure traps water almost like a gel, which means two things:

1. Brined meats are juicier when cooked.
2. Since they hold more moisture, brined meats are more forgiving of overcooking.

For instance, a turkey cooked to 165° F will taste okay and will be relatively moist, but it dries out quickly with every degree over.

A brined turkey, on the other hand, can reach all the way to 180° F without losing its finger-lickin' status. This rule applies equally to all pork cuts, all poultry and fowl, and, oddly enough, shrimp.

Orange Brine

This brine is equally good on all kinds of poultry and pork—and I like it best on pork loin or even pork chops. It's good for grilled pork tenderloin, too, but you might also consider basting the tenderloin on the grill with a combination of orange-juice concentrate mixed with the hot sauce of your choice.

Application: Brining

In a pot bring 2 cups of the stock, the salt, brown sugar, peppercorns, and bay leaves just to a boil. Stir to dissolve the sugar and salt. Add the remaining stock, the orange juice, and 2 quarts ice water, and pour into a 2-gallon bucket. When the mixture has cooled to below 40° F, add the meat in a cool place (to maintain a sub-40° temperature). Let it brine for at least 8 hours and up to 48. Remove the meat from the brine, pat dry with paper towels, and cook as desired.

Software:

1 quart vegetable stock, chilled

½ cup kosher salt

¼ cup dark brown sugar

1 teaspoon black peppercorns

2 bay leaves

1 quart orange juice, chilled

2 quarts ice water

Hardware:

Medium stock pot

2-gallon plastic bucket

Thermometer

Paper towels

A Dip For Mr. Dennis

Mr. Dennis is an old New England euphemism for the family pig. This brine is excellent for pork, especially chops, which can soak for as little as ½ hour to nice effect.

Application: Brining

Combine spices in a tea ball or tie them securely into a paper coffee filter and place in pot with salt and molasses. Add water and bring to a boil. Remove from heat and cool to room temperature. Remove the tea ball and discard the spices; pour the liquid into the bucket and add the meat. Allow the meat to brine for at least 6 hours or as long as 12 hours. Remove the meat from the brine, pat dry, and immediately cook as desired.

Software:

1 tablespoon juniper berries

1 tablespoon whole black
  peppercorns

10 whole cloves

1½ cups kosher salt

½ cup molasses

2 quarts water

Target cut of pork

Hardware:

Tea ball or paper coffee filter
  and string

Medium stock pot

2-gallon plastic bucket

Shrimp Soak

Brining improves both the flavor and especially the texture of shrimp—after a soak, these crustaceans are completely plumped up with moisture. I recommend broiling them right in their shells on a sheet pan.

Application: Brining

Bring 1 cup of water to a boil in a small sauce pan. Add the salt and sugar and stir until the crystals have dissolved.

Pour the mixture into the plastic bucket and add the ice. When the ice has melted, add the shrimp and allow to soak—½ hour for 21/25s, or up to 1 hour for the really huge shrimp that some people erroneously call "jumbo."

Remove the shrimp from the brine, pat dry, and cook immediately.

Software:

1 cup water

¼ cup kosher salt

¼ cup sugar

1 pound ice

1 pound shrimp, unshelled

Hardware:

Small sauce pan

1-gallon plastic bucket

That's 21 to 25 shrimp per pound

Grilled Mahi-Mahi, Ceviche-Style

Software:

4½ pounds skinless mahi-mahi
   filets

1 teaspoon kosher salt

½ cup diced red onion

¼ cup freshly-squeezed lime juice

¼ cup freshly-squeezed orange juice

1 tablespoon minced jalapeño
   pepper

½ cup chopped cilantro

¼ cup dark brown sugar, packed

¼ cup tequila

1 tablespoon olive oil

Hardware:

Non-reactive bowl

Charcoal

Charcoal starter

Long tongs

Saucepan

This mahi-mahi is a winner. It retains a super fresh-fish flavor and the sauce is tangy and spicy with a clean finish from the herbs.

Application: Marinating, Grilling, and a Sauce

Rub the filets with kosher salt and set aside. In a non-reactive bowl, combine the remaining ingredients except ¼ cup of the cilantro and the olive oil. Mix to dissolve the sugar, and add the filets to the bowl. Marinate for 2 hours, turning the filets once after 1 hour. Remove the filets from the marinade and set it aside. Pat the filets dry with paper towels and lightly coat with the olive oil.

Heat the charcoal and grill the filets over direct heat until they are just cooked through—opaque at the center but still moist. While the fish is grilling, add the reserved marinade to a saucepan and heat until it is reduced to about ⅓ cup. Using tongs, remove the filets to serving plates and divide sauce equally among them. Top with remaining cilantro.

Yield: 4 entrée servings

Marinated Vegetable Salad

Application: Marinating

Cut each vegetable into uniform pieces: trim the ends of the beans; trim the bottoms off the asparagus; floret the broccoli and cauliflower; cut the carrots into rounds; and peel the beet and cut it into wide matchsticks. One kind of vegetable at a time, drop them into a large pot of salted boiling water and blanch until crisp-tender. Pull a piece out every few seconds and check it. The broccoli should only take about 45 seconds, but the cauliflower might take more than a minute. Do the carrots next to last as they'll discolor the water, and finish with the beets. Do not blanch the onion.

As each vegetable is ready, remove them to an ice-water bath to stop them from cooking. This is very important; if you don't have an ice-water bath ready, the vegetables will continue cooking after you pull them out of the water and they'll get too soft.

Thoroughly drain, then put all the vegetables—except the broccoli and the onion—in an airtight plastic container and lightly season with salt and pepper.

In a mixing bowl, blend the tangerine, lemon, and lime juices. Add the vinegar, garlic, shallot, and mustard. Whisking constantly, add the oil in a thin stream to emulsify. Add the tarragon and pour over the vegetables in the container. They should not be drowning in the marinade. Refrigerate for several hours or overnight, turning the container periodically.

When ready to serve, add the broccoli and onions to the party. If you add them earlier, the onions will "bleed" pink on all the vegetables and the broccoli will turn gray from the acidity.

Yield: 1 huge platter of vegetables

Note: If you can't find tangerines consider using grapefruit; oranges aren't acidic enough to fully marinate the vegetables.

Software:

½ pound wax beans or green beans

1 bunch thin asparagus

2 broccoli crowns

1 head cauliflower

3 large carrots

1 golden beet about the size of a baseball

1 medium red onion, sliced Lyonnaise-style

Kosher salt

Freshly ground black pepper

Juice of 4 tangerines (¾ cup; see **Note**)

Juice of 1 lemon (2 tablespoons)

Juice of 2 limes (2 tablespoons)

¼ cup champagne vinegar

1 tablespoon chopped garlic

1 tablespoon chopped shallot

1 teaspoon Dijon mustard

¼ cup good olive oil

2 tablespoons chopped tarragon

Hardware:

Paring knife

Large pot

Spider or slotted spoon

Large ice-water bath

Large lidded airtight plastic container

Mixing bowl

Whisk

Software:

4 tablespoons soy sauce

4 tablespoons Worcestershire
    sauce

2 tablespoons red wine vinegar

2 tablespoons teriyaki sauce

2 tablespoons lemon juice

2 cloves of garlic, left whole but
    lightly crushed

1 tablespoon Dijon mustard

1 tablespoon extra-virgin olive oil

Target cut of meat

Hardware:

Lidded plastic container

Large zip-top freezer bag

Plastic straw

Rhapsody for Red (Meat)

This is a good marinade to use before any cooking method, but I prefer it for pieces that require a longer cook time—like lamb shoulder, which I marinate, sear, then wrap tightly in aluminum foil and cook for 2 or 3 hours at 300° F.

Application: Marinating

Place all the ingredients in a lidded container and shake vigorously to combine. Place along with target meat in a large zip-top freezer bag. Seal the bag until almost closed. Insert plastic straw in remaining opening and suck as much air as possible from the bag. Seal the bag completely and refrigerate 2 to 8 hours.

Remove the meat from the bag—do not rinse—and cook meat as desired.

Note: This recipe makes enough marinade for a single flank steak. For more or less meat, increase or decrease the amounts proportionately.

Spice Rubs

I recently bought a jar of spice mix. The jar in question bore a bright, shiny, full-color photo of a smiling celebrity chef. The back label (in black and white) listed six ingredients, the first of which was salt. I bought one jar of the chef's mix as well as new containers of each of the spices listed in the ingredient roster. Once home, it took me about ½ hour to replicate the mix. Using a pharmacy scale, I then calculated the amounts of each spice I used and the approximate cost. Now I know why the chef is smiling. I guess the people who buy this particular product assume the celebrity chef knows something they can never know and that knowledge justifies a 400 percent markup (make that 500 percent; those glossy, full-color photos are expensive). With the exception of Old Bay, chili powder, and the occasional curry powder, I try to steer clear of prepared spice mixes.

Don't get me wrong—I am a spice snob. I buy all my spices via the Internet or mail order. I know when I place an order with say, The Spice House or Penzeys Spices, I will get the best product available this side of the Spice Islands (see Sources). Sure, they might be a little pricey, but they're potent, which means I'll use less and therefore get more for my money. I avoid grocery store spices—there's just no way to know where they've been or how long they've been there.

Whenever possible I buy spices in their whole form. Like coffee, the minute a spice is ground it starts to lose its potency, so the less time that passes between grinding and use, the better. Whole spices also have a much longer shelf life than ground, so less gets thrown away. To grind spices, use a clean pepper mill, or spice or coffee grinder (see Spice Rules, page 193).

If the spice in question is a seed (such as cumin, coriander, or sesame), I always toast them before grinding. This activates or "opens up" the essential oils that give the spices their distinctive flavors. To toast spices, heat a small sauté pan, preferably non-stick, over medium-high heat and add the spice. Keep the pan moving to avoid burning. Toast until the spice is fragrant, but not browned, and transfer it to a plate to cool thoroughly (if ground when hot, the spices can steam inside the grinder and get gummy).

HERBS AND SPICES

When the leaf of a plant is used as a flavoring agent, we call it an herb. Most herbs can be used in either their fresh or dry state. I'm not a huge fan of dry herbs unless they're headed for a soup or pot of spaghetti sauce. That's because I can add them near the beginning of the cooking process. Try that with fresh herbs and you'll find that whatever good they have to offer will disappear. By the same token, adding dry herbs at the end of cooking doesn't work because the pieces have to rehydrate before they can contribute anything in the way of flavor.

When the dried seed, pod, root, or bark of a plant is used as a flavoring agent, it's a spice. Some plants render both. Cilantro, for instance, is a green herb most often found in Mexican dishes. The seed of the plant (technically fruit) is called coriander and most often finds itself in Asian fare…go figure.

A NOTE ON SALT

Don't be scared by the amounts of salt in these recipes. Although salt will season the meat, its main purpose is to enhance the texture of the meat and make it more receptive to smoke; a key point in the barbecue world.

ESSENTIAL OILS

Herbs and spices can bring flavor and aroma to foods because they contain powerful compounds referred to as essential oils, "essential" because they were once thought to hold the essence of the plant. These oils can be manufactured in just about any part of a plant: flowers smell pretty because of glands that produce oils in the base of the bloom; poison ivy makes you itch because of oils that spread out across the surface of its leaves. The flavor and aroma of spices are made possible by oil deposits in seeds (cumin), pods or fruits (nutmeg), bark (cinnamon), and even stems (sassafras).

In addition to flavorings, essential oils are used to odorize everything from perfume to paint. Essential oils also were the basis of many traditional medicines and were often used in dental products. (Remember the little bottle of clove oil Dustin Hoffman kept in his pocket after being "worked on" by Laurence Olivier in *Marathon Man?*)

Essential plant oils, whether from orange zest or coriander seeds, are highly volatile, that is they evaporate very quickly when exposed to the air. The problem is, you have to grind them to get their full flavor and aroma—and that's about as exposed to air as you can get. What can you do? (See Spice Rules.)

Although I'll keep whole spices like coriander around for up to a year and star anise and nutmeg even longer, ground spices and dry have a six-month life span at best. Buy some little circular labels at your local office Maxi-mart (usually located right next to the Mega-mart), stick one on the bottom of each container with an expiration date that's six months from the day you filled it. If the container's still full when that day comes, you might reconsider that spice's place in your kitchen.

And speaking of that place in your kitchen, proper storage of spices is key. That groovy spice rack with the retro glass vials may look spiffy but it's lousy food science. Spices hate light almost as much as they dislike air—so keep them tightly sealed and keep them out of sight. You also should fight the temptation to store spices in a drawer or cabinet near a heat source like an oven or dishwasher. Volatile acids vanish quickly in hot environments.

The Rub

Marinades can be wonderful, but when it comes to getting a lot of flavor onto meat quickly, spice rubs are the way to go. This is especially true if the meat in question possesses a relatively high surface-to-mass ratio (flank steak, skirt steak, chicken breasts, and tuna steaks are all good examples). And unlike marinades, rubs don't add to the preparation time of the meal.

Every single commercially available spice mix I've been able to get my hands on has listed salt as either the first or second ingredient. Salt content is a huge demon in the world of spice rubs and seasonings. Suppose you like the profile of a rub—say, its heat. You might think "I'll add more rub to make my food spicier." That seems logical, but it's also going to make it saltier.

That's why there is no salt in the ingredient lists of the recipes that follow. Add salt to the rub as needed—better yet, salt the food before you add the rub. Isn't it great to be in control of what you eat?

There's a reason why they call it a rub. Many recipes call for seasonings to be sprinkled onto the target food. But it's not enough. Once you've liberally sowed the surface, massage that rub into the meat—work it into those nooks and crannies. Most of this "first strike" will seem to magically disappear. Let it rest for a few minutes and the salt that first went onto the meat will pull moisture to the surface, providing fertile ground for another strafing of goodness. Depending on the concentration of flavor desired, this process can be repeated up to five times.

The choice of rub depends not only on the target food but on the cooking method as well. For instance, I wouldn't use the same rub on ribs that I intended to braise as a piece of tuna I intended to sear. For one thing, they have different flavor and texture profiles. The rub that is used on the Blackened Tuna Steak (page 36) doesn't need the assistance of fat to release its flavor, so it's perfect for the relatively lean fish. The pepper and chile flavors in the rub for No-Backyard Baby Back Ribs (page 168) not only foil the fattiness of the meat, but some of the ingredients (such as capsaicin, the hot stuff in chiles) are fat-soluble as well, so their flavor is actually activated by the fat as it cooks out of the meat.

If you intend to dry sear your target meat, you might want to avoid spices that turn bitter in the face of high heat, specifically black pepper and anything containing chiles, including bell pepper. Of course the blackening craze of the 1980s gave some folks a taste for burned, so if you like carbon…well, it's your food.

These rubs are easy to make, but you don't just get to throw all the spices together and be the hero. Most of the spices need to be toasted separately, then cooled thoroughly prior to being ground and mixed. This is a bit more work, but the result will be more pronounced flavors. Note that once toasted, spices will only keep for three months—and only if tightly sealed.

SPICE RULES

DON'T:
- buy spice sets just because you like the packaging.
- name music groups or any members thereof after spices.
- buy spices in bulk unless you've got a darned good reason…like you own a restaurant, barbecue competitively, or are working on a remake of *Dune*.
- store spices where you can see them.
- store spices near heat sources.

DO:
- buy whole (rather than ground) spices.
- keep an extra pepper grinder around for grinding small amounts of spice.
- keep an inexpensive electric coffee grinder around for grinding larger amounts of spice.
- make your own spice mixes.

Software:

½ part toasted ground fennel seeds (see **Notes**)

1 part toasted ground coriander seeds

½ part toasted ground cumin seeds

½ part toasted ground celery seeds

¼ part toasted ground white peppercorns

¼ part toasted ground black peppercorns

½ part toasted ground red pepper flakes

1 part dried, rubbed sage

1 part filé powder

1 part ground dried onion flakes

¾ part chile powder (I use passila; see **Notes**)

1 part confectioners' sugar

¼ part garlic powder

½ part ground cinnamon

Hardware:

Small sauté pan, preferably non-stick

Spice or coffee grinder

Mixing bowl

Airtight storage container

Chicken Rub

Rubs really need high heat to "activate" their flavors, so this is best used with recipes for seared, grilled, or roasted chicken. Here's one: rub a chicken breast with this spice mixture, then pan sear it, and slice the finished chicken into strips to serve over pasta.

Application: Rub

Toast the spices separately as described in Spice Rubs (page 191), using a small non-stick sauté pan, then grind in a spice or coffee grinder.

Combine all the ingredients in a mixing bowl, then transfer to an airtight storage container for up to 3 months. When you're ready to use the rub, add salt as necessary.

Notes: The measurements in all of the rub recipes are provided as ratios: just make sure you stick to one measuring device (thimble, ladle, dump truck) and the result will be perfect. I generally use a 2-ounce ramekin. For this Chicken Rub, use half a ramekin of toasted ground fennel seeds, 1 full ramekin of toasted ground coriander seeds, half a ramekin of toasted ground cumin seed, and so on. Note that these proportions are based on ground—not whole seed—quantities, so measure the spices after they're ground.

As far as chile powder is concerned, I try to always use those that are pure. For example, a powder that is made of nothing but passila chiles is better than a mixture of several varieties (along with who-knows-what other spices and fillers).

Fish Rub

This is great for grilling, broiling, and blackening all types of fish, and it's also good on shrimp, scallops, and lobster. Just keep in mind that rubs require high heat to "activate" their flavors.

Application: Rub

Toast the spices separately as described in Spice Rubs (page 191), using a small non-stick sauté pan, then grind them in a spice or coffee grinder.

Combine all the ingredients in a mixing bowl, then transfer to an airtight storage container for up to 3 months. When you're ready to use the rub, add salt as necessary.

Software:

½ part toasted ground fennel seeds (see **Notes**, page 194)

½ part toasted ground cumin seeds

1 part toasted ground celery seeds

¼ part toasted ground white peppercorns

¼ part toasted ground black peppercorns

¼ part toasted ground red pepper flakes

½ part confectioners' sugar

¼ part paprika

¼ part garlic powder

1 part ground dried onion flakes

1 part chile powder (I use guajillo; see **Notes**, page 194)

½ part filé powder

Hardware:

Small sauté pan, preferably non-stick

Spice or coffee grinder

Mixing bowl

Airtight storage container

Software:

1 part toasted ground coriander seeds (see **Notes**, page 194)

1 part toasted ground cumin seeds

½ part toasted ground celery seeds

¼ part toasted ground white peppercorns

¼ part toasted ground black peppercorns

¼ part toasted ground red pepper flakes

½ part confectioners' sugar

¾ part garlic powder

1 part mild chile powder (I use New Mexico; see **Notes**, page 194)

½ part ground dried onion flakes

½ part filé powder

½ part dried rubbed sage

Hardware:

Small sauté pan, preferably non-stick

Spice or coffee grinder

Mixing bowl

Airtight storage container

Beef Rub

This is great for pan-searing, grilling, blackening, or broiling just about any cut of beef. Just remember that rubs need a high-heat cooking method to "activate" their flavors.

Application: Rub

Toast the spices separately and grind them as described in Spice Rubs (page 191), using a small non-stick sauté pan and a spice or coffee grinder. Combine all the ingredients in a mixing bowl, then transfer to an airtight storage container for up to 3 months. When you're ready to use the rub, add salt as necessary.

Haste Makes Paste

A rub and a marinade in one, use this for roasts that will be broiled, grilled, or—roasted. It's not pretty (the paste will burn in places), but the meat will be delicious, especially if the meat is lamb. The paste will also make a mess of the grill (it will stick, but the meat won't). I usually fire up some extra charcoal and throw it right on the cooking grate just after I remove the meat. The charcoal burns off the offending residue and then falls through to the bottom grate—no muss, no fuss.

Application: Rub

Place the garlic in the bowl of a food processor and finely chop. Add the remaining ingredients and process to a pastelike consistency.

Rub the mixture over the entire surface of the target meat, cover, and refrigerate from 4 hours to 2 days. Cook as desired.

Do not add any more paste once the cooking begins.

Software:

4 cloves of garlic

10 mint leaves

1 tablespoon dark brown sugar

1 tablespoon kosher salt

2 teaspoons freshly ground black
   pepper

6 tablespoons strong mustard

Target meat

Hardware:

Food processor

Once used to smother the taste of spoiled food, now used to enhance natural flavors.

CHAPTER 8 | Sauces

All the World's a Sauce

By and large, most home cooks don't do sauce... and that's too bad. Traditional sauces are indeed scary—as all dinosaurs (even the cute ones) are. They're scary because they are not of our time. They are of a time when toqued Frenchmen walked the Earth, backed by armies of 14-year-old apprentices who probably didn't live to see 40 because the air in the kitchens, with their wood-burning ovens, would rot their lungs. The kitchens these culinary T-Rexes occupied bear no resemblance to the rooms we cook in, nor did the groceries that filled them. These guys worked with whole everything: they didn't buy a steak, they bought a side of beef. They didn't buy a fish filet, they bought the fish. They purchased cartloads of produce and had that army of apprentices at the ready to clean it all. This meant a lot of leftovers: meat scraps and bones and fish heads, carrot tops, mushroom stems—that sort of thing. Being clever and innovative, the ancient chefs didn't want to waste these items. They made sauces, and everyone was happy.

Fast-forward a couple hundred years and people are still buying books packed with recipes for the mother sauces and their archaic offspring. This makes about as much sense as going to the barber to have leeches slapped on a wart.[29]

Still, there are lessons to be learned from *les dinosaurs*. They made sauces out of leftovers and so should we, as long as the process doesn't require that you hire a brigade of assistants.

Most classical sauces fall into these extremely overgeneralized categories:

- Sauces based on stocks
- Sauces based on emulsions
- Sauces based on roux

A stock is a liquid in which collagen from animal bones and connective tissue has been dissolved and converted into a protein matrix called gelatin. Broth and stock are not the same thing. A broth is essentially any liquid that's had food cooked in it, be it meat or vegetables. Bones are not required for a broth, but they are for a stock. Thus, there is no such thing as vegetable stock.

An emulsion is a colloid[30]: two liquids, which do not like each other, are forced into a colloidal relationship via dispersion of one into the other in the form of microscopic droplets. Vinaigrette dressings are temporary emulsions; unless there is an emulsifier present (such as lecithin or Polysorbate 80, for instance, or pulverized vegetable matter, like mustard) vinaigrettes will always separate in the end. Mayonnaise and hollandaise are also oil-in-water emulsions (mayo is raw, hollandaise cooked), but they are more stable than vinaigrettes because of emulsifiers present in the egg yolks. Butter is an emulsion made up of water droplets in fat.

A roux is an equal mixture of starch (usually from wheat flour) and fat, which are mixed together and cooked. A flavorful liquid is then added and the starch particles, encased in the fat, are free to be distributed in the liquid. With the addition of heat, they

---

[29] If you find the analogy a bit overwrought, you've never messed up a consommé an hour before service in a French restaurant.

[30] Yes, this is legal. A colloid is any substance, either gas or liquid, in which tiny droplets of one substance are dispersed in another.

swell and burst, thickening the liquid. American gravy (the kind usually served at Thanksgiving), "sawmill" gravy, and most pan gravies are examples of roux sauces.

Stock

I don't make stock often, but when I do I always feel like I've gotten away with something, like I've pulled some kind of alchemical con job on nature.

Stocks have always provided a way to juice a little more value out of the ingredients on hand. Veal bones are a pretty terrific source of collagen, but I rarely have a cow carcass lying around the house. I do, however, have chicken bones, hen bones, and duck bones from time to time—and a freezer to store them in.

When I've got five or six racks of chicken plus a couple of duck carcasses, I break out my biggest pot and a pair of tin snips. Since smaller pieces mean faster collagen extraction, I break the frozen carcasses into pieces (if they're too tough, I use the snips) and add them to the pot. I add enough cold water to cover the bones (if your water tastes crummy, see Filter Your Water, page 136) and bring to a boil.

Now here's the screwy part. Collagen is not the only thing in the pot. Many other water-soluble substances will emerge from the bones once the water hits a boil. They will collect at the top of the pot and, since their presence serves to reduce the surface tension of the water, once water vapor starts to rise from the bottom, there's going to be a whole lot of foaming goin' on. Ever seen foam riding the waves on a windy day at the beach? Same stuff.

Many stock makers, wishing to discard this foam, turn to slotted spoons, ladles, you name it. I use one of those little square nets they use to catch neon tetras down at the pet store. As soon as I get a big netfull I unload it by turning it upside down under cold running water. After five minutes or so of defoaming, stop and watch. Odds are you'll be in the clear and can go ahead and toss in a couple of quartered onions, a couple of carrots split down the middle, at least three ribs of celery broken in half, and a palmful of black peppercorns. No green herbs yet. And no salt.[32]

> ### THE WHOLE BIRD
>
> One of the reasons I always buy whole chicken is to get the rack: the carcass, complete with wings, rib cage, and backbone.[31] There are, of course, other reasons to buy whole:
>
> - The less processing a food has undergone, the cheaper its per-pound price will be.
> - All things being equal, whole birds will keep longer than pieces will.
> - Many meat cutters hack the pieces apart instead of taking the time to separate them at the joints.
>
> So in buying a whole bird you pay less money and get all those great pieces to make stock with. I make stock only a few times a year, so I bag, tag, and freeze the bones as I gather them. (A chest freezer in the basement is a wonderful thing.)

As soon as it does, drop the heat so that you maintain a low boil.

---

[31] Bones from cooked chickens won't deliver as much collagen as those of raw ones because too many of the proteins have coagulated. Some folks like to roast the bones for flavor, but I'd rather keep my stocks neutral.

[32] The way I see it, stock is an ingredient and as such, shouldn't be salted until put to use.

SURFACE TENSION

It was in 1751 that Johann Andreas von Segner, a German physicist and mathematician, first introduced his ideas about the surface tension of liquids. Today, we understand that molecules at the surface of a liquid attract each other to create something that's been referred to as like a skin or a stretched membrane. (It's because of this tendency that some insects are able to stand on the surface of a pond.) Water molecules are so attracted to each other that when presented with a different environment, such as air, they will shape themselves into spheres to expose as few molecules as possible to that environment. It's easy to find an example of this phenomenon right at home in your kitchen. Check out a slowly dripping faucet. As the drops of water form, they sag or stretch out into almost a teardrop shape before falling.

Surface tension explains why pure water cannot be bubbled or persuaded to foam. And this goes not only for water but also for any pure liquid. To coax water into foaming, you have to break the tension by adding something that can work its way into the water.

Now here's where the simmering comes in. You want to drop the heat as low as you can and still have a few stray bubbles breaking the surface. It's not that boiling won't do the job, it's just that all that turbulence would break things up so much that you'd end up with a very cloudy stock.

How long to simmer? That depends on the volume of bones and water. I try to keep mine going for at least 8 hours, but then I'm greedy for the most gelatin I can get. You'll know it's over when you reach in with tongs and can easily crush the bones.

Big point: the more the water fills with gelatin, the slower gelatin is extracted—the water gets "full" so to speak. So be sure to replenish the water as it evaporates from the pot, so that the original level of liquid is maintained. If bones are poking out the top, they're not in the water, and they've got to be in the water if they're going to do your stock any good.

When the bones crumble in the mighty grip of your tongs, it's time to kill the heat and ponder your evacuation options. If you're making only a gallon or two, you can probably safely lift the pot to the sink, but straining it is going to be a genuine pain. And remember, as we discussed in an earlier section, steam is a very efficient conductor of heat—and so are your arms.

Since stock can be kept in a deep freeze for up to a year when properly sealed, and I happen to have a chest freezer, I make stock only a few times a year—and when I do, I make a lot. And when I need to move it, I fall back on a skill developed in my misspent youth. Now, I'm not saying that I actually siphoned gas out of my parents' cars so that I could fuel my Pinto and still have money for Big Macs, but . . . well, yes, that is what I'm saying.

Find a heavy rubber band (the type that markets put on bunches of broccoli works well) and use it to attach a single layer of cheesecloth over one end of a 6-foot length of ½- to 1-inch food-grade plastic tubing (see illustration, right). I use stuff from the hardware store, but if you want to be super safe, buy food-grade tubing at your local home brewer supply. (If you live up north you can use the same tubing that folks use to hook up their taps during maple season.)

Place another pot (if you can, go with one as big as the one you're siphoning from) at a lower level (in the sink, perhaps, with the pot of stock sitting on a hot pad on the counter). Set a fine-mesh strainer in the mouth of the empty pot. Hold the open end of the hose (without the cheesecloth) in your hand and, being careful not to block the opening to the pot, feed the cheesecloth-covered end of the hose into the pot of stock. Get as much of the hose in as possible; since the tubing was kept on a spool forever, it'll probably help you out by coiling like a snake.

When you have at least two-thirds of the hose submerged, use your thumb to block up the end you're holding and slowly extract the tube, making sure that the cheesecloth end stays all the way at the bottom of the pot.

Pull the tube down and hold it in the strainer. (I usually loop it under a rubber band on the handle so that I'm not stuck trying to hold both ends of the tube in their respective spots.) Now remove your thumb and behold. As long as you don't let the end of the hose that's submerged in the stock come to the surface, gravity and suction will transport the stock through the cheesecloth to the clean pot. (Yes, you can achieve the same end by sucking on the

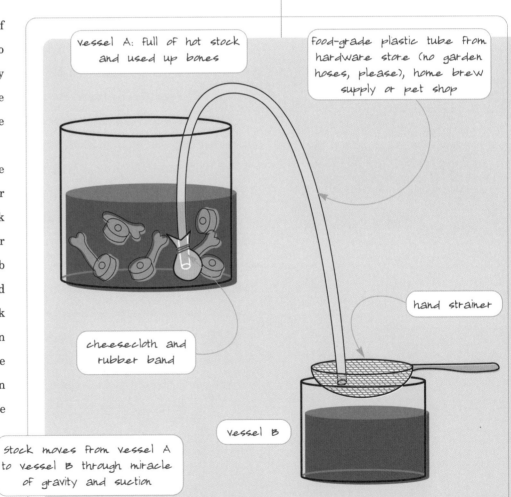

vessel A: full of hot stock and used up bones

food-grade plastic tube from hardware store (no garden hoses, please), home brew supply or pet shop

hand strainer

cheesecloth and rubber band

vessel B

stock moves from vessel A to vessel B through miracle of gravity and suction pipe, and yes, this is what I actually do, but neither me nor my publisher has any desire to be sued just because somebody gulps a big ol' mouthful of hot stock.)

Now take a look at the stock you've managed to move. If it seems relatively clear you don't have to strain further, but I usually do. Take four layers of cheesecloth and attach them to a colander with a couple of clothespins and strain into another container, preferably one with a lid.

Take a spoon and give the final liquid a taste. Feels kind of funny in your mouth, huh? Not thick, necessarily, but "full," with lots of body. That's the gelatin. Note the subtle chicken flavor. It's not overwhelming, and that's good because this stuff is going to work in a lot of different dishes and you wouldn't want everything to taste like chicken.

Now we switch to sanitation mode. You have a big bucket of germ food sitting there in the Zone (see page 261), and that just won't do. Put the container in the refrigerator and not only will it take forever to cool down, but everything else in the fridge will get hot.

If it's cold out, lid up the container and set it in the carport or garage until the temperature of the stock drops to about 40° F.

If it's not cold out, fill a heavy zip-top freezer bag with ice, seal it carefully, then float it in the stock. As soon as the ice melts, remove the bag, drain, and refill with more ice.[33]

Once the stock is cool there are more options. I usually freeze four or five ice cube–trays full. These stock blocks will be moved to freezer bags and used to mount sauces on down the line. The rest of the stock goes into 1-quart plastic containers. (I'm a Rubbermaid man, but Tupperware is darned fine, too.) The important thing is that the container be shaped so that a giant stocksicle can slide right out.

"It'll never slide right out," you say? It will if you lay a piece of butcher's twine or dental floss (unflavored, of course) down one side and up the other (see illustration). Think of it as a ripcord for the frozen liquid of your choice.

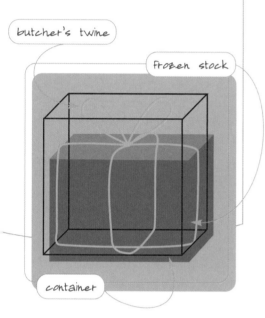

butcher's twine

frozen stock

container

[33] This is a really wonderful example of thermodynamics, and I just love thermodynamics. In this case the heat of the stock is moving into the bag. . . very groovy when you think about it.

Now what? Well, now you've got a full-bodied, flavorful liquid for any occasion. That pot of collards we were talking about? Use stock instead of water. And soup—everything in the kitchen can be soup if you have stock around. The best soup I've ever tasted was composed of leftover mushroom risotto, seared chicken thighs, parsley, and homemade chicken stock . . . delicious.

Pan Sauces

I blame the demise of pan sauce–making on non-stick pans. Sure, I've got a few myself but I only use them for eggs, crêpes, that sort of thing. The problem is that non-stick pans do not work with you when it comes to sauce making. Steel and iron pans are the sauce maker's friend because stuff sticks to them and that stuff is called *fond*.

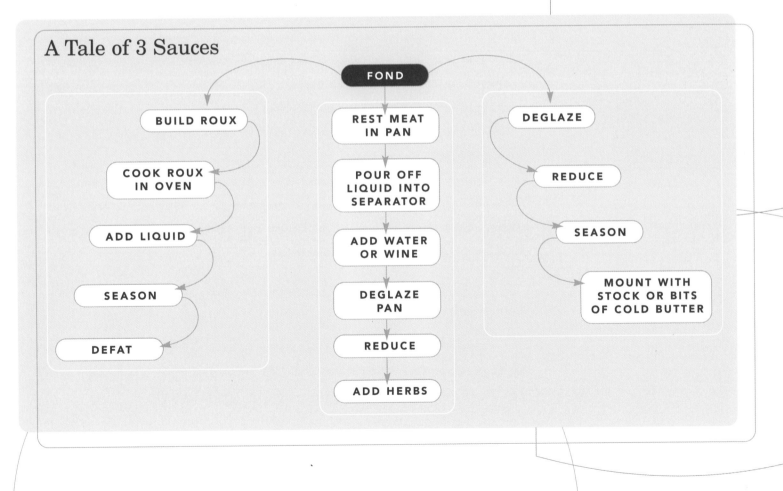

A Tale of 3 Sauces

FOND

BUILD ROUX → **COOK ROUX IN OVEN** → **ADD LIQUID** → **SEASON** → **DEFAT**

REST MEAT IN PAN → **POUR OFF LIQUID INTO SEPARATOR** → **ADD WATER OR WINE** → **DEGLAZE PAN** → **REDUCE** → **ADD HERBS**

DEGLAZE → **REDUCE** → **SEASON** → **MOUNT WITH STOCK OR BITS OF COLD BUTTER**

Fond is (of course) French, but the word derives from the Latin *fundus*, meaning "bottom" or "property." In modern usage it means the basis or foundation of something—as in a sauce.

Say you seared a steak in a pan, or roasted a pork loin in a roasting pan. Once you pull the meat from the metal, you notice that the bottom is covered with a dark and no-doubt nasty crust. Your first instinct is to toss that pan in the sink to scrub later. That would be a shame.

The first step to converting that grimy crust to a sauce is to decide what to do with any fat in the pan. You basically have two choices: build a roux or defat the pan. If the beast in question is a turkey or a roast that might be nice with a gravy, you would go the roux path, which we'll get to shortly.

A juicy flank steak or porterhouse, on the other hand, is not something that screams "gravy." There is enough richness in such meats to satisfy the tongue, so you're better off with a "lean" pan sauce, or one that has been finished with a little butter or an aged cheese like gorgonzola (or both, see Blue Butter, page 210). Unless you seared an incredibly lean piece of meat, odds are good that some fat exited from it and is hanging around the pan. If you pan fried or sautéed something—say, turkey cutlets—then there will definitely be a good bit of fat left hanging around.

Fat gets in the way of deglazing, that is, to add liquid to the hot pan in order to loosen and dissolve the browned bits of goodness stuck to the bottom of said pan.[34] Most recipes suggest simply burning off the fat, but that will probably send a lot of great-tasting juices with it. There are three strategies:

1. Pour off the fat, sacrifice the liquid, and live with it. You'll still be able to deglaze but oh, what a waste.

2. Allow the cooked meat to rest on a resting rack (see page 28) so that you capture any and all juices. Then remove the meat and place the bowl in the freezer for a few minutes. The fat will lift right off and you can return the juice to the pan.

---

[34] Even if you have no intention of making a sauce, deglazing is still a good idea because it's the best way to get cooked-on goop off the bottom of a pan. Just add enough water to the hot pan to come ½-inch or so up the side and let it come to a boil, scraping occasionally with a wooden spatula. The pan will come clean in no time.

3. My favorite method, especially for poultry, is to rest the meat in the pan, and then drain the collected liquid into a gravy separator. Add enough water and/or wine to the liquid to lift the oil well above the spigot of the separator. Then I use this liquid to deglaze the pan. Reduce by half over high heat and add a handful of parsley for the final minute and you have a simple, fresh *jus*.

What other liquid should you use to deglaze the pan? As long as it's a water-type liquid, the sky's the limit. Alcohols, be it wine or bourbon or beer or cognac, are favorites because they:

- are water-type liquids;
- contain a lot of flavor; and
- contain alcohol, which can dissolve and impart alcohol-soluble flavor compounds to the sauce.

Other deglazing options include everything from tea to Perrier, but unless I'm just cleaning the pan, I avoid straight water because it doesn't bring any flavor to the party whatsoever.

Add enough liquid to cover the bottom of the pan by about a ¼ inch.

Bring the liquid to a boil, scraping the pan often with a wooden spatula. Allow the liquid to reduce by half. By then anything worth keeping in the sauce will be dissolved. If no flour was involved in the cooking process you will be left with a thin liquid—not something that is going to cling to a forkful of meat and ride its way to your mouth. Here you have two choices. Add butter (tasty, glossy, thick, and fattening) or a touch of stock (tasty, glossy, thick, and fat-free). Or you can go with a combination of stock and a flavored butter like our Herbed Compound Butter (page 211). Add this, with perhaps some minced herbs, at the last possible moment, and stir or whisk to combine. You'll be amazed at how a sauce appears out of nowhere.

Tilt the pan so that the sauce collects at the base of the wall and spoon it onto the meat, not on the side. Don't pour straight from the pan, because you never know when

some brown bit on the bottom was actually a burned bit, which won't dissolve as readily as its unburned pan-mates. Spooning will prevent you from delivering burned crunchy things to the platter along with an otherwise perfect sauce.

Gravy

If the food in question is a large roast—a pork loin or a turkey, for example—a gravy might be appropriate. (My general rule is that unless the critter gets carved after cooking, gravy just wouldn't be right.) Gravy is a starch-thickened sauce. Traditional American gravies are based on either meat drippings or milk, thickened with starch. The word gravy comes from the Latin *granatus* or "full of grains."

The easiest way to make gravy is to take advantage of what is in the pan when the roast comes out of the oven: fond and a fat that's full of the flavor of the food you just took out of the pan. Of course, if the food in question was dredged in flour before being sautéed or pan-fried (you'd never dredge a food destined for searing, would you?) then you are already in possession of a basic roux, which you must take advantage of.

Choose Your Starch

Starches make great thickeners. When individual starch granules meet up with hot liquids, they break open, releasing long chains of glucose. If there's enough of them, they tangle up and trap liquid, thickening the sauce. But some starches work better than others in different applications.

Root starches, such as potato starch, arrowroot, and tapioca, thicken at relatively low temperatures, so although they're great for pie fillings and clear glazes, they thin out at higher temperatures and don't fare well when stirred. Therefore, they are not the wisest choice for gravies. That leaves flours and cornstarch. One advantage of using flour is that it starts to thicken before reaching a simmer, and if you keep it on a very low simmer the sauce will become smoother. Wheat starch is the most sauce-friendly starch, and the lower the protein the better. That means that cake or pastry flours work best—the resulting gravy will smooth out in half the time. All-purpose flour, a kitchen cupboard staple, is fine too, but don't use bread or whole wheat flour. And remember, sauces thickened with flour continue to thicken a bit as they cool, so don't make them too thick to begin with.

Cornstarch comes from the endosperm (the central portion) of the corn kernel. It's commonly used as a thickener and because it has the tendency to form lumps, is typically mixed with cold water to form a paste before being added to a hot mixture. Sauces thickened with cornstarch will be clear, as opposed to those thickened with flour, which will be opaque.

Roux Rules of Thumb

A roux isn't picky about the liquid it thickens; it only cares about how much of it there is to thicken. Three tablespoons of all-purpose flour will thicken 1 cup of liquid. As far as fat is concerned, 2 tablespoons of fat to every 3 tablespoons of all-purpose flour is a good rule to follow.

You can cook up a roux to suit your specific need. Varying in degrees of darkness—from white to blond to brick, depending on how long they're cooked—roux can be quite different from one another. The darker a roux gets the more color and nutty flavor it'll bring to a sauce. But the darker a roux is, the less thickening power it has. One ounce of white roux has the thickening power of 4 ounces of brick roux. Average roux cooking times are 5 to 10 minutes for white, 10 to 15 minutes for blond, and 20 minutes or more for brick.

Software:

1 teaspoon olive oil

3 tablespoons minced shallot

Pinch of chile flakes

3 tablespoons minced parsley
  (see **Note**)

2 tablespoons white wine

¾ pound unsalted butter, softened

¼ pound blue cheese at room
  temperature (Saga, Maytag, or
  Stilton are all good)

Freshly ground black pepper

Kosher salt, if needed

Hardware:

Sauté pan

Electric mixer with paddle
  attachment

Rubber spatula

Waxed paper

Plastic wrap

Permanent marker

Blue Butter

What all fashionable steaks are wearing this season—and for all the right reasons. It's tangy, creamy, herby, and easy, all at the same time.

Application: Sautéing

Heat the sauté pan and add the oil. Sweat the shallot for 1 to 2 minutes then add the chile flakes to toast. (The chile is here to add a slight background heat. It shouldn't be such a presence that the end result is spicy at all.) Add half of the parsley and toss to coat with oil then add the wine. Put the paddle attachment on an electric mixer and beat the butter for about 1 minute, then add the shallot mixture and the cheese and beat to combine. Add some black pepper and stop the mixer and taste to check the seasoning. If needed, add some more pepper and salt. (You may not need any salt, as blue cheese is pretty salty.) Fold in the remaining parsley, transfer the butter out onto 4 pieces of waxed paper and roll into four logs. Put in the freezer to harden and then remove the waxed paper. Wrap in plastic wrap and store in the refrigerator for use soon or store it the freezer for up to 4 months. Label the logs and production date using a permanent marker.

Yield: 1 pound blue cheese butter

Note: A word on parsley: it's grown in sandy topsoil, so it needs to be thoroughly washed. Wash it once or twice before chopping it and then put it in a container half full of water and stir it once. Then let it settle. Lift the clean parsley out of the water and squeeze to dry. There's nothing worse than herb and sand compound butter.

Compound Butters

Either of these butters can be used as cooking fats, or sauces—or just melted on a steak. You can substitute any herbs to make the herbed butter work for just about any application.

HERBED COMPOUND BUTTER

Application: Sautéing

Heat a sauté pan and add the oil; add the shallots and sweat for 1 to 2 minutes. Add the wine and cook until almost dry. Toss in the parsley and remove from the heat. Put the butter in the bowl of a mixer and attach the paddle. Beat the butter for 1 minute, then add the shallot mixture and season with salt and pepper. Mix to blend and taste; adjust seasoning. Fold in the basil. Transfer to 4 pieces of waxed paper and roll into 4 logs. Freeze to harden, then remove the waxed paper. Wrap tightly in plastic wrap and store in the refrigerator for up to 3 weeks or in the freezer for up to 4 months. Label the logs and production date using a permanent marker.

POACHED GARLIC COMPOUND BUTTER

Application: Poaching

Place the garlic in a small saucepan and add just enough oil to cover the cloves. Heat over a low flame (do not allow the oil to "boil"), until the garlic is caramel brown and soft, about 20 minutes. Drain off the oil and reserve (see **Note**). Allow the garlic to cool to room temperature. Place the garlic and the butter in the bowl of an electric mixer and blend, using the paddle attachment. Add the wine, salt, and pepper, then wrap and store as described above.

Yield: 1 pound compound butter

Note: The reserved garlic oil can be saved for other uses. Store in the refrigerator for no longer than 1 month.

Software:

For Herbed Compound Butter

1 teaspoon olive oil

4 tablespoons minced shallots

¼ cup white wine

2 tablespoons finely chopped parsley (see **Note**, page 210)

1 pound unsalted butter, softened

Kosher salt

Freshly ground black pepper

4 tablespoons basil cut into fine chiffonade

For Poached Garlic Compound Butter

3 heads of garlic, broken into cloves and peeled

Vegetable oil

¾ pound unsalted butter, softened

3 tablespoons white wine

Kosher salt

Freshly ground white pepper

Hardware:

Sauté pan or small sauce pan

Electric mixer with paddle attachment

Rubber spatula

Waxed paper

Plastic wrap

Permanent marker

Software:

For the clams:

40 littleneck clams

½ cup white wine

1 (8-ounce) bottle clam juice

For the sauce:

Olive oil

½ medium onion, diced

2 tablespoons minced garlic

¼ cup white wine

1 cup reserved liquid from
   steaming clams

Kosher salt

Freshly ground black pepper

¼ cup chopped parsley

2 tablespoons Parmesan cheese

1 tablespoon Poached Garlic
   Compound Butter (see page 211)

Hardware:

Heavy pot with lid

Steamer basket

Tongs

Large bowl

Fine-mesh sieve or cheesecloth
   or coffee filter

Small sauce pan

Wooden spoon

Clam Sauce (White)

Best served with linguini—and a great crusty bread for soaking up the sauce.

Application: Steaming, Sautéing, Simmering

Rinse the clams under cold water to remove any sand or mud. Commercial clams are usually pretty clean, but it's still good practice to wash them. Pour the wine and clam juice into the pot and set the basket in it. Place the clams in the basket in as even a layer as possible. Turn the heat to high and put the lid on the pot loosely or the liquid will boil up and over. Keep your eyes on the pot. Once the liquid is creating steam well, remove the lid. Using tongs, pull the clams out and transfer to a large bowl as they open. Once they've all opened, remove the pot from the heat. Strain the liquid and reserve for use in the sauce. Pull the clam meat from their shells.

For the sauce: Heat a small sauce pan and add some oil. Sauté the onion and garlic until fragrant. Add the wine and cook until almost dry. Add the reserved liquid and bring to a simmer. Taste and adjust the seasonings with salt and pepper. Toss in the parsley and cheese. Finish by stirring in the poached garlic compound butter and clam meat.

Yield: enough sauce for 4 servings of pasta

Clam Sauce (Red)

Most of the red sauces you come across in restaurants are something like Manhattan chowder poured over pasta. This one is more like a fresh tomato pan sauce with clams— best with angel hair pasta.

Application: Steaming, Sautéing, Simmering

Prepare the steamed clams following the method described on the opposite page.

For the sauce: Heat the sauté pan and add the oil. Sauté the garlic briefly, until just colored then add the chile flakes. After just a second, the oils in the chile flakes will be released—look out though, chile flakes can burn in a hurry. Add the tomatoes and cook until just softened. Add enough of the reserved liquid to make the sauce a consistency you like. Season with salt and pepper, add the herbs, then bring the sauce together by stirring in the poached garlic butter. Add the clam meat.

Yield: enough sauce for 4 servings of pasta

Software:

40 steamed littleneck clams
(see page 212)

1 tablespoon olive oil

2 heaping tablespoons minced garlic

Pinch of chile flakes

3 ripe plum tomatoes, seeded
and diced (about 1 cup)

About ½ cup reserved liquid from
steaming clams

Kosher salt

Freshly ground black pepper

1 tablespoon fresh basil, cut into fine
chiffonade

1 tablespoon oregano, leaves only

1 tablespoon Poached Garlic Compound
Butter (see page 211)

Hardware:

Sauté pan

Wooden spoon

Software:

5 egg yolks (the fresher, the better)

2 teaspoons lemon juice, plus more to taste

¼ teaspoon cayenne pepper, plus more to taste

1 teaspoon salt

1 teaspoon sugar (see **Note**)

1 stick unsalted butter, cut into tablespoon-size chunks

Hardware:

Small pot

Heavy metal mixing bowl large enough to sit on top of the pot with a couple of inches of lip to spare.

Balloon whisk

Dish towel

Hollandaise Takes a Holiday

I've suffered more failed hollandaise sauces than I can count. So I don't make it anymore. Instead, I make a lemon curd that is like hollandaise sauce, except that it looks better, tastes better, and clings to food better than any hollandaise I've ever made. And unlike the classic version, this sauce is cooked.

Application: Simmering

Place an inch of water in the pot, cover, and bring to a boil.

Place the egg yolks in the metal bowl and whisk vigorously until they lighten in texture and color. This is important, as it partially denatures (or unwinds) the proteins in the yolks, which will prevent them from curdling when faced with the lemon juice.

Add 2 teaspoons of the lemon juice, ¼ teaspoon of the cayenne, a pinch of salt and all of the sugar. Whisk until smooth.

When the water boils, reduce the heat to medium-low and place the bowl on top of the pot.

Whisk the egg mixture gently but continuously for about 7 minutes, or until it moves like very heavy cream (the whisk will leave a definite trail in the liquid).

Remove the bowl from the pot and set it on a dish towel (for stability).

Whisk the butter into the mixture 1 piece at a time, allowing each piece to melt almost completely before adding the next.

Taste, adjust seasoning, and serve immediately.

Yield: about 1 cup

Note: The most difficult thing about making hollandaise sauce is that it easily curdles. That is, the proteins become over-coagulated. Sugar molecules interfere with the process of curdling, so I invite a few to the party just to keep the peace. Low, controlled heat and frequent whisking do the rest.

Red Onion Tomato Jam

This is a tasty accompaniment to garlicky bread and fried calamari. It's also great on meatloaf instead of the traditional ketchup coating.

Application: Sautéing, Simmering

Heat a small sauce pan over medium-high heat and add the oil. Add the onions and shallot and toss to coat with the oil. Reduce the heat to low and allow the onions and shallots to sweat and caramelize for about 15 minutes, stirring often. They should be very soft and sweet-tasting. Add the tomatoes, brown sugar, vinegar and tomato paste. Stir to combine and cook until the mixture is thick and bubbly. Add the stock and reduce to thick bubbly consistency again. Season with salt and pepper. Remove from heat and set half the mixture aside. Purée the other half and fold it back into the reserved mixture. Fold in the basil.

Yield: about 2 cups

Software:

2 teaspoons olive oil

2 cups red onions, sliced
   Lyonnaise-style

¼ cup shallot, finely diced

2 cups seeded and diced tomatoes

3 tablespoons brown sugar

4 tablespoons balsamic vinegar

2 teaspoons tomato paste

1 cup beef stock

Kosher salt

Freshly ground black pepper

1 to 2 tablespoons basil, cut into
   fine chiffonade

Hardware:

Small sauce pan

Rubber spatula

Stick blender

Eggs are the plastic of the kitchen. There's very little they can't do.

CHAPTER 9 | **Eggs**

Eggs-cetera

Legend has it that each fold on a chef's toque, that tower of power that perches upon the pates of chefs worldwide, represents a method by which eggs may be cooked. A tall tale? Yes, but I'd buy it. The humble chicken egg is arguably the most versatile food on earth. It can be fried, poached, roasted, coddled, scrambled, pickled, boiled, and broiled. Were it not for the emulsifying power of the fatty yolk, we would have neither mayonnaise nor hollandaise, nor would we have custard. Were it not for the amazing foaming flexibility of the white's unique proteins, there would be no mousse, no meringue, no soufflé. In short, were it not for eggs, life as we know it would not exist—in the kitchen, or anywhere else for that matter.

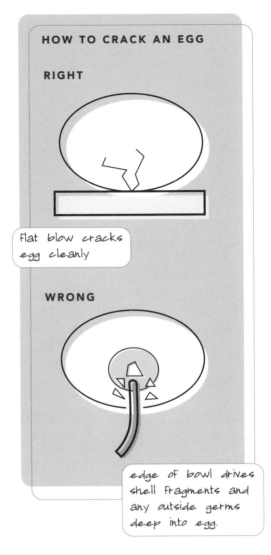

HOW TO CRACK AN EGG

RIGHT

Flat blow cracks egg cleanly

WRONG

edge of bowl drives shell fragments and any outside germs deep into egg.

An 8-inch pan is best for 1 to 2 large eggs.

All this power and versatility can lead to confusion when one simply wishes to cook an egg for eggs' sake. I finally came to terms with egg cookery when I realized that eggs are essentially liquid fish.[35] I admit, this is not an especially appealing idea, but it makes a lot of sense when put into practice.

Like fish, eggs don't like to be pushed around thermally. When exposed to the right temperature for the right amount of time, their proteins denature and then coagulate into a nice soft gel. But when pushed too far or for too long, these proteins turn into little chemical fists and wring all the moisture right out. That's why scrambled eggs often appear (and taste) like yellow bits of rubber floating in water.

Unlike eggs, fish have the advantage of being solid, which means they may be dredged, battered, or breaded. This gives the cook the ability to apply high heat and create a golden brown exterior. I have yet to see this work with eggs, though I've heard that recent advances in zero-gravity cooking look promising.

So, here are some rules for fish and eggs: fried eggs, eggs over easy, eggs sunny-side up, scrambled eggs, omelets, quiche, flan, custards,[36] and egg-based sauces such as hollandaise.

1. Heat a non-stick pan over the lowest heat your cook top can muster.

2. Add a small amount of fat to the pan using a basting brush for thin, even coverage. You can use either butter or oil or (my preference) a combination of the two. Why add fat to a non-stick pan? For one thing, I like to be able to slide my egg around to shape it while it cooks and to be able to flip it, and that requires lubrication. (Non-stick doesn't necessarily mean slick; see The Right Pan.) A little fat also helps to conduct heat evenly into the surface of the egg. Fat also improves flavor. Say you want your eggs soft and creamy but you also want a taste of golden brown—that nutty sweetness that only shows itself

[35] I would compare it to liquid chicken but chicken meat contains connective tissue and eggs do not. Technically speaking the chalazae is a connective structure, meant to keep the yolk centered in the egg, but since it's composed of nothing but twisted white (or albumen), it doesn't really count.

[36] The exceptions are starch-stabilized stirred custards such as pastry cream, which can, because of their starch content, be boiled to no ill effect.

when serious BTUs are involved. No problem. You can develop that flavor before the eggs even show up. Simply melt a pat of butter over medium heat. As soon as the foaming subsides, turn the heat up and hold it there just until you catch a whiff of something like roasted nuts. Kill the heat and let the pan cool down. Then cook the eggs over low heat. The browned butter will coat your eggs with Maillard goodness.

3. Unless you're using a very small pan—say four inches across—resist the urge to crack your eggs directly into the pan. Instead, break them into a small tea cup or ramekin. Why? So you can do this:

THE RIGHT PAN

Because they're high in protein, eggs can stick mightily to cookware. So when eggs are on the menu, grab a good nonstick pan. Eggs also hate high heat, so you'll need a pan that's a good conductor and is free of hot spots. As usual, a good place to find such cookware is at a restaurant supply store. Choose a thick pan that is heavier than it looks, and has a textured (not super-smooth) surface; it will last longer and release food easily. If you're cooking for two, an 8-inch pan is fine, but a 10-inch is even better. And remember, most commercial pans are oven-safe; just don't put them under the broiler.

Cracked into a flat pan, the egg runs out in all directions. This makes for a tough flip. It also results in a wide, flat egg that takes up a lot of plate space and is more likely to overcook.

Lift the handle 2 to 3 inches and slide the egg in with your other hand. The egg will pool at the forward lip. Hold in this position for 30 seconds or so and you will be rewarded with a compact, round egg that's easy to flip.

AGE MATTERS

Eggs have a multilayered construction. Besides the outer shell, there is a thin white or albumen, a thick albumin, the yolk, and the chalazae. This last item is basically a bungee cord of egg white that keeps the yolk (and the microscopic embryo that's attached to it) in place. These layers are separated by membranes, which deteriorate as the egg ages. That means that an older egg (say, one month old) is going to be a beast to cook over easy, because the odds are good that the yolk is going to crash when you turn it. On the flip side, this same egg would be a heck of a lot easier to peel if cooked hard, because the membrane between the outer white and the shell will be less resistant.

With the exception of sunny side up and scrambled, egg preparations get at least one flip, but knowing *when* to flip the flip is a little tricky. I like my eggs over easy, which means that the whites are nicely set but the yolk is lavalike: flowing, but not runny. I don't flip until the thick albumin immediately surrounding the yolk is almost opaque. Then I flip (see Age Matters) and count to 15 slowly. Then I flip again (so that the yolk is visible once again) and slide it onto a plate. At no point do I ever touch the eggs with a spatula— that just invites trouble . . . and yolk breakage. If I'm making a full-blown fried egg, I flip at the same time, but I let it cook a full minute more before plating. In other words, I always execute the first flip at the same state of doneness. What differs is how long I cook it on the second side.

There are, of course, exceptions to the low-temperature rule. Frittatas, soufflés, and meringes all require higher heat because they need to:

• expand. This requires one of two things: either water must turn to steam before the egg sets, or air bubbles physically trapped in the matrix must expand, again before the egg sets. Both scenarios require high heat.

• brown via the Maillard reaction. It's important to note that in this case other ingredients are always present. Eggs should never be left to face high heat alone.

Buying and Storing Eggs

Eggs are bathed, sanitized, dried, and then candled at processing plants. Specially trained workers can spot irregularities and mark a bad egg; the computer remembers that egg and removes it down the line. Eggs that pass muster are weighed by a jet of air and sent to the appropriate cartons.

A dozen medium eggs weigh a minimum of 21 ounces, a dozen large weigh 24 to 26 ounces, a dozen extra-large have to tip the 27-ounce mark, and a dozen jumbo are a robust 30 ounces. At only 15 ounces per dozen, the peewee size don't find their way to the breakfast table and are used instead for industrial purposes.

Egg size doesn't necessarily correlate to egg quality; a grading system serves that purpose. Egg grading is voluntary, and falls under state statute, but many egg processors leave the chore to on-site USDA inspectors. The different grades of eggs are AA, A, and B. Double-A eggs are your freshest eggs. The white is firm and stands up when the egg is cracked open and the yolk is rounder. The difference between AA and A is mainly the age of the egg: an A-grade egg is just a little older than an AA. (So, somebody could buy a dozen AA eggs, take them home, leave them in the refrigerator for a couple of weeks, and they would drop to grade A.) A B-grade egg is good and clean on the outside but when twirled in front of the light you can see the shadow of the yolk. The reason you see the yolk that plainly is because the membranes have broken down. So, when you crack it into your pan or onto a plate it's going to run out.

Eggs usually make their way to your market within a week of being laid and are a staple item that pretty much flies off the shelf; old eggs are a rarity. The Julian date (not the "use by" date) tells you when a carton was packaged. It will be a number between 1 and 365, representing the day of the year on which it was packaged.

When you peek into a carton of eggs checking for cracks, also check to see that the eggs are cold. A room-temperature egg ages more in a day than a refrigerated egg ages in one week. Keeping the fridge at or a little below 40° F will help keep eggs fresh. So will keeping eggs in their carton toward the back of a shelf. The nice little egg shelf found on many refrigerator doors is cute, but that door spends too much time open, hanging out and heating up. Plus, shelf bins promote drying and breakage.

RISK FACTOR

One in ten- to twenty-thousand eggs may be infected with *salmonella*, and even if an egg were infected, the *salmonella* level would probably be too small to harm a healthy adult. It's advisable, however, that older folks, expectant mothers, young children, and anyone with immune system problems steer clear of undercooked or raw eggs. That means passing on sunny-side up eggs, homemade mayonnaise, hollandaise, eggnog, and classic Caesar salad.

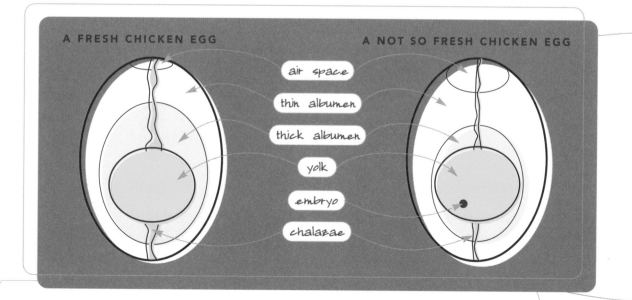

A FRESH CHICKEN EGG — A NOT SO FRESH CHICKEN EGG

air space
thin albumen
thick albumen
yolk
embryo
chalazae

Scrambled Eggs

Ask a French chef to scramble you a few eggs and you're likely to see him whisk a few eggs together with a bit of heavy cream, then cook them in a double boiler over simmering, not boiling, water. I'm often annoyed by the persnickety extra steps that French cuisine demands, but this time I must agree. It's not that it's impossible to make good scrambled eggs straight in a pan, it's just that the double boiler guarantees that the cooking will be done at a steady temperature and at a relatively low rate of conduction.

Don't forget to garnish. A sprinkling of fresh herbs, especially chives, does wonders for scrambled eggs. The best plate of scrambled eggs I ever had (far better than the best omelet I ever had) was finished with truffle oil and sprinkled with finely minced red onion and a dollop of caviar.

Application: Simmering

Pour an inch or two of water into a heavy sauce pan and bring to a boil. Lower the heat until bubbles just break the surface (okay, I'll say it: a simmer). Place a heavy metal bowl over the sauce pan and put the butter in the bowl. Make sure that the bottom of the bowl doesn't come anywhere near the water below.

In a separate mixing bowl, whisk the eggs together with the cream and salt. You don't have to get this completely smooth, but the more homogenized the mixture, the smoother the finished eggs will be.

When the butter has melted, add the egg mixture to the heated bowl. Now, when and how you stir with a plastic spatula will go a long way toward determining the final texture of the eggs. The desired action isn't so much stirring as it is scraping. As the egg cooks on the surface of the bowl, scrape it away so that a fresh coating of the egg mixture can come into contact with the metal. These sheets of cooked egg form lumps known as "curd." Continuous scraping will result in a very fine curd while less frequent scraping produces larger curd. The choice is entirely yours, and you should play around with your technique a bit until you find one that suits your taste. As soon as there is no liquid left in the bowl, pull it from the heat, and move the eggs onto a plate. The eggs may not look done, but they'll continue to cook and will be just right by the time you take your first bite.

Yield: 1 serving (see Note)

Note: I consider 3 eggs a single serving. To increase, double the recipe for each additional diner.

DOUBLE BOILERS

I think that America's general disdain for double boilers comes from the fact that many pot manufacturers insist on making them despite the fact that they are useless, silly uni-taskers that can't even do the one job that they're meant to do.

Figure A. Just look at this silly thing. You can't get a whisk, spoon, or spatula into the corner. The entire side is in contact with the bottom pot. Remember conduction? Heat's going to move right up the side of the bottom pan into this vessel. Worst of all, this vessel has no other use that I can find except take up space and collect dust. Silly, I tell ya.

Figure B. Ah, logic. A metal mixing bowl is whisk and spatula friendly. Contact with the bottom pan is minimal, and the edge of the bowl extends well beyond that of the pan. This may not seem like a big deal, but that span gives heat a place to dissipate and it prevents steam from condensing and rolling down into the food, which is especially important when dealing with chocolate, which will seize into a gnarly mass at the mere mention of water.

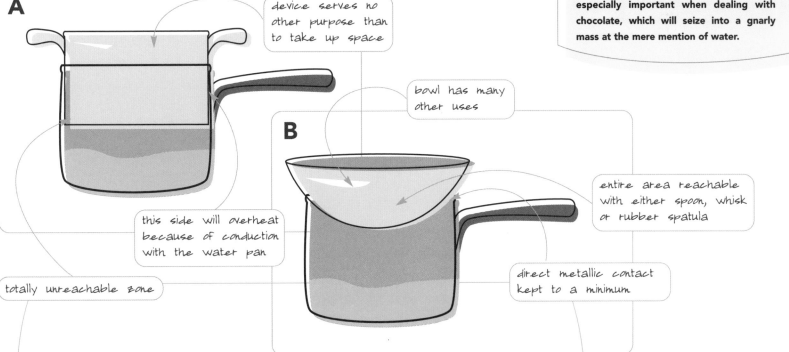

A
device serves no other purpose than to take up space

this side will overheat because of conduction with the water pan

totally unreachable zone

B
bowl has many other uses

entire area reachable with either spoon, whisk or rubber spatula

direct metallic contact kept to a minimum

Poached Eggs

Software:

2 to 4 large eggs

1 teaspoon kosher salt

1 teaspoon vinegar (see **Note**)

Hardware:

1 to 4 small, low-sided custard
cups or teacups

10-inch non-stick sauce pan or
sauté pan, with a lid

Kitchen timer

Slotted spoon

Once they invented cooking, the French set out to name everything involved—and poaching is no exception. *Poach* comes from the French for "pouch" or "pocket" and refers to the shape of an egg cooked in barely simmering water. I suppose it's right that the method be named for the dish, because there is nothing as sublime as a properly poached egg.

Many cooks prefer a deep-water method that allows the egg to form more of a...well, pouch. I prefer this shallow-pan method because it produces a more horizontal—and therefore more plate-able—*oeuf*. My favorite way to serve poached eggs is on top of a salad of bitter greens. Poached eggs can also be cooked ahead of time. Simply move the cooked eggs straight from the pan to a bowl of ice water and hold them there for up to 8 hours. Bring them back to heat in a quick (no more than 1 minute) bath in simmering water.

Application: Poaching

Break the eggs into small custard or tea cups.

Pour enough water into a 10-inch non-stick sauce pan or sauté pan to come halfway up the side of the pan. Bring to a boil over high heat.

When bubbles start to beak the water's surface, stir in the salt and the vinegar.

Slide the eggs gently into the pan by holding the cups as close to the surface of the water as possible. Arrange them at twelve, three, six, and nine o'clock.

As soon as the whites start to turn opaque, remove the pan from the heat and cover with the lid. Set your timer for 3 minutes. When the timer goes off, gently lift the eggs from the water onto a plate with a slotted spoon, and serve.

> Three minutes produces eggs the way I like them, but everyone is different. Experiment a bit with your timing.

Yield: 2 servings

Note: The older the eggs, the more "thin" albumen there's going to be. This is the part of the egg that feathers out creating something that looks more like a Portuguese man of war than a pouch. The vinegar will help a bit by coagulating any proteins it finds wandering about, but you'll still be better off poaching the freshest eggs you can get your hands on. If you prefer a low-acid vinegar, such as rice wine vinegar, increase the amount used to 1½ teaspoons.

Cocktail-Hour Egg Stack

This is one of my favorite scrambled egg variations, and a great way to use up leftovers.

For filling each layer:

¼ cup sautéed onions, mushrooms, or peppers; tomatoes; avocados; crumbled or grated cheese; anchovies; cooked meats (sausage, bacon, grilled chicken, and so on, crumbled or diced); spinach; roasted garlic cloves; or anything you like or have on hand

For the spread for each layer:

2 tablespoons flavored cream cheese, sour cream, tapanade, flavored mayonnaise, guacamole, pesto, salsa, mustard, anchovy paste, tomato sauce, or anything you like or have on hand

Application: Broiling

Preheat the broiler.

To make each egg layer, in a mixing bowl whisk together 2 eggs with ¼ cup of milk. Heat a 10-inch non-stick sauté pan under the broiler for 2 minutes, remove, then add 1 tablespoon of the oil. Count to ten, then pour in the egg mixture and allow the bottom to set. Season with salt and pepper and add the filling ingredient of your choice. Set the pan about 6 inches under the broiler for 1 to 2 minutes (depending on the toppings) to finish cooking. Using a large spatula, slide the layer onto a serving plate and add the spread of your choice. Repeat, stacking one layer on top of the other, until you have at least 6 layers. Slice as you would a pie and serve warm or at room temperature.

Yield: 6 servings

Software:

For the 6 egg layers:

12 large eggs

1½ cups milk

6 tablespoons olive oil

Kosher salt

Freshly ground black pepper

Hardware:

Mixing bowl

Whisk

10-inch non-stick sauté pan

Aluminum foil to cover pan
   handle, if necessary

Spatula

Hard-Cooked Eggs

For Baked Eggs
Software:

2 to 4 dozen large eggs

Hardware:

Baking sheet

Large mixing bowl

Oven-proof gloves

For Steamed Eggs
Software:

1 to 6 eggs

Hardware:

Sauce pan with lid

Metal steamer basket

Tongs

Large mixing bowl

When you think about it, a hard-cooked egg is just about the most convenient food in the world. It comes in its own single-serving container, a container in which it not only can be stored for long periods, but cooked as well.

So why don't we eat more of these delicious devices? Well, somewhere along the line someone decided that they're bad for us (a gross misstatement) and anytime we hear the word boil, associated with a food, our expectations go down, as does the care we take in cooking it.

Sure, you can place any number of eggs in a pot, cover with cold water, bring to a boil, and cook for 12 minutes, but why? We've already established that a pot of boiling water is a very violent neighborhood. I like hard-cooked eggs a lot, so I have favorite methods for cooking both large and small numbers of them. Baking is great for large numbers of eggs, and steaming is the way to go with just a few eggs.

Application: Baking

Position the oven racks in the center of the oven, then place the eggs on the racks. Place a baking sheet pan in the bottom of the oven (just in case an egg breaks). Set the oven to 325° F, and bake for 30 minutes. When the eggs are done, fill a large bowl with ice water and move the eggs into the bowl. Peel the eggs (see **Note**) as soon as they're cool enough to handle, then return them to the ice water to thoroughly chill.

Application: Steaming

Pour 1 inch of water into a sauce pan and place a metal steamer basket inside the pan. Bring the water to a boil over high heat, then place the eggs in the steamer. Cover the pan and lower the heat to medium-high. Cook the eggs for 12 minutes, then, using tongs, remove them to a large bowl of ice water. Peel the eggs (see **Note**) as soon as they are cool enough to handle.

Note: I usually find steamed eggs to be a little easier to peel than baked eggs, but just barely. I think the difference may be that the small amount of egg white that's pushed out of the pores is left to caramelize on the surface of the baked eggs, but is continuously washed away by the steam and therefore doesn't gum up the works. The fact that the shell of the baked egg gets significantly hotter during cooking than the shell of the steamed egg may also be a factor. Still, I prefer the slightly creamier texture of baked eggs to steamed. I imagine it's because the dry heat moves into these eggs more slowly than the steam heat does. Still, both methods beat the tar out of boiling.

Of course, you can't enjoy hard-cooked eggs without peeling them. And, as usual, there is a best way to accomplish this.

Take an egg from the bowl of cooling water and gently tap it against a counter or the side of your sink. Rotate it as you go, with the intention of cracking as much of the surface of the shell as possible. When you've cracked everywhere there is to crack, take the egg and roll it gently between the palms of your hands. This will help to loosen the membrane just under the fragmented shell.

Now turn the egg until you find where the air space was. It will be easy to spot because there will be a convenient gap between the shell and the white beneath. Submerge the egg in the cold water and start peeling from this spot. With practice you'll be able to take the entire shell off in a long strip—just like peeling an orange.

Pickled Eggs

Software:

**For "Dark and Lovely"
   pickled eggs:**

2¼ cups cider vinegar

¾ cup water

1½ tablespoons dark brown sugar

1 tablespoon granulated sugar

1½ teaspoons pickling spice

¼ teaspoon Liquid Smoke (see **Notes**)

1 tablespoon salt

¾ teaspoon chile flakes

1 dozen large hard-cooked eggs,
   peeled

For "Classic" pickled eggs:

2¼ cups apple cider

¾ cup champagne vinegar

1 tablespoon salt

2 teaspoons pickling spice

6 whole cloves garlic

1 dozen large hard-cooked eggs,
   peeled

Hardware:

Sauce pan

1-quart jar with lid, preferably

glass, but not metal

I ate my first pickled egg on a dare (come to think of it, a lot of my "firsts" were dares). When I was in ninth grade, my friends and I used to walk every morning to a little store near the school to sugar-load and flirt with trouble. (We looked so cool in our Starsky and Hutch–inspired fashions.) Anyway, there was this big jug at the end of the counter that looked like it had been left behind by a traveling side show. Dark, alien-looking ovals lurked therein, along with—rumor had it—a dead chicken. Well, one day big talk led to big money (three bucks if I remember correctly), and I found myself in possession of an embalmed chicken embryo mummified in waxed paper. Prepared to die, I took a bite. I've loved them ever since. The "Dark and Lovely" eggs will turn that way because of the Liquid Smoke.

Add all of the ingredients except the eggs to a sauce pan. Bring the mixture to a simmer and cook until the salt and/or sugar dissolves. Place the eggs in a 1-quart jar and pour the hot mixture over the eggs, making sure to cover them completely with liquid. Let cool to room temperature, then put the lid on the jar. Refrigerate for 4 weeks (see **Notes**) before serving.

Yield: 1 dozen pickled eggs

Notes: Liquid Smoke is a liquid seasoning made from hickory smoke concentrate. It is available in most supermarkets—look in the barbeque sauce section.

Although the high acidity of the liquid in both recipes should keep any bad bugs away, please keep these refrigerated. They should keep for about 2 months once pickled.

Deviled Eggs

If you're making hard-cooked eggs, why not serve them deviled?

In a small mixing bowl, using a mixing spoon blend together all of the ingredients except the eggs and paprika. With a sharp knife, split the eggs lengthwise and remove the yolks to a separate mixing bowl. Mash the yolks with a fork and then blend in the mayonnaise mixture. Refill the egg whites with the mixture, smoothing the top with the fork. If you really like tradition, sprinkle some paprika on top.

Yield: 2 dozen deviled eggs

Software:

½ cup mayonnaise

2 tablespoons minced onion

2 tablespoons minced celery

¼ cup chopped fresh parsley

1 teaspoon dry mustard

¼ teaspoon salt

¼ teaspoon freshly ground white pepper

¼ teaspoon celery salt

12 hard-cooked eggs, peeled

Paprika (optional)

Hardware:

2 mixing bowls

Mixing spoon or rubber spatula

Sharp knife

Mom's Egg Salad

Egg salad is another great use for hard-cooked eggs. Pumpernickel is the only acceptable bread to use for an egg-salad sandwich.

With a chef's knife, coarsely chop the eggs and put them in a mixing bowl. With a wooden spoon, fold the remaining ingredients into the eggs. Chill the mixture in the refrigerator for at least 1 hour to let the flavors blend.

Yield: Filling for 8 sandwiches

Software:

12 hard-cooked eggs, peeled

⅓ cup mayonnaise

1 tablespoon freshly squeezed lemon juice

1 teaspoon celery salt

½ teaspoon salt

½ teaspoon freshly ground white pepper

1 cup finely diced celery

Hardware:

Chef's knife

Mixing bowl

Wooden spoon

Why is this chapter at the end of the book? Because it's the only application by which food actually cooks itself.

CHAPTER 10 **Microwave Cooking**

Catch a Wave

What the heck happened to my Mars bar?

—Dr. Percy Spencer

If appliance makers are correct, some 96 percent of American homes contain at least one microwave oven. Most of these are employed in the warming of coffee, the popping of popcorn, and the occasional "nuking" of frozen foods. When you consider what this technology is capable of, this seems a lot like using an aircraft carrier to pull a waterskier. Sure, it can do the job, but that's not the point. The microwave oven can do some amazing things—the trick is to understand how it works well enough to know what to feed it.

But first, some history. It began, as these things often do, with a guy in a lab coat. The guy was Dr. Percy Spencer, and the lab coat belonged to the Raytheon Corporation. One day in 1946, Dr. Spencer was futzing about with a new kind of vacuum tube that (it was hoped) would revolutionize the radar industry. It was called a magnetron tube, and, after working on it awhile, Doc Spencer decided it was time for a snack. He reached into his lab coat pocket for a chocolate bar and found that it had turned to mush. It's been a short leap from that melted candy bar to the distinctive hum heard at 3:00 A.M. in 7-Elevens across the country.

When I set out to understand the microwave, I hunted up an industry expert who prefers to remain anonymous.

Me: Uh, what's a microwave?

Expert: A form of electromagnetic energy.

Me: Hmm. What's electromagnetic energy?

Expert: Waves of electrical and magnetic energy that move together through space.

Me: I see.

Expert: Sure you do. Let me draw you a picture.

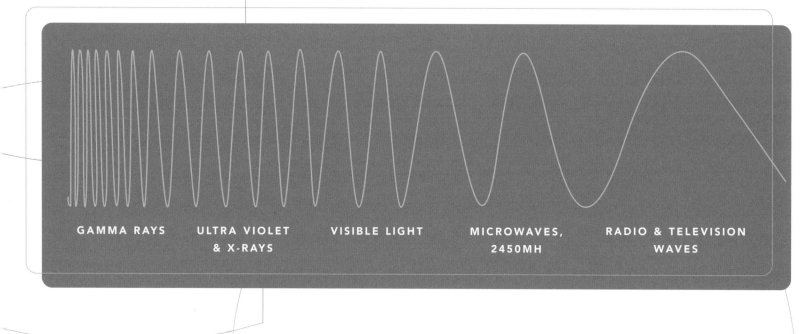

GAMMA RAYS   ULTRA VIOLET & X-RAYS   VISIBLE LIGHT   MICROWAVES, 2450MH   RADIO & TELEVISION WAVES

Me: Ah, yes. So how do you make one of these wavy things?

Expert: Well, you create an electromagnetic wave any time you feed an electric current through a conductor, such as a copper wire. But that kind of energy stays very close to the wire. However, if you oscillate it at a rapid rate...

Me: Oscillate?

Expert: Reverse polarity.

Me: I knew that.

Expert: When you do that, the electromagnetic field breaks free and a wave moves outward like ripples on a pond. In microwave ovens we use a device called a magnetron tube to create and direct these waves.

Me: Are they dangerous?

Expert: If you're inside the microwave.

Me: That's not really what I meant.

Expert: You have to remember that these are non-ionizing waves. They're not that much higher in frequency than television and radio broadcast waves, which we're exposed to all the time.

Me: Ionizing?

Expert: When the frequency of a given radiation reaches millions of cycles per second, that means it's packing considerable energy—enough to pass through you and onto a photographic plate. With enough exposure, such waves can ionize or change cell structure—even your genetic structure, which explains why too much tanning can lead to skin cancer. Of course, the sun's rays lose a lot of oomph while traveling millions of miles to the earth.

Me: What if the thing making the waves was close?

Expert: How close?

Me: Hiroshima close.

Expert: Let me put it this way, there's a big difference between being hit in the head by a beach ball thrown by a three-year-old child and a fastball thrown by a major-league pitcher.

Me: Okay, so what do you say to the charge that microwaves don't cook food?

Expert: That's right. Microwaves don't cook food, because food exposed to microwaves cooks itself.

Me (as I scratch my head): Perhaps you could elaborate.

Expert: Microwaves are a little odd because although they can pass straight through substances like glass and most plastics, they are actually absorbed by chemicals in food that have asymmetrical molecules.

Me: Like?

Expert: Like most fats, sugar, and especially water—that's the big one. (Pausing I recall the Mickey Mouse-hat concept.) When these molecules absorb the waves, they begin to vibrate. This vibration causes friction with nearby molecules, and that friction creates heat—the heat that does the actual cooking.

Me: So you can cook anything in a microwave oven that contains enough of those compounds.

Expert: Yep.

Me: Okay, I got it. What about the old sales tagline about microwaves cooking food from the inside out?

Expert: Microwaves still have to penetrate food, but some foods are easier to penetrate than others. For instance, microwaves can't penetrate a beef roast by more than a couple of inches.

Me: So you can't cook a roast in a microwave oven?

Expert: Yes, you can. It's just that the waves only penetrate so far. The core of the roast would cook by conduction—the old-fashioned way.

Me: Okay. Got it.

Expert: I'm not sure that you do, but I have to go.

Me: Okay. Bye, Dad.

Expert: Please don't call me at work again.

Superheating

So, from this enlightening conversation we come to understand that anything containing water and/or fat and sugar can be cooked via microwave energy. That would seem to include just about every food on earth. The problem is a lot of the flavors we expect from food come to us via the Maillard reaction, which as we all know only results from contact with very dry high heat. Since the microwave oven itself doesn't get hot, the Maillard reaction cannot be evoked. The water that's on the surface of and inside the food can't rise above 212° F (at sea level), and that's just not good enough. In fact, the only way to brown something in the microwave oven is to—carefully—get metals involved. For instance, there are certain prepared foods that one puts inside a foil-lined sleeve before letting the waves do their stuff. That foil contraption is designed to get super hot and brown the burrito . . . or whatever. But designing such a device yourself can lead to fire and/or permanent damage to the inside of the oven, so don't try it.

Fire can result from the super-heating of flammables such as popcorn bags. When appliance manufacturers test microwave ovens for fire containment they often use microwave popcorn as the fuel—and just to make sure there's a fire, they insert a 10-penny nail in the bag. Since it's dense and significantly longer than the microwave's wavelength, the nail gets really, really hot. This is one reason microwave oven manufacturers usually discourage the use of metal containers or cooking utensils in microwave ovens.

There's another reason. Even if the metal device doesn't get hot enough to start a fire, it can become so electrically charged that if it comes close enough to the wall or floor of the oven it can arc. The resulting "lightning" can badly mar the oven.

Foods not to microwave:
Eggs in the shell (the same principal as popcorn, but a lot more forceful and a lot more messy).
Shellfish: ditto

The Great Popcorn Controversy

I wish to defend myself against charges of microwave abuse. A couple of years ago on a certain television program, I made microwave popcorn from scratch, using plain popping corn, a little olive oil, and salt in a small paper bag sealed with not one, not three, but two standard office staples.

Well, despite the fact that I had tested this in no fewer than ten different ovens, and despite the fact that the product was delicious and cheaper than dirt, I received tons of angry mail. People were just sure that their houses would explode.

No. Relax. It's okay.

As long as you're using a microwave oven with a turntable and you don't place the bag where the staples can rub against one of the walls, nothing bad will happen. This is because staples have very little mass and they are shorter than the microwaves themselves, which means they're basically microwave "invisible." So don't be afraid to try the recipe on the next page.

Beyond the Burrito

Okay, back to the point. Since the outer surface of foods can't get hot enough to brown, there's no real reason to doom foods that benefit from tasty crusts to the mediocrity of microwave cooking. But there are plenty of foods that don't depend on such action.

Microwaves (the waves not the ovens) set certain molecules into motion, creating friction and therefore heat. Since water and sugar are two of the substances most affected, fruits would seem to be prime m-wave candidates, especially when a sauce is the desired result.

When it comes to microwave ovens, round containers always outperform rectangular vessels. And because the waves bounce around the cavity of the oven, I like taller rather than shorter vessels.

Homemade Microwave Popcorn

I've made this stuff six ways from Wednesday and until recently I always tossed the kernels in oil before placing them in the bag. But the more I learned about microwaves, the more I started to think this might be unnecessary. After all, the stuff that does the popping (water and plenty of starch) are on the inside of the kernels. The kernel itself doesn't need to brown, so why bother with the added mess? I ran a quick test batch and never looked back.

Although many home poppers advocate the use of other culinary oils in place of butter, I just can't break with this tasty tradition. However, I do like a sprinkle of cheese now and then. Oh, and if you're interested, toss a tablespoon of dark brown sugar in the bag sometime.

Application: Microwave Cooking

Pour the popcorn into a paper bag and fold the top of the bag over twice to close (each fold should be ½ inch deep; remember, the kernels need room to pop).

Seal the bag with 2 staples only, making sure to place the staples at least 2 to 3 inches apart (see page 236 for more on metal in the microwave oven).

Put the bag in the microwave oven and cook on high power for 2 to 3 minutes, or until the pops are 5 seconds apart.

Remove the bag from the oven and open it carefully, avoiding the steam. Pour the popcorn into a bowl and drizzle it with the butter, then toss with salt and cheese, if desired.

Yield: 6 to 8 cups popcorn

Software:

⅓ cup popcorn

2 to 3 tablespoons melted butter

Popcorn salt[37] to taste

1 tablespoon Parmesan cheese, finely grated, or other "cheese sprinkle" (optional)

Hardware:

Small paper bag (standard lunch size is fine)

Stapler (use exactly 2 staples—no more no less, see page 236)

Microwave oven with a carousel (important for even popping)

Large mixing bowl

---

[37] This is one time kosher salt just won't do. Popcorn salt is very fine, so it sticks readily to the popped kernels. If you can't find it in your local Mega-mart, go with (hate to say it) table salt.

Tomato Sauce Rosie

1 tablespoon olive oil

2 tablespoons thinly sliced garlic

2 tablespoons minced shallot

1 cup diced yellow onion

½ teaspoon chile flakes

1 (14-ounce) can unseasoned
  tomato sauce

1 (14-ounce) can unseasoned diced
  tomatoes

2 heaping tablespoons basil, cut
  into fine chiffonade

¼ cup chopped fresh parsley

2 teaspoons sugar

Kosher salt

Freshly ground black pepper

Hardware:

1½-quart microwave-safe glass or
  ceramic dish

Microwave oven with carousel

Plastic wrap

There are times when you want to slowly simmer a sauce all afternoon on the cook top. And then there are the times when you just want to eat something. The microwave oven is here to help—so let it.

Application: Microwave Cooking

In a microwave-safe glass dish, combine the oil, garlic, shallot, onion, and chile flakes. Put the dish in the microwave oven and cook on high power for 1 minute.

Remove the dish from the oven, add the tomato sauce and the diced tomatoes, then tightly cover the dish with plastic wrap. Pierce the film twice to allow steam to escape, return the dish to the microwave oven and cook on high power, for 2 minutes. Allow the dish to rest, covered, in the oven for 2 minutes, then remove, take off the plastic wrap, and stir in the basil, parsley, sugar, and salt and pepper to taste. Serve over your favorite pasta.

Yield: Approximately 3½ cups sauce

Rosie, of course being the Jetsons' robotic maid and cook. I'm pretty sure the ol' girl had a microwave oven in her midsection so she could cook this while ironing Judy's school uniforms.

Bourbon Apple Pear Sauce

This sauce can be served hot or chilled, over ice cream, or pound cake, or anything you like.

Application: Microwave Cooking

Combine all the ingredients except the bourbon and lemon juice in a microwave-safe container, loosely cover (to allow steam to escape), and cook in the microwave oven on high power for 10 minutes. Allow the dish to rest in the oven for 10 minutes more.

Remove the star anise. With a sieve, drain the liquid from the fruit into a small bowl, and set aside. Return the fruit to the container and use a potato masher to mash to your desired consistency.

Add the reserved liquid and the bourbon to a small sauce pan and cook over medium heat until the liquid is reduced to a near-syrup consistency. Fold the sauce into the fruit. If the sauce is too sweet, add a little lemon juice to taste.

Yield: 3 cups

Software:

2 Granny Smith apples, peeled, cored, and diced

4 Taylor Gold pears (or your favorite variety), peeled, cored, and diced

1½ tablespoons honey

2 tablespoons butter

½ teaspoon cinnamon

1 piece star anise

½ ounce bourbon

Freshly squeezed lemon juice to taste (optional)

Hardware:

1½-quart microwave-safe container with lid

Fine-mesh sieve

Small bowl

Potato masher (preferably the grid kind)

Small sauce pan

Beef Cuts

Although the beef critter may be the same from coast to coast the traditions of butchering them are not. For instance, in the Northeast the chuck and round are most often cut into whole muscle roasts, meaning bullet-shaped cuts in which the grain runs the length of the meat. In the South, the chuck is most often cut into big slabs or steaks containing cross sections of many different muscles. The best way to keep straight on such matters is to find yourself a good butcher. This may mean abandoning your local Mega-mart.

CHUCK

Chuck Roast

Blade Roast

Arm Roast

Ground Beef

RIB

Rib Roast

Rib Steaks
(Delmonico)

Rib Eye Steak

BRISKET

Corned Beef

Texas BBQ

SHORT PLATE

Short Ribs
(continued from ribs)

Skirt Steak

SHANK

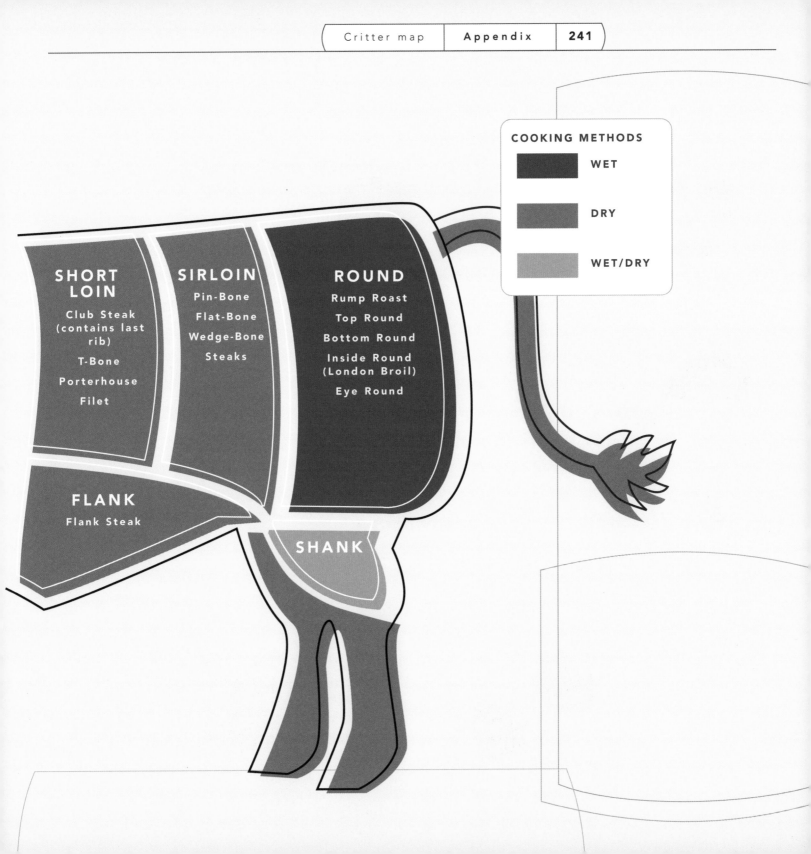

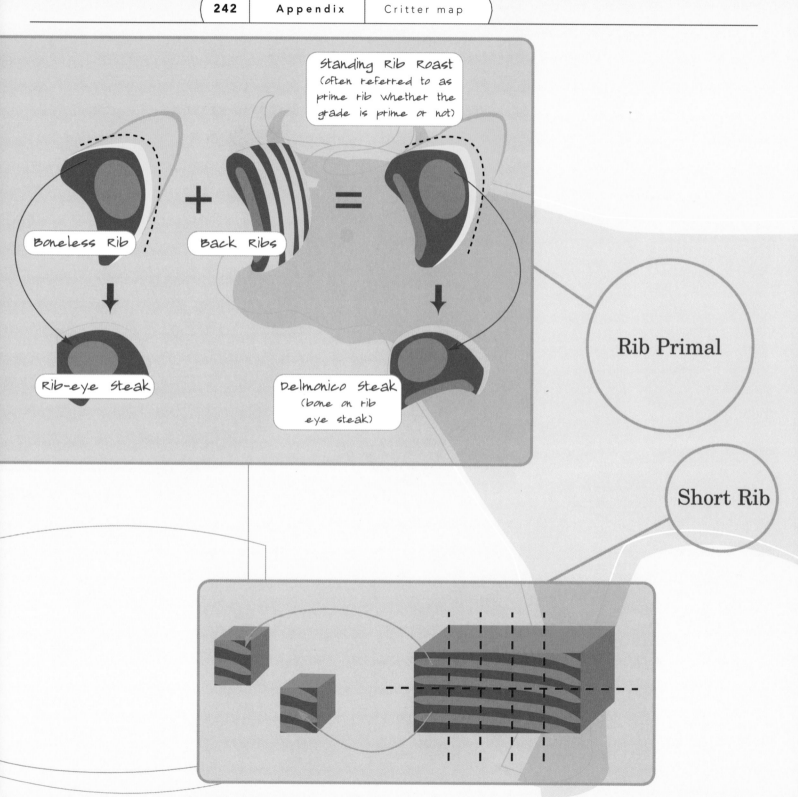

Standing Rib Roast
(often referred to as prime rib whether the grade is prime or not)

Boneless Rib

+

Back Ribs

=

Rib-eye Steak

Delmonico Steak
(bone on rib eye steak)

Rib Primal

Short Rib

Loin Cuts

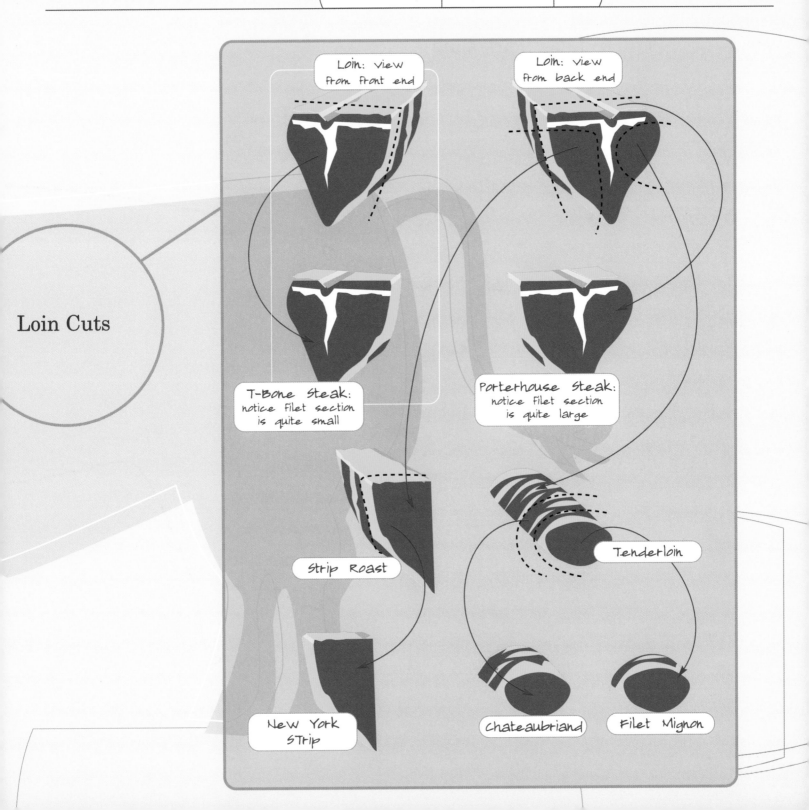

Loin: view from front end

Loin: view from back end

T-Bone Steak: notice filet section is quite small

Porterhouse Steak: notice filet section is quite large

Strip Roast

Tenderloin

New York Strip

Chateaubriand

Filet Mignon

Pork Cuts

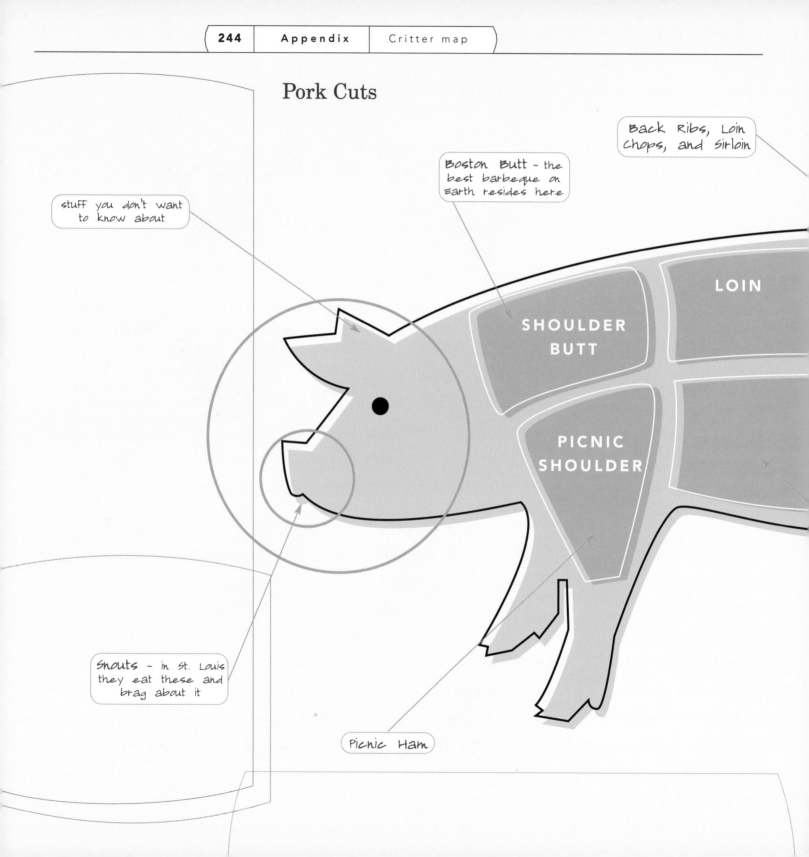

Back Ribs, Loin Chops, and Sirloin

Boston Butt - the best barbeque on Earth resides here

stuff you don't want to know about

SHOULDER BUTT

LOIN

PICNIC SHOULDER

Snouts - in St. Louis they eat these and brag about it

Picnic Ham

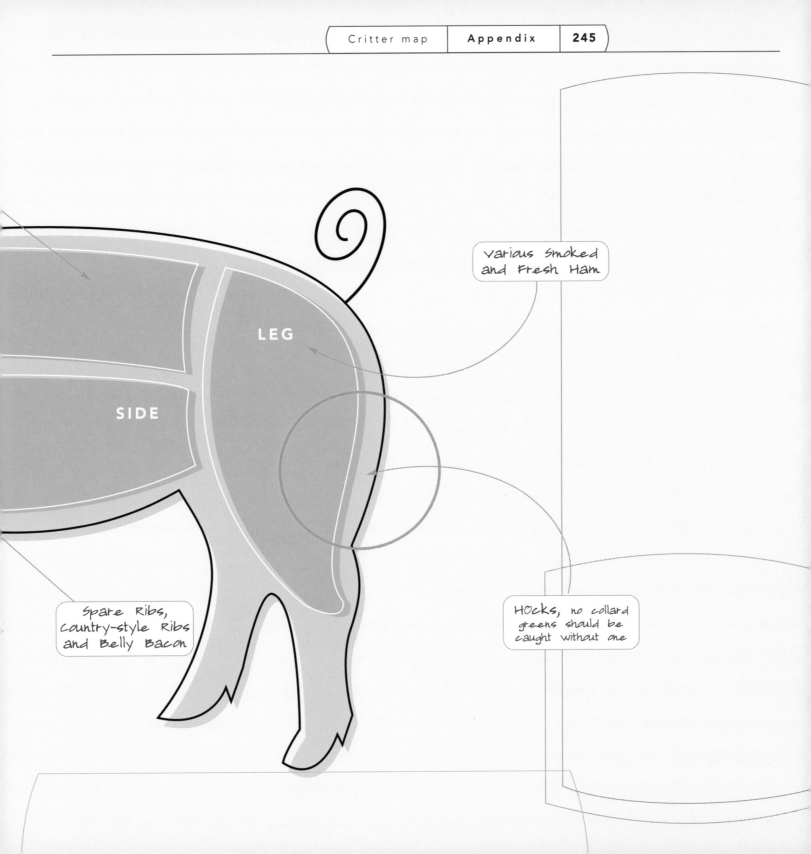

The Basic Culinary Toolbox

The word gadget derives from the French *gachette* or "piece of machinery." It's a cool word and I dig the way it sounds, but I'm not too fond of the modern connotation, which smacks of infomercial hucksterism rather than the Yankee ingenuity that produced marvels like the ice-cream churn and the space shuttle. The fact that the word is most often used in association with devices intended for culinary use is a sad statement indeed. In an effort to save time, calories, energy, and so on, people turn to gadgets; then when they find no satisfaction in them, stick them in a drawer. Eventually, there are so many gadgets there's no room to cook. What we need is less gadgetry and more tools. Tools are serious things, meant to last and to be employed in a wide range of applications. Good tools are rarely cheap, but there aren't many that you absolutely have to have either. Here are some thoughts on a few essential tools.

Knives

I used to have a lot of knives: five or six boning knives, chef's knives in every size from 4 to 14 inches, and even three or four different paring knives. Why so many? Because I didn't know what I was doing and I thought that my mediocre swordsmanship could somehow be improved by a great number of tools. Since I also didn't know how to take care of knives properly, I spread the abuse out among the lot. Now I'm down to five knives. I use an 8-inch Asian-style cleaver, a semiflexible boning knife, a French-style paring knife, a serrated electric knife, and a 12-inch cimeter, which I mostly use to cut the backbones out of chickens and to break down large fish and beef sub primals. The cimeter and the boning knife are stamped-blade knives made by Forschner, the Swiss Army knife folks. The electric knife is specially made for fish cutting and came from a sporting goods store. It's an ugly thing with a two-tone blue-and-gold chassis, but it has several different blades, two speeds, and it cost less than thirty bucks. My paring knife came from France and cost about thirty bucks. The cleaver was handmade by the only American-born master of

ROCKWELL

The relative hardness or softness of a knife is reflected in the Rockwell of its metal. The Rockwell scale is a 100-point scale used to rate the hardness of minerals, metals, and ceramics. Diamonds have a Rockwell rating of 100. Most high-end HCS knives come in between 55 and 58, while carbon steel knives are softer, at 51. Some of the new ceramic knives on the market boast near diamondlike hardness, which their manufacturers claim give them a longer-lasting edge. I find their lack of heft annoying, and the fact that they break like a plate when dropped is especially painful given their car-payment-like price tags.

Japanese blade making and cost more than two hundred smackers. If I had to choose one knife to live the rest of my cooking days with, this would be the one.

To be of real use a knife must be sharp, but it must possess the correct heft, shape, and balance for the job. Most of all, it must suit the hand holding it. Before you buy, you should know what you're looking for (and at), how and from what it's made, and the reputation of those who made it. Once you get it home, you should know how to store it, use it, and maintain it.

Metal Matters

When it comes to metal, there are basically two choices: carbon steel or alloys referred to as high-carbon stainless steel. Stainless-steel knives are widely available but impossible to sharpen, and quality knifesmiths never mess with the stuff unless they're making pocket knives.

Steel is an amalgam of 80 percent iron and 20 percent other elements. In carbon steel, which has been around for quite a while, that 20 percent is carbon. A relatively soft yet resilient metal, carbon steel is easy to sharpen and holds an edge well. No matter what the knife salesman tells you, no high-carbon stainless-steel blade can match carbon steel's sharpness. Carbon steel is, however, vulnerable in the kitchen environment. Acid, moisture, and salt will stain, rust, or even pit the blade if it's not promptly cleaned and dried after each use. (You should probably pass on carbon steel when outfitting the beach house kitchen.) Slicing even one tomato with a new carbon steel knife will change the color of the blade. In time, it will take on a dark patina that some find charming, others nasty.

Most professional-grade knives on the market today are high-carbon stainless steel. This is an alloy of iron and carbon combined with other metals such as chromium or nickel (for corrosion resistance), and molybdenum or vanadium (for durability and flexibility, respectively). Although the exact formula varies from brand to brand, HCS knives possess some of the positive attributes of both carbon steel and stainless steel. The edge will never match that of carbon steel, but neither will it corrode. The trade-off is acceptable to the great majority of the folks who happily use them.

KNIFE-BUYING TIPS

• **Steer clear of sets.** They may save you a buck or two but they're rarely worth the savings. Besides, they usually come with knife blocks, which take up space and are impossible to clean. Even if you like blocks, don't buy a set. You're better off buying your blades one at a time so that you get exactly what you need.

• **Shop around,** prices vary widely.

• **Never buy a knife that you haven't tried out** on a cutting board. If the clerk gives you flack about this, walk away.

Construction

There are three ways to make a blade: forging, stamping or cutting, or separate-component technology (SCT). This is the arena where cutlery marketing departments duke it out. It's also where you'll find the greatest delineation in performance and price.

The best knives in the world are hot-drop forged. A steel blank is heated to 2000° F, dropped into a mold, and shaped via blows from a hammer wielded by either man or machine. The stresses of forging actually alter the molecular structure of the metal, making it denser and more resilient. Forged blades are then hardened and tempered (a process of heating and cooling in oil) for strength, then shaped and handles attached. This requires dozens of individual steps involving many skilled technicians, a fact reflected in the selling price. Once upon a time, all Wusthof-Trident, J. A. Henckel, Sabatier, Lamson, and Chef's Choice knives were fully forged, but today most of these labels offer more economical stamped-blade lines too. If you're looking to make a friend for life, full-tang, forged knives are the only way to go. Of course, some friendships can be rewarding even if they don't last forever.

Stamped, die-cut, and laser-cut knives have long been seen as inferior to forged blades. The blade and partial tang is stamped like a gingerbread man out of cold-rolled sheet steel. A handle is affixed, and away you go. Cost is the advantage here; the bad news

A single forged piece of metal running from point to end of handle

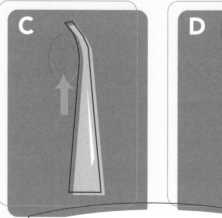

Figure A Sharp blade in "true". Figure B Sharp blade out of "true."

Figures C & D Honing steel pushing edge back into alignment.

is, without a bolster or full-tang, heft, balance, and the molecular advantage of full forging are nowhere to be seen. However because they're quite thin, many chefs often prefer stamped blades for fish and boning knives, which are usually employed in such a way that heft and balance don't really matter.

Separate-component technology is a new way for knife makers to get that great drop-forged look without going to all the trouble. SCT knives are pieced together from three separate parts. The blade and partial tang are stamped, then the bolster is formed from metal powder injected into a mold. SCT manufacturers claim this lets them use the perfect metal for each part rather than settling on one steel for the entire knife. The way I see it, even if the thing actually hangs together and even if the balance and weight are great, there's still no way a stamped blade's ever going to dice through the decades like a forged blade—it just doesn't have the molecular muscle. These imposters are tough to spot, so you'll have to find knowledgeable salespeople.

Maintenance

Most cooks who buy good knives ruin them within a year. Here are the best ways to accomplish this.

Store your knives in a drawer with a lot of other metal things. Every time you open or close the drawer your edges will knock up against things that will bend/man-

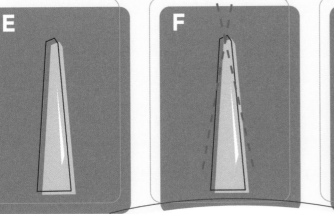

Figure E Dull blade. Figure F Dull blade showing angle of material to be removed. Figure G New edge after sharpening.

SHARPENING AND HONING

When a blade is sharp it looks like Figure A.

Given its thinness, it's easy for the edge to develop microscopic bends, even with light use: Figure B. At this point the knife is still "sharp;" it's just out of alignment and therefore not much good to the cook. Continued use at this point will only make things worse.

When frequently and properly applied, a honing steel, which is a good bit harder than the knife and is usually magnetized, can bring the edge back to "true" (Figures C & D). The key word here is "properly" and I'm convinced that (like shooting pool or writing poetry) this is one of those things that just can't be taught on paper, as it requires the guidance of a skilled practitioner. My advice is to find a professional knife sharpener in your area who can sharpen your arsenal once or twice a year. Ask this person to sell you a steel the right size for your knives and show you how to use it.

I give a knife a stroke or two with the steel nearly every time I use it.

TYPES OF CUTS

• To mince is to cut food into very small pieces.

• To chop is to cut food more coarsely than a mince.

• To dice is to cut food into tiny cubes, approximately ⅛- to ¼-inch square.

• To cube is to cut food into ½-inch square pieces.

• To julienne is to cut food into matchstick-thin strips, about ⅛-inch square, of various lengths.

• Chiffonade is from the French for "made of rags" and refers to food cut into very thin strips (see illustration).

• Lyonnaise-style is in the manner of the city of Lyons, France. Onions sliced Lyonnaise-style are cut lengthwise from top to root, rather than across (see illustration).

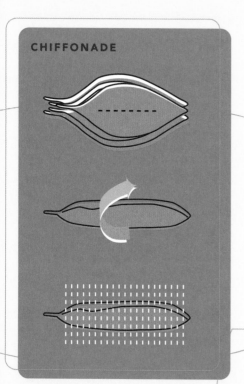

CHIFFONADE

gle/mash the fine edge into something resembling a tuna-can lid. Thus impeded, your blade will require a great deal of force to actually cut anything. And a dull knife with a lot of force behind it is about as safe as a shark with a chainsaw.

Wash your knives in the dishwasher. If banging against plates (which have Rockwells far in excess of carbon steel) isn't enough to do in the blade, the harsh chemicals of the wash and the ovenlike heat of the dry cycle will quickly grant your once smooth handle the topography of a dry lake bed. The fissures will soon fill with kitchen gunk—if the handle doesn't fall off first.

Cut on a glass cutting board. Just think of it: a metallic edge with an average Rockwell of 58 coming into repeated perpendicular contact with a surface with an average Rockwell of 98. I simply cannot imagine a better way to render a blade useless. (See Cutting Boards, page 259.)

Sharpen your knives yourself. Sharpening devices are the darlings of the kitchen gadget industry, so you'll have no trouble finding one in your price range to tickle your fancy. Count on the silliest-looking designs to effect the quickest destruction. As far as sharpening stones go, they may not look silly but they require considerable skill and experience to master and they're a pain to maintain. Hone your knives often but never sharpen them—leave that to the pros.

If you use a honing steel, be sure to use it improperly. If you need an example, find yourself a restaurant that has a big window that looks into the kitchen. Sometimes, when they know you're watching, they'll run their knife up and down the steel very rapidly. This is indeed horrible for the blade, but to the layperson it looks cool, which is why they do it.

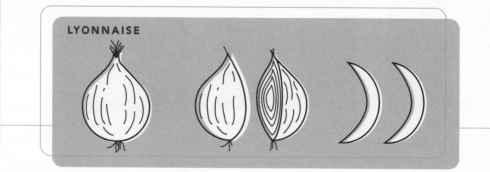

LYONNAISE

Storage

Deciding where and how to store a knife is a big deal to both the blade and your fingers. I like magnetic bars because they don't take up a lot of space and if there's any moisture left on a knife it will air-dry, but these are not usually recommended if you've got kids, pets, or homicidal tendencies. Storing knives in a drawer is fine as long as the drawer in question contains some device that will keep the blades separate and stable. Counter blocks are okay, but they rarely match up to an eclectic collection, and they tend to take up a lot of space. The best idea I've seen lately is a long skinny slot cut into the top of a butcher block deep enough for the knives to simply line up along the slot. Whatever device you choose, please make sure that the blades are completely enclosed. A friend had a rolling kitchen cart with a knife block attached to the side. One day he purchased a 12-inch slicer and put it into the block. Later that same day he reached down to the bottom of the cart for a pot, only to realize that the block was 11 inches long and had a completely open bottom. He had time to ponder this fact later as he sat in the emergency room.

Pots and Pans

Sometime during the last twenty years of the past century, the kitchen became the new living room. Not so much because cooking and eating are communal acts connecting us all via the collective rumblies in our tumblies, but because there was a lot of cash floating around and a plethora of expensive new kitchen pretties to spend it on. Suddenly kitchens that had never witnessed an egg boil were being fitted with five-thousand-dollar cook tops. And of course nothing befits a five-thousand-dollar cook top quite like a halo of silently shining geosynchronous sauce pans. Even I, with my two-hundred-dollar cook top, fell victim to pot-rack fever. Following several years of collecting I finally had to mount flying buttresses on my humble ranch house just to support the ceiling joists, which moaned at the butter melters, fry pans, sauce pans, sauté pans, Windsor pans, casseroles, stock pots, and griddles I had accumulated. Then came the day I dropped two C notes on a French potato pot. My family got together and applied some tough love, slipping in while

I was at Williams-Sonoma and taking it all away, leaving me with nothing but my great-grandmother's 12-inch cast-iron skillet. Some might call such intervention harsh, but once I quit my sobbing I found that I was free, finally, to cook. Really cook. My family slowly returned my pots and pans to me as Christmas and birthday presents, but in my new-found zen-lightenment I gave most of them away. To this day, my rack remains light. Here's the breakdown in order of importance.

12-Inch Cast-Iron Skillet

I recently got into one of those "What pan would you want if you were stuck on a deserted island" conversations you hear so much about. My 12-inch Lodge was the easy choice. Besides all the metallurgical and thermal reasons given in the Searing section, this remains a culinary chameleon. Not only is its shape versatile, the properly cured surface is hard and black and slippery as a newt in Vaseline.[38] I've even turned mine upside down and used the bottom as a griddle—oh yes, I have. I've used it as a flame-tamer, too, by placing other pans on top of it. I've baked biscuits in it, baked quiche in it, baked apple pie in it, I've cooked on campfires with it, and one particularly rough winter during my college years I managed to rip a gas heater off the wall, set it up on coffee cans, and fry bacon-wrapped prawns over it. Take care of that cast-iron skillet and it will never let you down.

What it's good for: this would take too long. What it's not good for: boiling pasta—that's about it.

5-Quart Casserole

This is a relative newcomer to my collection, but it easily replaces three different vessels in my life, thus allowing for more downscaling. It is essentially a small, heavy stock pot with two loop handles. Since I like finishing things in the oven I've never been much of a sauce pan fan—I don't like wrestling with straight single handles, which I think are pretty darned dangerous. Although this isn't a common piece, several companies make one (or something close). Mine was made by All-Clad, the Smith & Wesson of the pot and pan world, if you ask me. It costs more than just about anything out there, but you'll only have to buy it once, and since the pieces are so darned versatile you don't have to buy many.

Cooking was the only way I could get dates during college.

---

[38] There are those who will tell you that acidic items such as tomato sauce will rip a cure right off a pan. All I can say is I don't buy it.

What it's good for: a multitude of cook-top or oven applications, from soup beans to small batches of pasta, and steaming. What it's not good for: sautéing; pan-frying.

8-Inch Teflon-Coated Fry Pan

I like eggs and this is my egg pan. It cost me twelve bucks. I keep it wrapped in a couple of layers of plastic wrap when I'm not using it so that its surface won't scratch.

What it's good for: frying eggs; scrambling eggs; omelets; low-fat sautéing. What it's not good for: searing, or pan-frying.

3-Quart Saucier with Lid

In the deserted-island scenario, this one ran a close second to the cast iron. It's a hybrid pan, half skillet, half sauce pan and the design is perfect for reducing sauces that pool in the small-diameter bottom. (It's not called a saucier for nothing.) Its rounded bottom makes it perfect for roux-based sauces because there are no corners that a whisk can't get into.

What it's good for: all sauces from sawmill gravy to crème anglaise; reducing; rice (pilaf); simmering. What it's not good for: pan-frying; sautéing.

12-Inch Sauté Pan with Lid

The main difference between a sauté pan and a skillet is the angle of the walls, which flare out on a skillet or fry pan and are straight on a sauté pan, thus granting you more flat floor space to work. Another important feature of the sauté pan is the loop handle on the side opposite the straight handle—very convenient for moving the pan in and out of the oven. My sauté pan is also a clad piece with an exterior of stainless steel over an aluminum core. This is my pan-fry and pan-braise tool of choice.

What it's good for: chicken piccata; salisbury steak; fried green tomatoes; pan-frying in general.[39] What it's not good for: stir-frys; thin soups; eggs.

Dutch Oven

Another cast-iron number. Heavy but the best vessel around for slow cooking. It's got a wire loop handle for easy moving (or suspending over campfires, open hearths, and so on. Since it's so gosh-darned dense, it holds heat forever; if I'm taking a hot dish to someone's

---

[39] This only holds true for heavy-duty (read: expensive) models. Skimpy models are none too good for pan-frying because they don't heat evenly over a burner.

house, I'll take it in the Dutch oven even if I didn't cook it in there. (It never turns over in the car, either, which is a nice bonus.)[40] What it's good for: long-cooking stews; baked beans; pot roast. What it's not good for: sautéing.

10-Inch Stainless-Steel Fry Pan

Another clad pan, like the sauté pan, but this one has sloping walls that allow for single-handed food turning via the "toss."

What it's good for: sautéing. What it's not so good for: eggs (they stick); pan braises (there's not enough flat floor space); soup (it's too shallow).

8- to 12-Quart Stock Pot

Making stock is cheap and easy—if you have a stock pot. Cookin' up a mess of greens or boiling water for pasta also requires a large vessel. You can spend a mess of green on a clad stock pot, but such models are prohibitively expensive and more than a little heavy. My favorite is stainless steel with a thick pad of metal welded onto the bottom.

One More Pan

Even if you're positively certain that you haven't a single pot or pan to your name, as long as you have an oven you probably do: just about every oven constructed in the free world comes with its own broiling pan. That's right, that funny-looking enamel-coated thing with the funny little grate. Never used it? You should. It's the perfect device for broiling. Not only does it keep food up and out of whatever juices might hinder the browning process (and broiling is about nothing if not browning) it allows said juices, including flammable fats, to gather in the pan below, where they can be rescued and put to good use. I wouldn't say that it's the most-used pan in my kitchen, but it is the most-oft-used pan that didn't cost me a thin dime.

A Few Words on Lids

Heavy, well-seated, with sturdy handles. Have one for every pot or pan you own. Since not all vessels come with lids, a unilid is a great idea—and it takes up less space, too.

---

[40] There is currently a resurgence in Dutch-oven cooking out West and in, of all places, Japan.

Stuff with Wires

Electric Skillet

An electric skillet is a must-have because of its versatility. It's got a vast, open, non-stick plain just begging for pancakes, fried eggs, bacon, free-form crepes, pan-seared steak, and more. The thermostat keeps the oil at just the right temperature for frying, too. And best of all, even top-of-the-line models rarely cost more than thirty dollars. When shopping, look for a 12-inch model with a calibrated thermostat, sturdy design, and a tall, tight-fitting lid with an adjustable steam vent.

If I want a steak and it's too hot in the kitchen already and I don't have time to fire up the grill, I'll take my electric skillet out on the screened-in porch and sear away from the comfort of my lounge chair. Not all out-of-kitchen cooking experiences have to involve a grill. I'm a big fan of electricity. Besides my electric skillet I have a nice big electric griddle, and a crockpot—and an electric fryer—and a toaster—and a toaster oven—and a microwave. With the exception of the microwave all the items in this list come in stove-top models. What I like about the electrical angle is control and convenience. All these devices come with thermostats, so I don't have to fiddle too much with heat maintenance.

Tool Talk

Tongs

There's a reason restaurant cooks call tongs their "hands." There's an awful lot of hot stuff in the kitchen, and there's no better device for manipulating that stuff than spring-loaded tongs. I advocate having two pairs: a short pair for the kitchen and a long pair for the grill. Go for blunt scalloped edges, which will give you purchase without tearing; avoid those with locks, which lock up on you only when you don't want them to. For easy storage, slip tongs inside the cardboard tube from a roll of paper towels to prevent them from opening. Tongs need not be expensive and restaurant supply stores carry them in every size imaginable.

Cooling Rack

I have a large heavy-duty rack that fits over a large baking sheet and spans my sink. It would be hard for me to overstate my affection for this medievally simple device. Besides cooling baked goods, I use this rack as a draining area for fried foods as well as foods I'm purging, such as eggplant or cabbage for slaw. I ovendry tomatoes on it, and on the rare occasion when I make fresh pasta I lay it on this rack to dry. When dry-aging beef in the fridge, my rack keeps it out of its own juices. When rack hunting avoid those with unidirectional wires and go with a heavy wire weave. Be sure to look for racks that have a tightly woven grid and are designed with support underneath to prevent sagging when weighted.

Heat-Resistant Rubber Spatulas

These are actually made of silicone rubber and although they're a little pricey, you could stir lava with them. My favorites, made by Rubbermaid, have red handles signifying their heat-friendly nature. I see no reason to ever scramble eggs or stir a custard without one of these devices.

Heavy-Duty Stainless Steel Bowl With a Nearly Round Bottom

Heavy-duty means 18/8 or 18/10 stainless-steel construction. The ratios refer to the percentages of the components in the steel. In the case of 18/10, you've got 18 percent chromium (lending corrosion resistance and luster) and 10 percent nickel (a soft metal added to steel to give it malleability). Seeing those fractions embossed on the bowl means that you've got good stuff. Also, look for smooth rather than rolled edges, which often signal an easily warped vessel. Although you want the bowl to be stable on a counter, the rounder the inside of the bowl the better. And the nearly round bottom is important because then the bowl and the whisk share the same profile enabling the whisk to do its job easily and well.

Digital Scale

Volume measures are fine for liquids and small amounts of dry goods (a tablespoon or two) but if you want precision you must weigh. There are basically three types of scales: balance, spring and digital. Balance scales are accurate and durable, but darned expensive and tricky to read. Spring scales, which utilize springs and levers are widely available and affordable but leave much to be desired in the realm of accuracy, especially when it concerns amounts less than 3 ounces. Digital scales assess weight by electronic current, are highly accurate, and easy to read and operate. Most switch effortlessly back and forth from standard to metric and include a "tare" function, the ability to weigh several ingredients in the same bowl by zeroing or canceling out the weight of each ingredient (not to mention the container) after it's added.

Thermometers

Just about everything that happens in the kitchen concerns temperature, which is why you need five thermometers.

Keeping your refrigerator as close to 38° F is really, really important (see Cleanliness is Next to…, page 260). Unfortunately the temperature controls in most refrigerators rely on a scale calibrated not by degrees but by alphanumerics—which aren't that useful for me since I have no idea how cold "B" is. A small alcohol-bulb style thermometer will allow you to manage the chill in your chest. I prefer those that hang off the back of a shelf far better than stand up models, which are always getting knocked over or blocked.

To tell the temperature of your oven, a mercury thermometer works best—but oven versions are tough to find. Coil-style oven thermometers are the next best thing. I like this style for the oven because they're fairly accurate at standard oven temperatures and are easy to read through even dingy door glass.

You'll also want an instant-read thermometer. They come in analog form, but I say why tinker with mechanics when you can have digital. Besides the fact that they're far more accurate and durable, the sensors are located at the tip of the stem. The mechanical sensors in analog models are usually a good inch up the stem, which can make shallow readings all but impossible. Be sure the version you buy has a stem long enough to reach the center of a large roast or loaf of bread. Unlike traditional meat thermometers, instant-read digitals are not meant to stay in the oven during cooking. For that you'll need a probe thermometer.

Probe thermometers are the best thing to happen to cooking in a few hundred years. They're like instant-read thermometers with brains and long-range remote probes that can stay in the food throughout cooking. For mindless meat roasting, simply insert the probe into the deepest part of the meat and set the on-board alarm to go off when the target temperature's reached. No opening and closing the oven door, grill lid, or smoker hatch. Make sure you buy a model with at least a three-foot probe wire and if possible, a range of 0 to 500° F.

Because mercury is a great conductor, mercury thermometers are amazingly fast and accurate and that's a good thing to have when frying or making candy. Most frying/candy thermometers clip right onto the side of your pan and have the high temperature range necessary for these types of cooking. Look for one with a strong cage around the bulb and clear calibrations regarding candy stages (the "ball" system). Unlike most thermometers a well-cared-for mercury model will last forever. I have one that I inherited from my grandmother and it's still dead-on.[41]

Salad Spinner

Moisture in your salad greens is good, but moisture on the greens is bad. Using centrifugal force, a good salad spinner is the best way to dry greens fast. The difference between the various types usually revolves around the drive mechanism. There are three main styles. The crank type has a habit of moving itself right off the counter as it spins, while the pull cord (or lawnmower) type is inclined to bring spinning greens to an abrupt halt and has a cord that can fray and break. But the pump type with a brake is a good choice since it tends to remain balanced as it spins. Also look for a sturdy basket that doubles for other things, like a colander. I also use mine for drying hand-cut fries before introducing them to the oil—a crucial step for splatter-free frying.

---

[41] Needless to say, mercury is really, really poisonous. If you do manage to break the thermometer during use, for the love of all things not genetically mangled, throw out the food.

Cutting Boards

To make your knife blade last, cut on boards of wood or plastic. Not quite as tough as butcher boards (made of dozens or hundreds of pieces of wood cut across the grain and then glued together), but lighter and a lot cheaper, are edge-grained boards. Beware thin specimens; they tend to warp. Buy a good solid kiln-dried maple cutting board, the biggest one you can stand on end in your sink. It won't be cheap but cared for it'll last for years and years. Only cut foods that are safely consumed raw on a wooden cutting board. Raw meat should be cut on plastic. Since they are non-porous and on the slippery side, plastic boards are inhospitable to bacteria. You can label your plastic board for poultry on one side and meat and fish on the other. Cutting boards are one of the most frequent causes of cross contamination in the kitchen. To disinfect boards, rub them with white vinegar, rinse and air dry. Plastic boards can be sanitized in the dishwasher, but never put a wooden board in the machine.

In addition to boards that aren't properly cleaned, wobbly boards are also dangerous. The simple solution to this problem is shelf liner. It makes a super non-skid surface; just put a piece underneath your board and you're good to go.

Spray Bottles

An inexpensive, dime-store item, the spray bottle is handy to have around. And when you buy one, buy three. One for oil, one for vinegar, and one for cleaning solution (and mark them clearly). Spritz a pan, dress a salad, and clean up with ease.

Side Towels

Last, but not least, side towels. These gems are simple, inexpensive things that make work in the kitchen much more pleasurable. A quick wipe with a damp one cleans your work space in a jiff and more importantly, a dry one makes for the perfect protective device when reaching for a hot handle. They're little things that make a big difference.

GOT BLEACH?

When it comes to cleaning up, I bet you have just what you need even without resorting to fancy specialized products. Got bleach? It's found in four out of five U.S. households, has been a staple for ages, and hasn't changed a hair since its introduction in 1916. Household bleach (including Clorox) is not chlorine. It contains no more chlorine than table salt. And it kills germs. Bleach, however, can be an irritant to both skin and eyes so it makes good sense to use a spray bottle.

Whatever tools I handled (including knives and the cutting board) get rinsed with a sanitizing solution composed of 1½ teaspoons Clorox bleach per pint of water. *Campylobacter jujuni*, an especially nasty germ, differs from *salmonella*, which requires a large colony to make you sick, because *C. jujuni* can do it with just a handful of organisms. The American Red Cross recommends ¼ cup of chlorine bleach per 1 gallon of water. Clorox, a sodium hypochlorite bleach (which breaks down into little more than salt water once it's done its killing/cleaning), breaks down the proteins in cell walls, rendering bacteria and the like good and dead. When I'm done in the kitchen, I spritz all the surfaces (and the clean cutting board) lightly with the same solution and leave it to dry. (See page 259 for notes on cutting boards.)

Cleanliness is Next to...

The word sanitation comes from the Latin *sanitas* and it doesn't mean garbage man, it means "health." As it applies to food, sanitation means keeping food safe for the eater. A discussion on food and cooking that ignores sanitation is like a discussion on mountain climbing that omits the mention of ropes. Cooking is fun, but not if you or someone you've fed ends up sick.[42]

Right now, your kitchen is a veritable megalopolis of microscopic organisms, and your refrigerator is downtown Germville. That's just the way it is, and you're just going to have to deal with it. Oh sure, you can write your congressman or you can protest to industry—or you can take responsibility for your own safety. Besides, who do you think is going to take care of you and yours?

a. You **b.** Politicians **c.** Big business **d.** None of the above

If you answered **b** or **c**, you'd better start saving up sick days, and if you said **d** you'd better just eat out. . . no strike that: most restaurant workers know even less about food safety than you do. If you answered **a**, you're darned tootin'.

Bad Bugs

There are zillions of different microorganisms in, on, and around food, but the ones that can render ill those who consume them are in a club all their own. They are the pathogens and they come in five basic flavors: bacteria, viruses, parasites, molds, and yeasts. The last two actually play a crucial role in much food and beverage production, but they can also spoil food (though they rarely make us sick). Viruses can make you very sick indeed, but since they can only survive in living tissue, they only rear their ugly little heads in shellfish.[43] Parasites like *Trichinella spiralis* in pork used to be a problem but have been all but eradicated in swine populations through proper feed management.

[42] The United States sees some forty thousand reported cases of *salmonella* each year, and more than one thousand of those result in death.

[43] Shellfish harvesting is very tightly regulated. Merchants are required to display bed tags from each shipment that tell where and when the harvest took place. If any problems become associated with the batch, health officials can quickly track it to the source.

Bacteria are by far the most troublesome and include the big three: *Salmonella*, *E. coli*, and *Clostridium botulinum*, the instigator of botulism. The first two set up shop in our digestive tracts and wreak havoc. The third is itself actually harmless, but its waste is a potent toxin that loves to attack respiratory systems.[44]

Although individual needs differ, most microorganisms require:

• Water

• Food

• A pH between 4.6 and 7

• Temperature between 40° and 140° F (known hereafter as "the Zone")

• Air (though some, like *botulinum*, do not)

The **water** content of any food is referred to as its "water activity." Most—but not all—bacteria, molds, yeasts, and the like require a relatively damp environment, which is why meats and fresh vegetables spoil quickly, while dry goods don't.

Food for microorganisms can be anything from nearly pure sugar (as in the case of mold on jam) or protein (meat). In any case, the food has to be dissolved in water in order for bacteria to digest it; cured hams can hang around a smokehouse for a couple of years without rotting.[45]

PH refers to the acidity of a given substance. The scale goes from 0 to 14, with 1 being eat-your-face-off acidic (remember the acid scene in *The Fly*?) and 14 being eat-your-face-off alkaline (remember the lye scene in *Fight Club*?). Limes rate a 2, baking soda rates an 8.1, and distilled water is dead neutral at 7. Almost all foods are slightly acidic, which is just what bacteria like. But they don't like an environment under a pH of 4.6, which is why raw fish prepared ceviche-style will keep a heck of a lot longer than raw fish that's, well, raw. Which is not to say that you'd want to leave ceviche hanging around that long (see Acid, page 262).

THE ZONE

The temperature range from 40° to 140° F is referred to as the danger Zone because most bacteria multiply readily within this window. And that's not good, because the more of these little bugs there are, the more likely you are to get sick—and of course the quicker the food's going to spoil. You might argue that the bacteria that accumulate in a piece of raw chicken left on a counter for 5 hours may indeed be killed by proper cooking, but why run the risk? Also, that piece of chicken will leave a lot of bacteria on everything it touches, thus increasing the chance for cross contamination. Outside the Zone, bacteria advancement slows radically, or even stops altogether (although some bacteria can remain active well below the freezing point).

[44] *Botulism* is especially ugly because it is an organism that produces resistant little spores that can withstand temperatures well in excess of the boiling point of water. *Botulinum* also thrives in anaerobic environments like sealed vacu-pouches and cans.

[45] It's interesting to note that although smoke has preservative powers and tastes great, the main reason it was used for curing in the United States is because it's an excellent fly repellant.

ACID

The strange case of fresh mayonnaise: Fresh mayonnaise is made with raw egg yolks, and that should tell you right off the bat that if you're going to risk eating something that may, could, just might have a touch of *salmonella* in it, the very least you should do is get it in the fridge lickety-split, right? That way the cold and the acid in the vinegar can kick microbial butt, right? Wrong. Freshly made mayo is better off sitting on your kitchen counter for 8 to 12 hours after it's made. How can this be? Turns out that acid is a very good disinfectant because acid coagulates proteins, and when cells get their proteins coagulated, they curl up and die. Acid assassinates best at room temperature. Nobody knows why. But if you refrigerate that golden goo right away, the best thing that will happen is the bacteria inside will stop reproducing. They won't be nuked, however, as they would on the counter. So when it comes to acid, colder is not always better, sanitationally speaking.

What You Can Do

At the Market

If you've never taken a close look at your market, take time to do it, because it doesn't matter how carefully your food is raised and processed if it's mishandled in transit or at the market itself. Some things to check for:

General cleanliness Dark, dingy, or dirty stores are generally run by dark, dingy, or dirty management and should be avoided.

Meat department If there are open cases, check a few meat packages. Are they tightly sealed? Do you see any leaking juices? Are the cases themselves clean? Are thermometers present? If not, bring one in and take the cases' temperature yourself (an instant-read will arouse less suspicion, as you won't have to stand around and wait for it to register). If it's 40° F. or higher, mention it to the department manager. If he or she doesn't jump, show them your thermometer and drop a reference to the article you're writing for the local newspaper. That'll put a chill in 'em.

Look in any closed cases Meat should be on clean trays, and there should be thermometers aplenty. Fish should be on lots of clean, well-drained ice. Now close your eyes and smell the air—really smell, the way Hannibal Lecter did when he was trying to figure out what perfume Agent Starling was wearing. If you smell anything other than clean, there's a problem somewhere.

Dairy and egg case Again, check your thermometer. If you really want to know, stick the probe right into an egg (yes, you'll then have to buy the carton). If it doesn't read 40° F. or below, tell somebody, and if they don't do anything about it, buy your eggs elsewhere.

Produce department Most folks don't think of fruits and vegetables as being high-risk foods pathogenically speaking, but because of their high moisture content and neutral pH, most of these make excellent bacteria resorts. And don't forget that produce does grow in dirt, and dirt is full of . . . you got it. I remember seeing a couple of very serious guys in white jackets rush into a produce department and remove every single alfalfa sprout in the place;

alfalfa sprouts are major *salmonella* carriers (though not as bad as turtles and iguanas).

My favorite fresh market keeps all its produce on big carts that roll into giant walk-in refrigerators each night. During the day, highly perishable vegetables like broccoli and spinach and the like are kept on nice clean ice. There are no misting systems. I hate mister systems: I've yet to see a vegetable that actually likes to get wet once it's been harvested. This has less to do with pathogenic trouble than good old-fashioned rotting. Greens and things lose their turgidity when exposed to long periods of surface moisture and that turns them to goo. Of course if the misting system is dirty, then it can become contaminated with pathogenic organisms. That means that every time it goes off, your prospective dinner gets a germ bath. Want to scare the produce manager the way you did the meat folks? Take a water sample from the mister. Tell him or her you're sending it to the lab for analysis. If he or she says "fine," don't bother sending it. If he or she develops a sudden facial tic find another market. Remember, it's your food.

Transportation If you're planning to buy perishables, bring a cooler to the market with at least one if not two cold packs inside. It just doesn't make sense to take food that's been properly stored, walk it around a nice warm market and then out to a car trunk you could bake biscuits in. If your cooler is too big for your cart then at least have it standing by in the trunk for the ride home. Your frozen goods will stay that way, your veggies won't wilt, and your meats will stay safely out of the Zone. You too will enjoy the freedom to go to the video rental place on the way home without having to calculate the *Listeria* growth rate in your fresh fish.

At Home

Once the groceries are home, three major issues face the cook: temperature abuse, cross contamination, and contamination by the human animal.

Temperature control

Foods whose temperature fall in the 40° to 140° F Zone are vulnerable to bacterial colonization, so proper refrigeration is key. Most folks have no idea what temperature their

BRINGING MEAT TO ROOM TEMPERATURE

I like to rest meat out of the refrigerator for a half hour before cooking so that there will be less difference between the temperature of the meat and the temperature of the oven. But if there are any doubts about how well the meat was handled prior to purchase, there is a small chance that the inside of the meat could be contaminated with pathogens that would only be killed were the meat to be cooked to a very high temperature.

For instance, you buy your T-bone steak off the back of a truck because the price is good. The guy who cuts the steak used the same knife to cut up a chicken. If he cut the steak correctly this would technically not be too much of a worry as long as the entire steak surface came into contact with very high heat—as in grilling.

But suppose he was not only a dirty cutter, but a sloppy one and he poked his knife through the steak. Now the inside of the meat is contaminated as well. And if you like your steak cooked medium rare, those bugs won't be killed.

And by pulling that meat out and placing it on the counter (and in the Zone) for a half hour, you create an environment in which those few microscopic nasties could grow into quite a powerful army.

But if you buy your meat from reputable sources—and practice safe handling at home—I feel that the danger is amazingly and perhaps incalculably low. To a healthy adult I'd say "go for it," but then I'd also say "eat steak tartare."

HOW LONG IS TOO LONG TO KEEP CANNED FOODS?

Canned foods should be stored in a cool, dry place. Never put them above the stove, under the sink, in a damp garage or basement, or any place exposed to very high or very low temperatures. Foods high in acid, such as tomatoes and other fruit, can be safely kept for up to 18 months; low-acid foods such as meat and vegetables are okay for 2 to 5 years. Canned meat and poultry will keep best for 2 to 5 years if the can remains in good condition and has been stored in a cool, clean, dry place.

While extremely rare, a toxin produced by *Clostridium botulinum* is the worst danger in the realm of canned goods. Never use food from containers that show possible botulism warnings including: leaking, bulging, or denting; cracked jars or jars with loose or bulging lids; canned food with a foul odor; or any container that spurts liquid as it is opened. Even a minuscule amount of *botulinum* toxin can be deadly.

refrigerator maintains, but you don't have this problem because you read the section on thermometers (page 257). Of course, the Zone gets abused on the other end as well. Take that big pot of beef stew you just finished simmering.

Wow . . . looks like a good gallon of stew. That's a heck of a lot of mass, upwards of 15 pounds of 200° potential germ chow. Once you spoon out a few bowls for you and yours, what will you do with the rest? Leave it on the counter to cool down? Okay, but that could take 12 hours or more, and most of that time will be spent in the Zone. Not worried? Figure you nuked all the bacteria during cooking? You may have gotten most of them, but trust me: you didn't get them all. And of course there's the air, the serving spoon, the finger that you used to pull out the sage leaves, that sort of thing. Remember the *Jurassic Park* rule: life will find a way no matter how clever you think you are.

So you should put it in the refrigerator, right?

That's a bad idea for a couple of reasons. First, even the best refrigerator models are designed to keep things cold, not make them cold. Sure, you can chill a few beers, but it could take ten hours or more to chill that stew. And since the stew is so hot, it will raise the temperature in the box, thus nudging every food present into the Zone—and that's not good. What you need is a way to cool the stew before it gets filed in the chill chest. If it's cold out—say, 35° F—you could certainly set the pot out on your deck, patio, or carport. That will cut a few hours off the time in the Zone, especially if it's windy, but it will still take several hours. If you could increase the surface-to-mass ratio, thus exposing more stew to more cold air, you'd be onto something. So pour your stew into the largest, flattest pan you have. A couple of baking pans or a large roasting pan should do nicely. If you're afraid bugs may come to call during this alfresco chill, simply cover with plastic wrap, but push the wrap down right onto the surface of the stew.

Okay, so what if it's July?

There are several methods for "shocking" food down to a safe temperature quickly. Soup and stew pots may be placed directly in a sink full of ice water (not just ice: conduction, remember?). Frequent stirring will bring more hot food in contact with the side of the pot, and since heat always moves toward cold, the heat will abandon the soup for the ice slurry.

If no sink is available, you can also fill a large zip-top freezer bag with ice, suck out all the air, and push it right down into the goo. This method has the added advantage of being able to capture any fat that happens to stick to the side of the bag and solidify. When the ice melts, either in the sink or the bag, take the food's temperature. If it's not close to 40° F, start over again. You'll be surprised how quickly the food cools down.

Of course, not all big hot foods are soupy or stewy. Large pans of braised dishes, large roasts, and the like can't really be stirred, and bagged ice is impractical. For these I break out my trusty cooler, fill the bottom with a couple inches of ice, sprinkle the ice liberally with salt, and place the roasting or braising pan right on top. (As any home ice-cream cranker can tell you, salt can melt ice without raising its temperature, creating a liquid that's actually colder than the freezing point.) Check in an hour or two and your thermometer will most likely clear you for fridge access.

Cooking

Improper cooking is the big daddy of thermal transgressions. It's the one most often associated with large outbreaks of both *salmonella* and *E. coli* in this country. As important as proper cooking is, there has been some overreacting out there of late. A government Internet site I checked out recently stated that poultry must be cooked to a final internal temperature of 180° F, while another site suggests that all fresh pork cuts be cooked to 170° F. Both seem pretty silly since *salmonella* dies instantly at 165° F (14 minutes at 140° F will do the job too), and *trichinae* (the parasites responsible for trichinosis) die at 170° F. Here's how I temp stuff.

- All poultry, game birds, stuffed meats and any previously cooked foods that are being reheated need to hit 165° F to be extra safe. (I usually take this reading from the thickest part of the meat, sometimes the breast, sometimes the thigh.)
- Pork (non-ground) should be cooked to 150° F.
- Beef steaks can be cooked to desired doneness.

- Rolled roast needs to be cooked to 130° F and should be held here for at least 1 hour before serving.
- Fish should be cooked to 140° F.
- Ground beef should be cooked to 155° F.
- Ground pork should be cooked to 160° F.
- Ground turkey should be cooked to 170° F.

Cross Contamination

The leading cause of food-borne illnesses in home kitchens, cross contamination happens any time you give bugs a way to get from one place to another. Following is a possible scenario:

You come home from the market and the only place to put that raw chicken is on the middle shelf in the fridge. Unbeknownst to you, there is a small hole in the bag and some of the juice runs out. It pools at the back edge of the shelf, then a few drops run down the wall of the refrigerator, into the crisper drawer, and onto a loosely wrapped head of lettuce. Since your refrigerator's running at an average of 45° F, this meager collection of bacterial pilgrims sets up a village, which within a few hours becomes a thriving metropolis. You take the lettuce out of the fridge, cut it into wedges on your cutting board, and build a salad, which you then set on the buffet half an hour before your guests arrive. Meanwhile, you cook the chicken to an internal temperature of 165° F, killing any *salmonella* or *campylobacter* that may be present. But you then cut it up on the very same cutting board with

> Unless you've tested it with a thermometer— see page 257.

THAWING

Thawing's a funny thing because it's just like cooking inasmuch as it's all about bringing a piece of food into thermal equilibrium with its surroundings. All the principals of cooking apply: temperature, conduction, convection, radiation, and density. When I tell folks that a block of ice will thaw faster under cold running water than in a 200° F oven, they think I've been in the nutmeg again (see Toxins). But it is indeed true. Cold water may be cold, but it's dense, it's a good conductor, and if it's running it's got convection on its side. The hot oven has temperature and radiation on its side, but unless you have the broiler on, that won't be enough. So in order to keep thawing food (say, a frozen Cornish game hen) in the Zone for the shortest time possible, either thaw it in the refrigerator (slow but safe) or tightly wrapped and submerged in cold water up to 70° F that's circulating somehow.

the very same knife you used for the lettuce, thus recontaminating it. Two or three days later, you start getting nasty letters from your friends written on hospital letterhead.

Had you placed the raw chicken in a container (say, a baking dish) and placed it on the bottom shelf, you wouldn't be forced to wear a giant red S across your chest.

Human Contamination

Consider the strange case of Mary Mallon, a cook who worked in households from Long Island to Manhattan in the early years of the twentieth century. Mary gave a nasty form of salmonella to dozens if not hundreds of people without actually getting sick herself. Mary is known to history as Typhoid Mary not because she had the audacity to touch food with her hands (something I'm a big fan of), but because she didn't wash her hands well enough or often enough. This drama repeats itself in homes and restaurants across America with alarming frequency. And all because we fail to do something most of us should have learned in kindergarten.

Hand-washing is a really big deal, and you should do it often while handling food, but there are a couple of other things you can do to keep your mitts in sanitary condition.

- Make sure you can turn the water on (hot and cold) at your kitchen sink without touching the taps with your hands. Touch the chicken, touch the tap, wash your hands, turn off the tap with your hand—you might as well have skipped the whole darned thing. If you have a single-lever model, make sure you can work it with the back of your wrist or your elbow. If you prefer a separate knob for both hot and cold, go with wide paddles that can be operated by the forearms. Or you can do what many restaurants do and install foot pedals or waist-level "lean-in" buttons.

- Make sure your soap dispenser can be pumped without direct hand contact.

- You can get latex gloves at any drugstore. They're great for handling raw meat or for cutting chile pods or garlic, which can leave some nasty compounds on your skin. When you're done working, just throw them away. (Make sure you get the ones that contain talcum powder for easy on and off.)

TOXINS

Toxins are poisons that cannot be neutralized by heat (or sanitation practices, for that matter). Aside from the aforementioned botulinum toxin, there's scrombrotoxin in fish and cheese, which causes scrombroid poisoning, a nasty, itchy, vomity kind of thing that usually isn't fatal. Not so for tetrodotoxin, which one might encounter in even a small nibble of a badly prepared piece of fugu, or blowfish. I like the Centers for Disease Control description:

"Tetrodotoxin is heat-stable and blocks sodium conductance and neuronal transmission in skeletal muscles. Paresthesia begins 10 to 45 minutes after ingestion, usually as tingling of the tongue and inner surface of the mouth. Other common symptoms include vomiting, lightheadedness, dizziness, feelings of doom, and weakness. An ascending paralysis develops, and death can occur within 6 to 24 hours, secondary to respiratory muscle paralysis. Other manifestations include salivation, muscle twitching, diaphoresis, pleuritic chest pain, dysphagia, aphonia, and convulsions. Severe poisoning is indicated by hypotension, bradycardia, depressed corneal reflexes, and fixed dilated pupils. Diagnosis is based on clinical symptoms and a history of ingestion. Treatment is supportive, and there is no specific antitoxin."

I especially like the "feelings of doom" part. Granted, you're not likely to stumble across bad fugu completely unaware (although three California chefs nearly died in 1996 when a coworker brought some prepackaged fugu back from Japan), but many common plants contain poisons. Apple seeds and peach pits contain a chemical of the cyanide family and can flat out kill

continued on next page

you if you chew up and swallow enough. (Don't worry: swallowing an apple seed or two won't hurt you. A couple hundred maybe, but what are the chances of that happening?) Raw or undercooked fresh red kidney beans can deliver a dose of phyto-haemagglutinin to the system and reward you with 4 to 6 hours of extreme abdominal distress. Nutmeg contains a toxin that is also a powerful hallucinogen; it produces very bad headaches in those who try to take advantage of it.

Then there's honey intoxication, which results from eating honey containing rhodo-dendron nectar. Said nectar contains grayantoxin, which can play havoc with your central nervous system for a day or so (it's rarely fatal, if that makes you feel any better). Then there are mushrooms. Think that's a chanterelle in your yard? Be sure—very sure—because if you're wrong, you may end up with your liver dissolved into a pool of goo, which I'm told doesn't feel very good. Or maybe you'll be lucky and latch onto some 'shrooms containing muscarine, in which case you'll probably just sweat out several pounds of water in a few hours, throw up, and take a nap. Either way, never gather wild mushrooms unless you're operating under the guidance of a skilled, educated, experienced, and preferably old mushroom hunter.

• Never wipe dirty hands on a kitchen towel—you might as well blow your nose on it. By the same token, never use a dirty towel to dry clean hands—you might as well blow your nose on them.

Speaking of your nose, sneezing and blowing are two of the best ways to introduce unwanted germs into your food. Coughing is good, too. And I hope I don't have mention the bathroom, right?

Organically Challenged

It's become clear in recent years that microorganisms inside livestock can become resistant to the sub-diagnostic doses of antibiotics that are often (in fact, usually) given to livestock in this country. Now this doesn't mean they become super-bugs, capable of shooting webs or turning into rubber—they still die at proper cooking temperatures. The problem is cross-contamination in the kitchen. If you're not diligent, you could end up with a strain of bug that won't respond to the first few drugs that are tried. This is not good news. As a result, I'm starting to look seriously at switching to organic and naturally raised meats whenever I can, not for flavor as much as for safety.

Want to keep up with developments in food safety? Check out www.fda.gov. They've got it all.

Sources

U.S Food & Drug Administration, Center for Food Safety & Applied Nutrition: Foodborne Microorganisms and Natural Toxins (informally known as the "Bad Bug Book"). Available for downloading at http://www.cfsan.fda.gov/~mow/badbug.zip

The Educational Foundation of the National Restaurant Association: Applied Foodservice Sanitation, 4th Ed. (1992)

McGee, Harold: On Food and Cooking: The Science and Lore of the Kitchen. New York: Fireside, 1984.

The Top 5 Activities to Be Pursued by a Cook

Number 1: Keep up with Family

Food is heritage. It's what makes "me" into "we." Besides, even if you don't like your family, everybody likes food. I keep a book of family recipes. They're not all good, but a few of them are classics for my clan and I'd hate to lose them.

Number 2: Travel

Whether you drive to the next county or the next hemisphere, nothing says where you are like the food you find along the way. When it comes to eating, beware the tourist guidebooks. Seek out the local favorites.

Number 3: Cook

Yes, this is fairly obvious, but the truth is, most of us cook as a means to an end: eating. What I'm suggesting is that you cook to cook. And keep a record of what you cook and what you thought of it before, during, and after the process.

Number 4: Taste

Remember, flavor is a noun, taste is a verb, and it's one we often forget to bother with. We'll spend hours preparing food that we gulp down in minutes as if we're afraid a band of hyenas might pass through and wrestle it away from us. So chew your food and taste it. If you're with other people, stop talking for a minute and just taste. If you're by yourself, turn off the TV, put down the book, and enjoy your interface with planet Earth. And I'm not just talking about fancy fare here. I'm talking about that ballpark frank, that cup of coffee, that Milky Way bar. Heck, if you're going to have to work off the calories, doesn't it make sense to enjoy them to the fullest?

Number 5: Read

Cooking and food connect to everything: history, art, literature, physics, chemistry, math—you name it, food's got it. So, the more you read about food, the smarter you get about everything.

A Selected Reading List

Although I've never counted, I'd guess I have a few hundred books dealing with food. These are the titles that never seem to make it from my table back onto the shelf.

Outlaw Cook, John Thorne

For my mind and money, John Thorne is the best American food writer alive and *Outlaw Cook* is the *Physiology of Taste* of our time. Part cookbook, part meditation, Thorne looks at everything from appetite to meatballs to the virtues of not being a very good cook. This is the book I reach for when the thrill is gone.

Cookwise, Shirley O. Corriher

Shirley is a hero and a friend and not only is her book full of delicious and reliable recipes, the text and illustrations explain exactly why they are delicious and reliable. Applicable food science for the cook who really doesn't want to look at electrospectrographs (not that there's anything wrong with that).

On Food and Cooking: The Science and Lore of the Kitchen, Harold McGee

Scholarly, scientific, badly dog-eared. This is the book cooks are talking about when they refer to the "bible." Until McGee got his nerdy self into the kitchen, cooks did things for no other reason than that they had been trained to do so. McGee changed that by explaining ingredients and methodologies via science. His sequel, *The Curious Cook,* is a companion piece that takes a close look at specific issues from poaching to the perfect sorbet, which no one but McGee would ever have the patience to quantify. At nearly 700 recipe-free pages, this is not an easy read, but it is an indispensable one for any cook who wants to know "why."

Gastronomic Me, M.F.K. Fisher

The first time I saw Fisher's photo on the back of her wartime treasury *How to Eat a Wolf*, I fell into a heavy crush. She could cook and eat and write—and she looked like Grace Kelly. Boy, do I wish I could have shared just one meal with this woman and then sat around to talk about it. Not only was Fisher the first modern food writer, she was a woman and not a chef, which makes her writing even better. Her work reads as if it were written yesterday afternoon. Nobody before or since has written as thoughtfully about eggs.

The Joy of Cooking (1962–1975 editions), Irma S. Rombauer

The only book on Earth that tells you how to make marshmallows *and* skin a squirrel.

The New Food Lover's Companion, Sharon Tyler Herbst

The subtitle says it all: *Comprehensive Definitions of Nearly 6,000 Food, Drink, and Culinary Terms*. I keep mine in a cool little zippered carrying case designed for Bibles and I take it everywhere. Although I like to act like I know everything, it actually does.

The Food Chronology, James Trager

Name a year, and Trager has charted its food-relevant events, broken down into classifications such as science, politics, economics, energy medicine, religion, and so on. There are several great books on food history, but most of them spin their pages on analysis. Trager just says what happened, when, and to whom and what. A food history Jack Webb would have loved.

The Visual Food Encyclopedia, edited by Serge D'Amico and François Fortin

In addition to thorough histories and technical information, this weighty tome sports more than 1,200 entries with excellent color illustrations. When you need to know what spirulina looks like, you'll have the answer right on your bookshelf.

The Frugal Gourmet, Jeff Smith

This was my first cookbook. I don't care what he does or did in his personal life. Everything in here worked back then and still does.

The New Southern Cook, John Martin Taylor

I don't usually buy cookbooks, especially regional ones, but this came to me as a gift. Once I tried a recipe, I cooked everything in it. Taylor has both knowledge and respect for Southern cooking, but he isn't afraid to take modern approaches. The recipes are dead-on and never fail.

The Time-Life Good Cook Series, Richard Olney, editor

This multivolume series from the 1970s covers everything from *Classic Desserts* to *Salads* to *Sauces*. Whenever I don't understand a procedure involving a classic dish (a common occurrence), I go to these books. They feature extremely accurate and easy-to-follow photo-steps to teach basic procedures, which are followed up with zillions of recipes. This series has been out of print for a while now, but thanks to the Internet you can find them used.

The American Century Cookbook: The Most Popular Recipes of the 20th Century, Jean Anderson

Those who do not cook their history are doomed to repeat it, which isn't always a bad thing.

Fish and Shellfish, James Peterson

For my money the best seafood book around. Peterson is a teacher rather than a chef, and I appreciate the difference.

Just Before Dark, Jim Harrison

The guy who wrote *Legends of the Fall* and *Wolf* is also a helluva food writer in a Hemingway kind of vein. His tastes run rich (foie gras, sweetbreads, half-rotted pheasants), but he writes about these foods with such gusto, such machismo that you want to go out and buy a couple of chest freezers and fill them with stuff you killed. Harrison used to write a column in *Esquire* called "The Raw and the Cooked," and it was there I first read a review of Thorne's *Outlaw Cook*.

Sources

The following are sources for some of the items mentioned in this book and others that aren't mentioned, but are in stock in my house at all times.

Bragg Farm Sugar House

Route 14 North P.O. Box 201

East Montpelier, VT 05651

(802) 223-5757

(800) 376-5757

www.central-vt.com/web/bragg

Bragg Farm maple syrup amber grade B—delicious. This is a true secret ingredient, and I use it as a foil for salty or hot flavors in a lot of dishes.

The King Arthur Flour Company, Inc.

P.O. Box 876

Norwich, VT 05055

(800) 827-6836

www.kingarthurflour.com

For King Arthur Special Bread Flour for Machines; great for loaves, lousy for biscuits.

Lodge Manufacturing Co.

P.O. Box 380

South Pittsburgh, TN 37380

(423) 837-7181

www.lodgemfg.com

Louisiana Gold Hot Pepper Sauce

Bruce Food Corporation

P.O. Drawer 1030

New Iberia, LA 70562-1030

(800) 299-9082

www.brucefoods.com

Neese Country Sausage

1452 Alamance Church Rd.

Greensboro, NC 27406

(800) 632-1010

Fax: (336) 275-0750

Neese's sausage is North Carolina's finest. Their liver loaf is good, too.

Old Bay Seasoning

McCormick & Company, Inc.

211 Schilling Circle

Hunt Valley, MD 21031

(410) 527-6000

www.mccormick.com

Penzys Spices

18900 W. Bluemound Road

Brookfield, WI 53045

(262) 641-0999

(800) 741-7787

Fax: (262) 785-7678

www.penzeys.com

St. Ives Coffee Roasters

966 Dorsey Street

Gainseville, GA 30501

(800) 767-JAVA (5282)

Fax: (770) 287-3396

I'm still looking for the perfect bean, perfect grind, and perfect roast, but I am getting close because St. Ives Coffee Roasters is getting close.

See's Candy Shops, Inc.

(retail outlets across the United States)

Mail Order: (800) 915-7337

www.sees.com

Keep your fancy European confections—my sweet teeth belong to the little California company that Mary See started back when women wore buns and shawls.

Shiner Bock Ale

The Spoetzl Brewery

603 East Brewery Street

Shiner, TX 77984

(361) 594-3383

www.shiner.com

Sierra Nevada Brewing Company

1075 East 20th Street

Chico, CA 95928

(530) 896-2198

Fax: (530) 893-1275

www.sierranevada.com

The Spice House

1031 N. Old World Third Street

Milwaukee, WI 53203

(414) 272-0977

Fax: (414) 272-1271

www.thespicehouse.com

Vermont Butter & Cheese Company

Websterville, Vermont 05678

(800) 884-6287

www.vtbutterandcheeseco.com

The White Lily Foods Company

218 East Depot Street

Knoxville, TN 37917

(432) 546-5511

www.whitelily.com

For White Lily Self-Rising Flour; great for biscuits.

Metric Conversion Charts

Weight Equivalents

The metric weights given in this chart are not exact equivalents, but have been rounded up or down slightly to make measuring easier.

Avoirdupois	Metric
¼ oz	7 g
½ oz	15 g
1 oz	30 g
2 oz	60 g
3 oz	90 g
4 oz	115 g
5 oz	150 g
6 oz	175 g
7 oz	200 g
8 oz (½ lb)	225 g
9 oz	250 g
10 oz	300 g
11 oz	325 g
12 oz	350 g
13 oz	375 g
14 oz	400 g
15 oz	425 g
16 oz (1 lb)	450 g
1½ lb	750 g
2 lb	900 g
2¼ lb	1 kg
3 lb	1.4 kg
4 lb	1.8 kg

Volume Equivalents

These are not exact equivalents for American cups and spoons, but have been rounded up or down slightly to make measuring easier.

American	Metric	Imperial
¼ t	1.2 ml	--
½ t	2.5 ml	--
1 t	5.0 ml	--
½ T (1.5 t)	7.5 ml	--
1 T (3 t)	15 ml	--
¼ cup (4 T)	60 ml	2 fl oz
⅓ cup (5 T)	75 ml	2½ fl oz
½ cup (8 T)	125 ml	4 fl oz
⅔ cup (10 T)	150 ml	5 fl oz
¾ cup (12 T)	175 ml	6 fl oz
1 cup (16 T)	250 ml	8 fl oz
1¼ cups	300 ml	10 fl oz (½ pt)
1½ cups	350 ml	12 fl oz
2 cups (1 pint)	500 ml	16 fl oz
2½ cups	625 ml	20 fl oz (1 pint)
1 quart	1 liter	32 fl oz

Oven Temperature Equivalents

Oven Mark	F	C	Gas
Very cool	250–275	130–140	½–1
Cool	300	150	2
Warm	325	170	3
Moderate	350	180	4
Moderately hot	375-400	190-200	5-6
Hot	425-450	220-230	7-8
Very hot	475	250	9

Epilogue

Unless you're one of those folks who check out the ending of a book first, you've probably plowed through almost three pounds of paper to reach this spot. Thanks for sticking with it. I hope it didn't take as much work to read as it did to write it.

In the end, I certainly don't expect you to remember every manic message contained herein, but there are a few things I hope you take away for the long term.

Although the act of cooking involves a great many things, at its core it's about the marriage of food and heat. Being a good cook means understanding the food enough to know how to apply that heat. Do you deliver a massive dose via cast iron or do you dole it out slowly via water in a warm oven? Therein lies the core question of cooking. Everything else is secondary.

Just as voltage is but one factor in determining the potential of an electrical current, temperature is but one factor in determining the potential of heat. The mode of transmission, radiation, conduction, and convection are as crucial to the equation as the temperature itself. That's why you can stick your hand inside a 500° F oven but not into 200° F.

Searing is, in the residential milieu at least, the fastest way to get heat into food. The primary goal: browning via the Maillard reaction (for meat) and caramelization (fruits and vegetables). Depending on their size and shape, target foods may be seared until done or finished by another method. Since searing takes place in a dry pan, no flour or other coatings should be employed. Certain spice rubs, however, are definitely allowed.

Don't fear the fryer. Since it takes a lot less energy to bring a pound of oil to 350° F than it does to boil a pound of water, fat is an amazingly efficient cooking medium. What's more, frying adds flavor because it delivers enough of a thermal punch to create browning, something water just can't do. And remember, when done correctly, most of the cooking fat stays in the pan. What constitutes correctness?

- The temperature of the cooking fat must be kept high enough so that the water under the surface of the food boils. Miss this mark, and fat will invade the food with a vengeance.

- Don't crowd the fryer.

- All excess dredge or batter should be removed prior to frying.

- Once cooked, fried foods must be thoroughly drained.

Buy yourself a grill that can be controlled. Better to load it up with burning charcoal and choke it back via air control than to not have enough heat to begin with. Lubricate grillables with only enough oil to give the seasoning something to hold on to. This is less than you think. If the grill grates are dirty, the grill is useless. Grill by zone. Most foods, be they animal or vegetable, fare best when moved between areas of direct and indirect heat. Buy good charcoal and use a chimney starter so that you can add burning coals to your fire. I've never believed in adding cold charcoal to an existing fire.

When pan frying, you'll rarely need as much oil as you think. What looks like a pitiful puddle in an empty pan will rise considerably once the food moves in.

A successful sauté depends on high heat, a small amount of oil, and constant movement. Pan crowding is the number-one problem facing the sauté. Work in batches if you're in doubt. Remember, if you see liquid bubbling in the bottom of the pan, you're not sautéing you're boiling. And since water-type liquids can't move past 212° F, your food won't brown no matter how hot the pan was when you started.

Water is tricky stuff. Don't turn your back on it.

Despite new "smart" appliance designs, it's still darned difficult to maintain a constant and gentle simmer on a cook top. So whenever possible, I move my simmerables off the stove and into the oven. Evaporation is inevitable, so keep hot liquid nearby to maintain the liquid level.

Braising is nothing more than simmering something that's been seared in as little liquid as possible. Maintain food-liquid contact by cooking in the smallest vessel possible or (my favorite) an aluminum foil enclosure set inside another pan. Cooking in aluminum is perfectly safe (yes, even when acidic foods are concerned), though foods cooked in foil should be removed from the foil as soon after cooking as possible.

Due to the way in which collagen converts into gelatin, meat braises and stews are always better the next day. I know of no exceptions.

Buy a pressure cooker, read the instructions, and then use it often.

Homemade stock makes sense—and sense is what I like making best.

If there's something left in the pot when the cooking is done, there's a sauce waiting to happen. The same goes for leftover marinades—just make sure you always bring them to a boil before serving.

If you're using flour to thicken a sauce, remember that it won't thicken until it the liquid in question reaches a boil. Cornstarch thickens at much lower temperatures, as do arrowroot and potato starch.

Give your microwave oven another chance.

Buy the biggest cutting board your sink can accommodate.

Unless it's got a rapid-cool section, your refrigerator was designed to keep things cold, not make them cold. So don't expect it to chill a pot of hot soup and keep everything else in it out of the danger zone.

Buy a pair of spring-loaded tongs and don't pay more than ten bucks for them.

Thermometers are tools, as are your tongue, nose, and fingers. Your brain is also a tool, so don't run with scissors (or knives), and think before you cook.

> Now you know, and
> knowin's half the battle.
>
> —GI JOE

Acknowledgments

The author wishes to acknowledge the works of those who inspired this one—as well as those the author just couldn't have done it without.

Professional

John and Matte Thorne: food writers (Outlaw Cook provided the spark for just about everything I've done); Shirley O. Corriher: food teacher and writer (her book Cookwise is the best of the last decade); Harold McGee: food-science deity (every time I thought I was breaking new ground, I found his footprints); Patrick Matecat: chef and darned fine teacher; New England Culinary Institute: darned fine culinary school; Sother Teague: chef and brother in arms; Stacey Geary: editor (on my end); Marisa Bulzone: editor (Stewart, Tabori & Chang); Michael Kann: chef and writer; Athalie White: marketing manager; Paul Nuesslein: recipe tester; Eileen Opatut: Food Network program director—a wonderful client; Dana Popoff: producer of Good Eats.

Personal

DeAnna Brown: wife (behind every writer there's...) / executive producer of Good Eats; Zoey Brown: daughter / beacon of light; Matilda: dog; Steve Markey: friend since forever; Phyllis Sauls: Mom and recipe tester.

Random

W. Shakespeare: dead but good writer; Coffee: beverage; Knob Hill Bourbon: ditto; Little Debbie Nutty Bars: delicious treat; Beef; Apple Computer: manufacturers of the Macintosh G4 powerbook on which book was written; Steely Dan: band / source of good vocabulary words; Airstream: makers of fine travel trailers and my office; All Clad Cookware: who have given me free stuff and lots of it; Lodge Manufacturing: sole keepers of the American cast-iron flame; Weber: makers of the best charcoal grill known to man; General Electric: most of the recipes herein were tested in and on their Profile gas range, a very reliable piece of ordnance indeed.

All illustrations are based on sketches by Alton Brown. Illustrations on pages 14–15, 18–19, 26, 29, 46–47, 58–59, 88, 97, 108–109, and 240–245 copyright © 2002 Campbell Laird. All other illustrations by Allyson C. McFarlane, Branda E. Rasmussen, Galen Smith, Paul G. Wagner, and Jed Weinstein.

Published in 2002 by
Stewart, Tabori & Chang
115 West 18th Street
New York, NY 10011
www.abramsbooks.com

Library of Congress Cataloging-in-Publication Data
Brown, Alton, 1962–
    I'm just here for the food / by Alton Brown.
      p. cm.
   ISBN 1-58479-083-0
    1. Cookery. I. Title.
TX651 .B728 2002
641.5--dc21   2001054936

The text of this book was composed in New Century Schoolbook and Avenir

Edited by Marisa Bulzone
Designed by Galen Smith and Allyson C. McFarlane
Graphic Production by Pamela Schechter

Printed in England by Butler & Tanner, Ltd.

14th printing

Stewart, Tabori & Chang is a subsidiary of

LA MARTINIÈRE
GROUPE